ALSO BY DAVID THOMSON

The Whole Equation

The New Biographical Dictionary of Film

In Nevada: The Land, the People, God and Chance

The Alien Quartet

Beneath Mulholland: Thoughts on Hollywood and Its Ghosts

Rosebud: The Story of Orson Welles

4-2

Showman: The Life of David O. Selznick

Silver Light

Warren Beatty and Desert Eyes

Suspects

Overexposures

Scott's Men

A Biographical Dictionary of Film

Wild Excursions: The Life and Fiction of Laurence Sterne

Hungry as Hunters

A Bowl of Eggs

Movie Man

NICOLE KIDMAN

Birthday Girl

NICOLE
KIDMAN

David Thomson

Alfred A. Knopf   New York   2006

THIS IS A BORZOI BOOK
PUBLISHED BY ALFRED A. KNOPF

www.aaknopf.com

Knopf, Borzoi Books, and the colophon are registered
trademarks of Random House, Inc.

Library of Congress Cataloging-in-Publication Data
Thomson, David, [date]
Nicole Kidman / by David Thomson.—1st ed.
p. cm.
Includes bibliographical references and index.
ISBN 1-4000-4273-9 (alk. paper)
1. Kidman, Nicole, 1967– 2. Motion picture actors and actresses—
Australia—Biography. I. Title.
PN3018.K53T56 2006
791.4302'8092—dc22
[B] 2006045234

Manufactured in the United States of America
First Edition

Photographic Credits
Corbis: 68, 79, 268; Getty Images: 127; The Kobal Collection:
frontispiece, 34, 96, 158, 169, 196

For all the actresses in French cinema

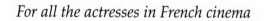

Spotted with tears, licked by flames, hair cropped short, dirty as a street urchin, still she stops crying for one moment to watch pigeons alight on the church cupola. Then she dies.

We have kept one of her tears, which rolled down to us, in a celluloid box. An odorless, tasteless, colorless tear, a drop from the purest spring.

—Luis Buñuel, 1928, on Falconetti in Carl Dreyer's *La Passion de Jeanne d'Arc*

CONTENTS

NICOLE KIDMAN

Strangers

I am talking to an Australian, a woman, about Nicole Kidman, and the crucial mystery is there at the start: "I've known her twenty years, and I've spent a staggering amount of time with her, but I feel I don't know her. Because what she gives you is what you want. A lot of actors are like that. They don't exist when they aren't playing a part."

This book is about acting and about an actress, but it must also study what happens to anyone beholding an actress—the spectator, the audience, or ourselves in any of our voyeur roles. And the most important thing in that vexed transaction is the way the actress and the spectator must remain strangers. That's how the magic works. Without that guarantee, the dangers of "relationship" are grisly and absurd—they range from illicit touching to murder. For there cannot be this pitch of irrational desire without that rigorous apartness, provided by a hundred feet of warm space in a theater, and by that astonishing human invention, the screen, at the movies. And just as the movies were never simply an art or a show, a drama or narrative, but the manifestation of desire, so the screen is both barrier and open sesame.

The thing that permits witness—seeing her, being so intimate—is also the outline of a prison.

This predicament reminds me of a moment in *Citizen Kane*. The reporter, Thompson, goes to visit Bernstein, an old man who was Charlie Kane's right-hand man and who is now chairman of the board of the Kane companies. Thompson asks him if he knows what "Rosebud," Kane's last word, might have referred to. Some girl? wonders Bernstein.

"There were a lot of them back in the early days . . ." Thompson thinks it unlikely that a chance meeting fifty years ago could have prompted a solemn last word. But Bernstein disputes this: "A fellow will remember a lot of things you wouldn't think he'd remember.

"You take me," he says. "One day, back in 1896, I was crossing over to Jersey on the ferry, and as we pulled out, there was another ferry pulling in, and on it there was a girl waiting to get off. A white dress she had on. She was carrying a white parasol. I only saw her for one second. She didn't see me at all, but I'll bet a month hasn't gone by since, that I haven't thought of that girl."

Bernstein seems to be single—to all intents and purposes he was married to Charlie Kane. I daresay some beaverish subtextual critic could argue that the girl in the parasol stands for the sheet of paper on which the young Kane sets out his "Declaration of Principles." Yet the reason why the anecdote (and the actor Everett Sloane's ecstatic yet heartbroken delivery of it) has stayed with me is that it embodies the principle of hopeless desire, and endless hope, on which the movies are founded. Of course, most little boys (even those of an advanced age) feel pressing hormonal urges to satisfy desire. And I would not exile myself from that gang. Still, there is another calling—and film is often its banner—that consists of those who would always protect and preserve desire by ensuring that it is never satisfied. For those of that persuasion—and it is more than merely sexual—there is no art more piquant than the films of Luis Buñuel, one of which is actually entitled *That Obscure Object of Desire*. (In that light, let me alert you not to miss this book's vision of *Belle de Jour* as if Nicole Kidman had played in it. In fact, I have dreamed this film with such intensity that it matters to me more than many films I actually have to see.)

Anyway, the subject of this book is Nicole Kidman. And I should own up straightaway that, yes, I like Nicole Kidman very much. When I tell people that, sometimes they leer and ask, "Do you love her?" And my answer is clear: Yes, of course, I love her—so long as I do not have to meet her.

Now, that proviso could be thought hostile; it might even conjure up possibilities of an aggressive streak, a harsh laugh, or even a regrettable body odor in Ms. Kidman that one would sooner avoid. That's not what

I am talking about, and it's nothing I have ever heard suggested. I suspect she is as fragrant as spring, as ripe as summer, as sad as autumn, and as coldly possessed as winter. Much more to the point, you see, I am suggesting that getting to know actresses is a depressing sport. The history of Hollywood could be composed as a volume of melancholy memoirs all made ruinous when Alfred Hitchcock, say, actually met Tippi Hedren, or whomever. Actors and actresses are seldom marriageable and too little thanks has been offered to the profession for the steadfast way in which its members sacrifice themselves to each other. It is as if they understood the spell put upon them and knew that anyone raised in any other craft or system would collapse with incredulity if confronted by the endless fascination performers only find in themselves. They go to the altar—they do not alter.

Laboring with movies for six decades now, I am coming to the conclusion that this medium has been steadily misunderstood. Yes, it has some semblance of being an entertainment, a business, an art, a storytelling machine—and so on. But all of those semirespectable identities help obscure what is most precious and unique, and what is absolutely formulated by the simultaneous presence and denial on the screen: that a movie is a dream, a sleepwalking, a séance, in which we seem to mingle with ghosts. And here is the vital spark: whenever we seem within reach of these intensely desirable creatures, their states and moods, we ourselves resemble actors as they come close to redeeming their terrible vacancy by assuming parts, or roles.

In other words, acting and being at the movies are mirror images, and they are the persistent, infectious forms of nonbeing that have steadily undermined the thing once known as real life in the last hundred years. So the study of acting is less a record of creative process or artistic eloquence; it is a kind of drug-taking, very bad for us—yet absolutely incurable. I daresay this sounds a touch odd or obscure at first—or maybe it is just alarming—but it will creep up on you as this book proceeds. It is an insidious process, such as ought to be banned everywhere by churches, schools, parents, and the law (all those institutions that claim to be looking after us). On the other hand, it has entered the bloodstream; it goes on and on—and some would say we are hopelessly lost to fantasy already, and so thoroughly immersed in desire that something like real, practical improvement (surely a good thing?) has been befuddled.

And yet there is something enormously positive and creative that can come from it, a mixture of calm and insight. It is to see that we can entertain the idea of strangers in our minds—if only by wanting to be them, or be like them. The movies are about beholding strangers and in the process losing touch with those real people one happens to meet and has the chance of knowing. I believe now that I learned to fall in love by watching actors and actresses, and that is not a wholesome training. It is one that prompts a rapid dissatisfaction with the thing or the person present, or possessed. Their charm can never compete with the allure of the unattainable. Thus, to follow desire is to give up the ghost on relationship. Just as you reflect on that, and consider how far it is a restlessness that has you in its grip, you will remember from so many life lessons that it is also a very bad thing. This is very dangerous territory, even if most of us are already there—in other words, there is still a weird kind of polite respectability that is possible in life from denying it.

Let me tell you a story that helps explain this. In my last book about the movies, *The Whole Equation*, I was feeling my way toward this point of view, and I included a chapter, "By a Nose," which concerned Nicole Kidman in *The Hours*. I offered it as a testament from a fan, a love letter, from someone in the dark to one of those beauties in the light. As a matter of fact, she was not my true favorite. Indeed, I feared in advance—and I still think it likely—that if I were to write about my real favorites, my movie sweethearts, I would be rendered speechless and helpless, because the fantastic intimacy is too great. So, yes, I do like Nicole Kidman, but not quite as much as Catherine Deneuve, Julia Roberts, Grace Kelly, and Donna Reed (I am tracing sweetheartism back to when I was about eleven).

Nevertheless, when Michiko Kakutani reviewed *The Whole Equation* in the *New York Times*, she saw fit to call my "crush" on Kidman ridiculous. (You see how brave authors must be.) Well, maybe, but I am owning up to it, because I think it is the only way to get at things that need to be said (somehow in all the turmoil of desire, I have retained the semblance of some educational purpose). Going to the movies and believing may be foolish, or worse. It may be crazy. But I think even book reviewers have been formed by its risk.

At the moment, as I try to write this, just behind one layer of my computer screen there is an AOL home page in which I have the chance to catch up with the diet secrets of Jessica Simpson and Denise Richards. There are their pictures—lean yet carnal—Jessica and Denise, would-bes who maintain a presence not always in movies, per se, or shows, but in celebrity newsbreaks, in fashion follies, dietary secrets, and scandal scoops. That supporting atmosphere is as old as movies, but it is more intense now just because of the Internet. Moreover, one of the most intriguing things about Nicole Kidman is that at least one of her ample size ten feet is firmly planted in that electronic wasteland. Nicole can be great and serious. She is an Oscar winner. Sometimes you can believe she might play any part. But she is also heart-and-soul a sexual celebrity, someone who, close to forty, is not just ready or eager but proud to give her sexy come-hither look to some magazine. Her appetite for life is not snobbish, or elitist, not ready to act her age. I mean, we do not see Vanessa Redgrave or Meryl Streep or Miranda Richardson (her colleagues as actors) in glamour pictures, not these days. Yet on the Internet you can get a lubricious roundup of every nude or seminude scene Nicole has ever done. You may know the curve of her bottom as well as you know your child's brow. Nicole does expensive perfume ads; she does eye-candy covers; she will drop her clothes if only to air out that elegant Australian body (she does wish she were a few inches shorter, with those inches added on her breasts—but there you are, she is very human). That's another reason why the world, for just a few years, has been crazy about her. How can I put it? Let's just say she has not flinched from the duty of a great celebrity to be on public display. There are thousands of hits on her every day, not real hits, blows to the body, but the hits of our day, the fantasy contacts, the "I want to know more about Nicole" pressures on the mouse.

I daresay that as she grows older she will become weathered, a great lined old lady like Katharine Hepburn, a mistress of the art of acting and of the cult of her own high-mindedness. But this book was conceived and composed while she was still *hot* and hittable, and likely to be in every tabloid and on every magazine cover because the rumor industry—our essential river of story—could not leave her alone. Even if she becomes that great old lady, Dame Nicole Kidman, in those greedy eyes of hers the hunger will persist for the good old days when she was in everyone's virtual bed. Millions more have had that palpable illusion help them make it through the night.

But note this, please. She is, as I write, in addition to everything else, a fun-loving thirty-nine-year-old with a cheerful eighteen-year-old's attitude. I mean, she has not grown up or old—she has been kept young by attention. She would like to go skiing; and for a moment at least she might like to go with you! One of the more hideous things about what happens to actresses and celebrities is that, somewhere around forty, the tissue-paper safety net dissolves and the star suddenly has to go from being a nymph to being an adult. Nicole's own name is already part of that terrible future, and I daresay she wakes up some nights screaming because she felt it was about to happen. (Not that I can be there to witness it—or stop imagining it.)

But just because of that vulnerability, it would be improper or cruel for a biography to grind too remorselessly close or fine. Let her live while she can. Why pretend to be censorious over every fleeting love affair, or any toke she might take? Let time take its course. Let her awkward teenage years off lightly, and know that, as with all actors and actresses, the idea of the real life is, anyway, the ultimate tragedy, the terminal desolation. They are too busy being the center of attention to have a life. So, I will be gentle and tender on passing over some things. If I elect to say little about the movie *Far and Away*, for instance, then understand that there are films made for no other reason than that the people involved were in love. It is their business. Sometimes it ends up looking like *Pierrot le Fou* or an Ingmar Bergman picture. Sometimes it's *Far and Away*—enough said. It is so very much more interesting to explore films not actually made, such as Nicole Kidman as Belle de Jour or Nicole Kidman in *Rebecca*. In a way, the best admiration we can give her is to imagine other parts she might play. That is adding to her creative soul.

One final word. You will want to know, "Did I talk to her?," no matter how ardently I have stressed the point about staying strangers. Well, at the very outset, I approached her through her representatives, asking for an interview. There was silence, and then there was a Well, yes, she is interested. But she was so busy . . . and time passed. So I began to write the book, and I had an entire draft done before hearing a word from her. What happened? Well, what do you think happened? One day in February 2006, my phone rang and I heard, "It's Nicole," as if she were a languid, superior, but amused prefect who had called a naughty boy to her study to see what he had been up to.

I think it's true: she tries to be what you want her to be.

Just Like Us: Not Like Us

I f pushed to the wall, would you sooner say "My wife is a very good actress" or "My wife is a rather poor actress"? If the case fits, please substitute "husband." We are talking about spouses, but deep down, these days, I can't get over the feeling that all these words—"wife," "husband," "spouse"—are out of order. Perhaps what I really mean is "lover," or "desired one." Many of us, particularly in middle age, are shy about saying those young words out loud. "Companion" comes up more and more these days, proud of its own correctness. But if you've ever reached out in the middle of the night to be sure that he or she, or anyone, was there, then "companion" doesn't seem adequate or accurate.

But consider "actress" a little more. You are going to tell me that in all your life you've never actually met or spoken to an "actress," a profes-sional—apart from the giggling girls in that school play. And it is in the nature of things, and something taken for granted that you, or I, never met Carole Lombard, Jean Harlow, Katharine Hepburn, Marilyn Mon-roe, Tuesday Weld, or Nicole Kidman. They seem profoundly un-meetable, because they are protected, and because they don't have time or boredom enough for commoners; because they don't quite see us. For most of us, I think, that unlikelihood is necessary: it's easier to entertain our desirous dreams without any risk of contact. In a way that's what the movies are all about, with the actor and actress like a parent, knowing the children are watching behind the dark curtain, but pretending not to notice. Because voyeurs hate to be identified. Their secret is their rapture.

By the way, I misled you a little in the last paragraph. I did meet Katharine Hepburn. I went to see her at her Manhattan house one day in the late eighties, to talk about David Selznick, the producer, the man who brought Hepburn to Hollywood in the first place. I suppose we got on, or she trusted me enough, because after an hour, she announced (this was her normal way of speaking), "Well, I think you should see Laura."

She meant Laura Harding, Hepburn's companion on that first train journey to California in 1932 and her long-term friend. The reason I needed to see Laura was because she and David Selznick had had a romance, which was not a well-known thing.

Whereupon Ms. Hepburn put in a call for her car and her driver, Jimmy, so that within a short space of time, and with a plastic tub of Hepburn's borscht, the three of us were en route to see Laura Harding in rural New Jersey, an hour away. By then, Ms. Hepburn and I were chatting about anything and everything, just like friends. She was kind, funny, direct, and very likable. She was full of her vivid character. I felt drab and fake beside her.

As you come out of the Lincoln Tunnel on the Jersey side of the Hudson River, there is an amazing array of highway intersections. And it was there that our car blew a tire. Jimmy was as calm as could be. He pulled over onto the shoulder, asked us to get out and sit on the curb, and began to change the tire.

Thus, one of my best chats with Katharine Hepburn was in the unlikely position of sitting side by side on the low curb, shouting to be heard in the roar and slipstream of hundreds of passing trucks. It was not long before some of these trucks started honking their horns as they passed. I thought at first that they were marveling at two idiots sitting so close to death. But that was not it. For Kate waved gaily back, and in truth she was being recognized and hailed. (Maybe the tire always blew at that spot?) You have to remember that Katharine Hepburn at this time, before she elected to sit looking at the wall, was still active and probably the most beloved woman in America.

And as the unlikely cavalcade passed by, she said to me, "They love me. I don't know why." She was radiant, sublime, transcendent, and it was plain that the "they" meant more than the truck drivers. It meant all of the rest of us. It included me. And I would not have argued one bit, just as I will always treasure my day with Kate and the very ordinary things like sitting on the curb and thinking to bring a tub of borscht for lunch. She was so normal—and Katharine Hepburn always took pride in that, in never putting on airs or letting her fame go to her head. At the same time, she was utterly extraordinary, because—without bothering with a script or learning lines—she treated everyone like an audience. It was her way of loving us.

Katharine Hepburn is the name Nicole Kidman often invokes as her idol or her model. She might have played her in Scorsese's *The Aviator* but for scheduling problems. It's easy to see how any actress might aspire to a working career that covered six decades, that never lost touch with the theater, that collected four Oscars, that is famous for a romantic involvement with Spencer Tracy marked by loyalty, sympathy, and support, and that made her so widely loved. And Kidman has a rich, muscular, "ordinary" side to her. She does not hide that Australian accent. She can come on very glamorous and then collapse in giggles—like the girl next door who was just trying on a famous older sister's gown. She cried at winning her Oscar, and turned away from us and the cameras. It was normal and human and touching. It seemed very real. But a stealth comes upon the real woman who is an actress who wonders whether she is acting naturally or acting, naturally. Before the age of forty, however much she might have tried to resist it, Nicole Kidman had some understanding of the nearly tidal force that makes her an idea in the sky, a real person over whom the most outlandish and ridiculous rumors gather, as if somehow an actress cannot help but be colored by the roles she has played. Or is it by that willingness, that need, that demand, that helpless calling, to be someone else? Being someone else is not what we are expected to find ordinary. Is it?

So ask yourself again: Would you rather be married to a good actress or a bad actress? Or, to put it in a slightly different way, a good liar or a bad liar? I know, those people who groan and sigh and blame themselves for being bad liars, they are the endearing ones, the ones you're more inclined to trust. Whereas the good liars are so smooth, so cool, so perfect, you never notice the lie until years later, perhaps . . . when the whole thing comes apart. There you are, it's an intriguing question, and one at the heart of many great works of art: Would you rather be married to someone who tells you the truth, or who lies kindly to you? Finding an answer can easily outlast your life. And maybe the dilemma is a little more pointed after a hundred years in which one of our formative influences—at the movies and on television—has been watching people act.

You'd have to assume that, as a species, we enjoy that pastime. I mean, a lot of us have spent four or five hours a day doing it most of our lives. Apart from being awake or being asleep, there aren't many things that so occupy us.

Now, I know, sometimes people are startled by this suggestion. Good Lord, they say, that doesn't have any real effect—it's not that we've become more like actors and actresses. I never argue, it's not worth the time. I just wait a moment or two until they say or do something for effect, as if they were playing themselves. Just watch yourself, and think about the subtle ways in which we know we are being watched, that we are in a play, that we too can get over awkward spots in life by putting on an act. You still don't believe it? All right, read on.

I misled you twice in that earlier paragraph. I met Tuesday Weld, too, and that was far more dangerous than sitting on a curb beside Katharine Hepburn as the eighteen-wheelers hurtled past. This was in 1983, when the San Francisco International Film Festival gave a tribute to Ms. Weld. I was forty-two then and she was thirty-eight: immediately that's a lot more dangerous, I suppose. And my wife was out of town.

Well, the tribute was in the hands of Leonard Michaels, a resident of Berkeley then, and a marvelous writer. Without ever having met Tuesday, Lenny adored her and admired her, so the Festival invited him to choose a program of clips from her career and to interview her on stage at the Castro Theater one Saturday afternoon. I was there, though I had not been involved in choosing the clips. I was there because I thought then, and think now, that Tuesday Weld was one of the great American actresses. Lord knows where she'd be in our esteem if she had called herself Susan Weld, her actual name.

The tribute did not go well. For reasons I never understood, Lenny had chosen nothing from *Pretty Poison* or *Play It As It Lays* or *The Cincinnati Kid*. There was a small but vociferous band of Tuesday fans in the front rows who became annoyed and vocal at these omissions. And Lenny had not interviewed a movie star in public before. Anyone who has been in that business will know what I mean. Movie stars like to be regular—they often yearn to be—but they are not. Tuesday Weld was plainly very nervous, yet more than that. I don't know her well enough to judge, but I suspect that once nervous or unsettled she can become very defensive. The failure of the interview owed a good deal to her mounting edginess, even if it might have been allayed at the outset. That and the rather modest-sized audience hurt her. It was plain that in the minds of the San Francisco filmgoing public, there lingered some doubt as to whether Tuesday Weld deserved a tribute.

Shortly after the interview, I received a phone call from the people who were doing their best to look after Ms. Weld. She was distraught; she knew it had gone badly; she needed reassurance. Was I available? I think that I was being asked this because Ms. Weld had seen the program note I had written, and liked it. I said that I was already invited to the dinner to be held that evening, at Prego on Union Street.

I arrived early as asked, and became Tuesday Weld's companion for that evening. Yes, I am using that word ironically, and out of difficulty. She was tense. Her hand was very cold. I know that because she insisted that I hold her hand. It did warm eventually. She fixed on me, and we talked. She was beautiful and smart, and she was a frightened woman gradually relaxing, or she was a woman (also frightened) putting on that performance. I did not bother to determine which, and I did not know the way to do so even if I had had the determination. People from the Festival occasionally whispered to me their appreciation of my "rescue" act, but no one gave any indication of guessing that I might, sooner or later, be in need of rescue myself.

For our conversation became warmer and more personal. We went from my showing an awareness and admiration of her career to her asking me my sign. I do not offer that with any attempt to be funny. A lot of Hollywood people, I have found, take signs very seriously. And I have found myself that if I am ever talking to a beautiful smart woman I take whatever she says seriously. It is natural, and one hopes to behave naturally in those circumstances.

Now, this is a book about one actress and about being an actress and a star; but, inevitably, it is also a book about our response to those things. For most actresses and all stars depend upon at least the notion that they are "reaching" all of us. Of course, that is no longer as true as it was: so many more people went to the movies in the twenties, thirties, and forties than do so now. Still, there are other ways in which the audience is touched: at home, by VHS and DVD (put like that, the technologies could be infectious diseases), by television "journalism," and by the steady way in which the media trust that we are obsessed with stars.

In fact, I think we are tricky, devious, and fickle. Yes, we like stars. In the last few years, at least, we have hurried off to see and be smitten by Michelle Pfeiffer, Meg Ryan, Julia Roberts, Elisabeth Shue, Nicole Kidman, Gwyneth Paltrow, Reese Witherspoon, Jennifer Lopez, Halle Berry, and so on. There are so many of them, and so many more who want to be in their places and who might do anything to be in their places. What does anything mean? Well, let's just say intense hoping and wishing and desiring.

But wait a minute. There are a couple of names in that list of stars who are already not quite as "alive" or as "fresh" as others. I admit, this is a delicate thing to talk about, for just as it is easy to celebrate success so it is edging toward bad taste to discuss its opposite—the thing called failure. But I need to be frank. Meg Ryan is no longer what she was.

Meg Ryan is nearly forty-three as I write, and I've heard a few people in the dark of theaters murmur that she looks it. Not that forty-three is the end of the world. But the movies are a street where young flesh is taken for granted: cellulite, varicose veins, double chins, wrinkles, narrowing eyes, hair losing its first color—all these are ordinary, normal things. But the audience does not approve of them. It likes perfect bodies, with breasts like young plums, and legs that are as shapely as the haunches of a Boxer dog. You can deplore this—as many women do—

but you should also recognize that you are part of the audience that has maintained for decades the pressing demand for the sexiest young flesh, with the most knowing smile, that Hollywood can find.

Meg Ryan was once the kid next door—and Meg Ryan plays an interesting part in the Nicole Kidman story. She had big popular hits (with Tom Hanks). She was liked. But then, as she grew older, her marriage to Dennis Quaid ended. Then there was the affair she had with Russell Crowe during *Proof of Life*. It's not exactly that the public blamed Meg, but I think she came out of the event poorly. And this coincided with a stage of aging where her looks suffered. She made several flops in which the camera was notably soft-focused. Then she made *In the Cut*, a property once bought for the movies by Nicole Kidman and at least considered by Nicole as a film she might act in herself. Meg Ryan let herself look older for the film and she was bravely naked in uncommonly unglamorous conditions. The film was a disaster. It might have even marked the end of Ms. Ryan's undoubted stardom or her image as "the girl next door," the orgasm we'd all like to share. (Acted orgasms are so much more emphatic.)

And this is not minor. For just as the young flesh comes, so it goes. And the audience that once loved to think of going to bed with X or Y, blithely consigns the same women to the scrap heap. The street has always resembled the trade of prostitution, and women are given no sentimental quarter there. They look the part, they play the game. Or they are yesterday. Elisabeth Shue is even more out of place than Meg Ryan in that list above. Shue, you could argue, was as beautiful as Ryan, or Pfeiffer or Kidman. And in *Leaving Las Vegas* she gave a magnificent performance. Still, her career didn't take. Just as she had made a lot of inconsequential films before *Leaving Las Vegas* (for which she was Oscar-nominated), so a lot more followed. Why? Well, she passed forty recently, and I suspect she had a weight problem that was difficult to control. Did she prefer to put more of herself into being a wife and a mother? Did she have poor advice or poor judgment? Did she not want "it" badly enough?

All of these matters are ways of defining Nicole Kidman, who will be forty in June 2007, who knows that the public that is crazy for her can turn cold the next minute, and who has all the same problems of deciding about advice, judgment, choice, and need. The race among actresses is very crowded and not entirely principled. So many are so very beautiful. So many can move you on screen—Meg Ryan's finest work by far is *In the Cut*. So advice and choice may be crucial. But the process I am outlining puts the ultimate stress on the very thing that— briefly, or whatever—ties us to one actress and not another: desire or need. And great need to act is not ordinary, even if great acting is the power to let us feel we're just like that.

Australian

Once upon a time the British assumed they had discovered Australia, so they assessed its great mass of intractable desert and its scattering of primitive native peoples and came to the conclusion that the place was fit for nothing but a penal colony. This is the kind of enormous, casual error that drives history forward.

Australia was so far from the rest of the world at the time of its discovery—the 1770s—that only the Arctic and the Antarctic were more distant. The general name for Australia and New Zealand in the mother country is "the antipodes," which means literally "the lands directly opposite," a phrase that speaks to emotional kinship or its absence as much as to spatial adjacency. The more common term used to describe the antipodes in Britain is still "down under." That's how British kids cherish the idea of digging a hole that might come out in Australia. But it's also a way in which the British think the worse of Australians—"down under" has a splendid air of moral superiority that hardly begins to realize that the British Isles are also "down under" Australasia. But this is in keeping with the understanding that Australia was first inhabited by convicts, their guards, and their whores. Having been raised in Britain, I know that there are three national types most thoroughly mocked or despised in Britain: the French, the Irish, and the Australians. And it is therefore appropriate that so many early Australians were of Irish descent.

This scorn is a great blessing to Australians in that it provides them with hostility, lack of sympathy, and the secure assumption of inferiority, things invariably associated with the development of high character and great work. This is a book about one Australian who was not prepared to be simply "down under." That way of describing Nicole Kidman gives ample warning that the ingenue was tall, strong, opinionated, determined, and talented. Far from a waif or a novice grateful to be taken on by an American star, she was ambition looking for an opening. No one should be surprised that she turned out smarter, stronger, and more interesting than American stars. Australians thrive on being patronized, even if that experience sometimes accounts for their rude vigor.

If there is a geographical and historical comparison to be made with Australia, it is California. With reasonable merit, California now considers itself one of the centers of the world: it has an immense, thriving economy; for a hundred years it has been the place that taught America and then the world to gaze at screens—first the movies, then computers; and in Los Angeles and San Francisco it has two unquestionably great and desirable cities. California is also the vegetable and fruit garden for America, and it is a state where wave upon wave of immigrants have taken root: not just Americans from the Midwest and the East, but Mexicans and other Hispanics, plus all the races of Asia. California has a very mixed racial composition, and modest racial harmony. Hispanics will soon have a majority in the state, and if blacks remain a dissatisfied minority, still there have been black mayors of both major cities (Tom Bradley and Willie Brown). As an anthology of landscapes, California equals all of America: it has a superb coastline, with many golden beaches that are empty; it has arable pasture, forest, rolling hills, and mountains as big as the mainland of the United States commands; it has great deserts, rivers, and lakes. What that meant, once upon a time, was that in California, Hollywood filmmakers could find every type of locale their scripts required.

But in 1770, say, California was not very much. Its cities were missions in the wilderness. The beauties of the country were largely unknown. And in southern California, especially, any explorer might have concluded that the prospects for settlement, let alone a new city, were restricted by the surrounding desert and by the difficulties in bringing adequate water to the coast. But Australia's desert looms over that of California.

California is a state of about 160,000 square miles, with desert, arid regions, or bare mountains occupying maybe half that area. Australia is and was almost 3 million square miles, of which two-thirds is uninhabitable. In other words, the size of the desert in Australia is more than ten times the size of all of California (and America is only 3.6 million square miles). Even the emotional power of space is greater in Australia. To this day, the cities of Australia are on the coast. The rare exception, Alice Springs, close to the center of the country, still has a population of only 30,000.

Australia was so unpromising, or so marked by penal colony status, that it grew far less quickly than California. The first Kidmans arrived there in 1839—by Australian standards, they were pioneers. Nicole looked back on the history and noticed above all "the guts" it must have required to make that voyage and to seek a new life in so strange and ungentle a land; guts or fierceness, or the urge to be different and dangerous. Australia grew slowly throughout the nineteenth century and was still largely dependent on immigrants from the British Isles. The attitude of the new colony was never as open as that of America or California. Nor was it as welcoming of people of different tongues or colors.

By 1900 the population of Australia was still only 3.8 million, no matter that there had been discoveries of gold and other minerals, and despite the evidence that the southeastern coastal strip, at least, was arable and ideal for cattle farming. Life in that area looked very much like the life in California—that's why the various films about Ned Kelly look like Westerns, as do those stirring Australian movies of the forties starring Chips Rafferty (maybe the first Australian film star), like *The Overlanders* and *Eureka Stockade*.

The two world wars had a profound impact on Australia. Australian regiments were formed and shipped overseas to fight the Germans in Flanders and North Africa and to protect Southeast Asia. That was a lesson to Australians that they had not escaped the European theater of dominance, and it was also a painful reminder that they could still be

called to die under British orders. It was not that Australia generally dis-
approved of either war—though there was a left-wing element that
wanted to put Australian interests first. After all, in the Second World
War, Australian ports in the north were bombed by Japanese planes.
The Torres Strait, separating the Cape York Peninsula from New
Guinea, is only a hundred miles wide. As this book is published, Nicole
will likely be making a film about northern Australia as war broke out.
Immediately after Pearl Harbor, and for some time, Australia felt threat-
ened by invasion—though whether that step actually appealed to Japan
is another matter. More to the point, many Australian servicemen were
captured in the fall of Singapore and Malaya. Many suffered and died in
Japanese prisoner-of-war camps, and many Australians were resentful
of the pomp and idiocy of the British officer class that might have con-
tributed to their capture. The two allies were not always friendly, and in
the years after 1945 and well into the 1950s books by Australians
expressed bitterness about the war and the burden of having been led
by "pommy bastards."

You may reckon, if you are American, that the animosity was rather
fabricated. Not so. I was seven, in London, and beginning to take serious notice of cricket when the first postwar tour by an Australian cricket
team occurred in 1948. There was history to this, of course. Since the
1870s, England v. Australia has been the most anguished highlight of
the cricketing calendar. And ever since 1882, that series had determined
the keeper of "the Ashes," a crude cup said to contain the ashes of a
burned cricket stump, the ashes of dismay and despair when Australia
beat England in a series.

Then, in 1932–33, that rivalry had become worse than bitter when
England toured Australia spearheaded by two fast bowlers—Bill Voce
(quick) and Harold Larwood (bloody fast and frightening). Cricket was
then a game in which a hard ball was bowled at a batsman at a speed
close to one hundred miles per hour, the batsman having pads on his
legs, gloves, a box for his groin, and no other protection. Under their
captain Douglas Jardine, the English team had Voce and Larwood bowl
short-pitched "bodyline" deliveries, more likely to hit the batsman than
his stumps. It was intimidation, and it worked. Australian batsmen
were struck and injured, including the world's master, Don Bradman,

the greatest batsman ever. England won the series 4–1, but they picked up Australian hatred along the way and there were diplomatic protests over the way the games had been played.

In 1948, still captained by Bradman, the Australians came to England with a great team that included two very fast bowlers—Ray Lindwall and Keith Miller—as well as a host of other fine players, and they took the series 4–0 against a good English team.

What has this got to do with Nicole Kidman? Well, in her youth, Bradman, Miller, and Lindwall were still alive and enormously honored in a game which Nicole played and took seriously. Furthermore, the Australian strength at cricket (it still goes on) was being underlined by their domination of tennis and swimming. By 1950, Wimbledon and other tennis tournaments began to succumb to Australian players—a long line of them: John Bromwich, Frank Sedgeman, Ken McGregor, Mervyn Rose, Mal Anderson, Ashley Cooper, the sensational kids, Ken Rosewall and Lew Hoad, Rod Laver, Roy Emerson, Fred Stolle, John Newcombe, Tony Roche. And by now, we are talking of players who were heroes during Nicole Kidman's childhood. Further, they had by then been joined by a line of women players that included Margaret Smith (taller even than Nicole) and Evonne Goolagong (that rare aborigine), who often challenged American command of tennis.

In Britain, a country that takes tennis very seriously, and which still had some lady champions in those years, there was an aggrieved air of the unfairness of it all—with all its sunshine, didn't Australia have an improper advantage at encouraging young cricketers, tennis players, and swimmers? Of course they swim, they live on the beaches, sighed the English, as people like Dawn Fraser began to win so many Olympic medals. There were other advances—at rugby, in track—as a country that still had under 15 million people in 1980 began to be noticed. Nicole Kidman was thirteen in 1980, and noticing. She was not an athlete, but not for want of trying. What's more, the same emergence of Australians was occurring in the arts and entertainment. By the 1950s it was clear that Australia had a great novelist, Patrick White—he would win the Nobel Prize in 1973 for books like *The Tree of Man* (1955), *Voss* (1957), and *Riders in the Chariot* (1961). White had actually been born in London, but Christina Stead was a native Australian. Sidney Nolan was hailed as Australia's first great painter. There was even an Australian play, *Summer of the Seventeenth Doll*, that flourished in London's West End. The great soprano Joan Sutherland was Australian. So was Olivia Newton-John. She had been born in Britain but she went to Australia and had her first great hit as Sandy in the movie of *Grease* in 1978, when Nicole Kidman was eleven.

Such novelties were another source of British patronage, of course; it was humbling to get a famous first at such staples of world culture. And the awards often sailed in the face of many eminent strivers in the past. But, again, these signs indicated the awakening of Australia. In London, by the sixties, an array of Australian talents were visible in entertainment: Rolf Harris on television, playing all those bizarre aboriginal instruments; Barry Humphries was introducing Dame Edna Everidge; writers like Germaine Greer and Clive James were becoming known.

And then there was acting and the movies. These days, not many people recollect that Errol Flynn was Australian—born actually in Tasmania, but as able to be Robin Hood as Custer or boxer Jim Corbett. From the age of ten, Peter Finch had been raised in Australia. Laurence Olivier discovered him there in the fifties. Thereafter, Finch moved with great speed from playing Aussies (in *A Town Like Alice*) to doing Oscar Wilde, English gentlemen, and full-blooded Americans—like newscaster Howard Beale, in *Network*, for which Finch won an Oscar in 1977.

Then, suddenly, a new wave of movies began to be made in Australia in the late 1970s. Bruce Beresford made *Don's Party* (1976) and *Breaker Morant* (1979); Peter Weir offered *Picnic at Hanging Rock* (1975), *The Last Wave* (1977), and *Gallipoli* (1981); Gillian Armstrong delivered *My Brilliant Career* (1979); George Miller made *Mad Max* (1979). In time, those directors and others like New Zealander Jane Campion would go away, to America. But in the space of a few years, Australian material had been identified, along with young actors like Mel Gibson (born in America but raised in Australia), Judy Davis, Sam Neill (from New Zealand), Jack Thompson, Bryan Brown, and Wendy Hughes.

Those names represent the first generation of new Australian actors, and Mel Gibson was plainly their one star and figurehead. Judy Davis is a great actress, but she never quite looked like a movie star. Nicole Kidman is the first Australian star actress, but she is herself the leader of a group or a generation that includes Cate Blanchett, Geoffrey Rush, Russell Crowe, Hugh Jackman, Eric Bana, Naomi Watts, Toni Collette, Heath Ledger, and how many others at a time when two of the most remarkable young directors in the world are Australian Baz Luhrmann and New Zealander Peter Jackson? Nor is it just that that group of actors has the confidence to play the world's heroes; they scoop up Oscars at the same time.

It is a vital point to see Nicole Kidman as part of this history and a very proud Australian, if only because it acknowledges a confidence, an ambition, and even an innocence that are no longer common in America.

Growing Up

S omeone the age of Nicole Kidman faces these prospects in life: she will be ten when *Star Wars, Saturday Night Fever,* and *Grease* open. She will come of age as Debra Winger, Meryl Streep, and Jessica Lange are the exciting women in film. She begins to think for herself in the short interval between the end of the Vietnam War and the coming of AIDS. She is precocious, pretty, and talented way beyond her local norms, and she begins her life as an actress while still in high school. She does not graduate from high school, which might have upset her academically inclined parents. Instead, that omission seems to carry their blessing. She comes of age when a lot of kids in the smart world go wrong, but she is in charge of herself. Her parents trust her—or they guess that there is probably not much point in standing in her way. Once the awkwardness of early teenage life has fallen away—and it has quite a distance to fall—there is a common sense and a drive in Nicole Kidman that bode well. (Though "drive" is not the word onlookers use. They speak of an ambition to match her father's wish, that she become the most beautiful and radiant actress who has ever lived.) Yes, *Flirting* is her last Australian film, or the last work of her youth, and in it she has surely grasped the sexual power she has in the world, but she is a wholesome flirt, and businesslike with it.

She is the first daughter and eldest child of Antony and Janelle Kidman, who married in December 1963—less than a month after the assassination of John Kennedy. Antony is descended from a long line of Australians. His grandfather Sir Sidney Kidman (who died in 1935) was a farmer's son who had arrived in Australia and become a significant landowner and stock farmer. Janelle Stuart had Scottish blood and her family had been in Australia only a few years. The young couple were in their mid-twenties when they married.

Not long afterward, they moved to Honolulu, where Antony was studying for his Ph.D. on a medical research scholarship at the University of Hawaii. Janelle had taken a job teaching nursing. Because they were living in the United States, the child born on June 20, 1967— Nicole Mary Kidman—could claim both American and Australian citizenship. She remembers being on her father's shoulders in holiday parades, waving two flags—the Australian and the American—and singing "Waltzing Matilda" and "I Wish I Was in Dixie."

Not that there was necessarily a pro-American sentiment in the Kidman household. By the time of Nicole's birth there were nearly half a million U.S. troops in Vietnam (and some Australians); the Kidmans were left-wing in their attitudes and gloomy about the foreign involvement.

Not long after Nicole's birth, the family moved to Washington, D.C., where Antony's work in biochemistry was carried on under a grant from the National Institutes of Health. Another daughter, Antonia, was born in Washington, and in 1971 the four Kidmans returned to Australia. All that Nicole would remember of D.C. was the winter cold, the occasional presence of snow, and the tumult of her parents being caught up in antiwar protests. "My mother would treat us as little adults," she told *Vanity Fair* in 2002. "We would discuss things. I was raised to think and to question. She wanted girls who were educated, aware of everything, and opinionated. So did my father. They wanted us to be sure of being able to speak out."

In Australia, they lived in the North Shore area outside Sydney, upper-class suburbia, with great views of the hills and the harbor as well as ample space for the family. It's a place where families organize their lives around their children's future—the school, the sports, the music and drama. Nicole was spoiled, but it was more than that: she was given every expectation of glory waiting for her.

Dr. Antony Kidman would establish the Health Psychology Unit at the Royal North Shore Hospital; that became the base for his expanding career as doctor, researcher, and writer. He was interested in the links between physical illness and state of mind, and in time he would be the author of several quite successful self-help books written for lay readers—*From Thought to Action; Managing Love and Hate; Tactics for Change*. As a nurse, Janelle joined her husband in creating a home that was clearly founded on the idea that intelligence, learning, and well-directed help could improve life for everyone. Dr. Kidman was not entirely orthodox or simply an academic, and it's worth pointing out that his positive view of health—that mind could surely assist matter—was not too far from the Scientology ideas that would inspire Tom Cruise.

Nicole remembers: "I was writing as a child. I couldn't understand why my mind was so dark. I had a strange relationship with death. I was captivated by the idea. I kept diaries, a journal. Oh, no one can read that stuff! I put curses on the covers of the books to scare people away. I burned most of them just before I got married. I'm very open to mystery. I like not understanding myself. People presume that's being sad—but I'm interested in our flaws. I believe we're all in the same struggle. I think my darkness came from the capacity to love. I felt I had too much love to give. I was struck by the desire to live and then the fear of it all being taken away. It's so precarious and vulnerable and dangerous. So I believe in the chance to be kind to people."

Nor can one underestimate the influence of this secure family background. Later on in life, Nicole would lament a certain stodginess in their lives: being fixed in Sydney, and going to just the same two schools all her life. A time came when she broke away—and it was a dramatic shift, going off to Amsterdam at the age of seventeen with a much older man. No one had much doubt in advance or in hindsight that Nicole would be getting a lot of sex, an exposure to drugs, and a general need to grow up fast there—and in taking the trip she had to drop out of high school. But her parents let her go, not without worry, but in the belief that they had raised her decently and that a part of that process was her having the right to decide. She survived, and was probably a lot wiser and smarter for it—as well as someone who had seen Rembrandt's great works in person.

Nicole had been sent to good schools—the Lane Cove Primary

School and then the North Sydney Girls' High School, a very "English" and expensive school, where the girls wore tartan blazers, white shirts, and navy skirts. And by the time she was thirteen, that left a lot of leg showing on Nicole, for she was already five feet nine inches. This was not becoming, at least not in her own eyes. The abnormal height was only part of her embarrassment. Nicole had profuse curling red hair that would not lie down or go straight. As a teenager, she was always trying out ways to control it and failing. And she was not happy. Worse still, her very pale, freckled skin reacted badly to sunbathing, so that the natural Australian location, the beach, was always difficult for her.

As a student, she was acceptable without being outstanding. Still, we know from her later life that she read *Mrs. Dalloway* (without enthusiasm) and *The Portrait of a Lady* (without really understanding it). But she liked *Crime and Punishment, Wuthering Heights,* and *Middlemarch,* and she had begun to keep diaries and notebooks of her own writings. Such things are not uncommon in imaginative teenagers, but the habits seem to have lasted and several people close to her have expressed the thought that one day Nicole Kidman will write something substantial. More than that, as a very young teenager she had played Blanche Du Bois in a school production of Tennessee Williams's *A Streetcar Named Desire.*

Did the school encourage her to "understand" that play? Who knows? It shows an adventurous school, and raises an intriguing possibility: Nicole Kidman is coming to a time of life when she might try Blanche again. That play still challenges audiences and actresses alike. In recent years, it has been tried, with mixed results, by Jessica Lange and Natasha Richardson, and in 1984, not long after Nicole's first shot at it, the role was performed on television by Ann-Margret, one of those icons on Nicole's imaginative horizon—and one of the stars she likes to imitate in photo shoots. But when she played the part, Nicole saw the movie and was deeply impressed by Marlon Brando—just as she was by James Dean in *Rebel Without a Cause.* Of course, there were actresses she loved, too: Katharine Hepburn, Ava Gardner, Ingrid Bergman, Vanessa Redgrave, Meryl Streep. But it's as true of Nicole as it is of many modern actresses that they have fed upon great male acting as well as performers of their own sex.

Playacting was clearly Nicole's forte well before she got to high school. She did nativity plays, and by the age of ten she was a weekend regular at the Phillips Street Theater in Sydney. This is the training ground that really formed her and led to work at an early age, and it was on a schedule carried out in addition to her regular schoolwork. Moreover, it was an education that allowed her to bypass the more obvious route for an aspiring actress in Sydney—NIDA, the National Institute of Dramatic Art, the school that has turned out so many Australian performers, not least Judy Davis, who would have been the famous young actress that a Nicole might look up to.

Born in Perth, and twelve years older than Nicole, Davis could never match Nicole's looks. But she was a sensation in Australia as a young stage actress, and her work at NIDA included *Miss Julie, Hedda Gabler,* and *Mother Courage,* which led to a film career that took off in 1979 with *My Brilliant Career.* Davis (fifty in 2005) still has a movie career, and I don't doubt but that she would be brilliant onstage again. But she has never quite made it as a star or outside Australia. So it's all the more worth stressing that Nicole's burgeoning career as a TV and film actress was what persuaded many people that NIDA for her would have been a waste of time. After all, by the age of twenty-five she had made it in so many other ways—and had incidentally courted the idea that she was very ambitious and not quite intent on acting for its own sake.

For instance, it was in theater, rather than at the beach, that Nicole began to find common ground with boys. This is not really surprising, but it is often omitted from books like this: that performers and audiences alike may have been helped to experience or think about sexual encounters by their involvement in plays—or play. For Nicole, a production of Frank Wedekind's *Spring Awakening* at the Phillips Street Theater was her first sight of young male nudity. And just as Nicole admitted to being very uneasy with her teenage self, so she remarked on the liberation of pretending to be people just a little more sophisticated or daring. The constant sexual edge in her acting—call it flirtation, if you will—is her way of understanding so much. By the age of eighteen, she was no longer a girl called "Stalky," but a very commanding young woman.

And so she was noticed. When Nicole was thirteen a young New

Zealand director, Jane Campion, was looking to make a short film, *A Girl's Own Story* (her graduation project at the Australian Film and Television School). She auditioned Nicole, loved her ability "for making things seem immediate and real," and wanted to cast her. But the headmistress at the high school refused to let Nicole have the time off. Still, Campion sent Nicole a note: "I hope one day we will work together. Be careful what you do, because you have real potential."

At about the same time, the director John Duigan noticed her at Phillips Street and asked her to make a screen test. "She was remarkably poised and very smart," he recalled. "She got to the kernel of things without pussyfooting around." In time, Duigan would cast her as the head prefect, Nicola Radcliffe, who helps two young lovers (Noah Taylor and Thandie Newton) in his film *Flirting*. That was done in 1989, and released after *Dead Calm*, but it shows a very polished and smooth-haired blonde in Nicole, as classy and composed as a young Grace Kelly.

By then, Nicole Kidman had an astonishing body of teenage work, suggesting that she spent at least as much time with her agent, June Cann, as with her schoolteachers. In 1983 she did a TV movie for children, *Bush Christmas*, directed by Henri Safran, about three kids who recover a stolen race horse. The same year, she did *BMX Bandits*, in which she is a teenage biker up against adult bank robbers. This material clearly resembles the cheerful, good-natured, and very high-minded feature films that run on the Disney Channel and which often star Hilary Duff. But don't expect to see Ms. Duff in *Mrs. Dalloway*. What Kidman was doing, I think, was work for real in the only way she found available.

She had eighteen Australian credits in all from film and television. Not all survive on video, and plainly some were mediocre. But time and again, she got good notices, and as the eighties wore on it was clear that much more adult parts were waiting. The best example of this was the miniseries *Vietnam*, which traced the history of Australia's participation in America's war. Nicole had a key recurring role, that of Megan Goddard, who went from schoolgirl to militant activist in the course of the series—or from teenager to woman. Terry Hayes was the head writer and the series was directed by John Duigan and Chris Noonan. *Vietnam* was a turning point for her in Australia, just as *To Die For* would be in Hollywood. The story involves a remarkable, long scene in which Megan on a phone-in show hears her brother at the other end of the line (he is a veteran calling in to challenge her case), and she breaks down. Kidman held the country in that scene. It would be a stunning audition piece as her career developed, and it is still among her most moving scenes. *Vietnam* aired in 1986 and provided enough income for Nicole to get her own apartment.

Two other projects from 1989 deserve to be mentioned: *Bangkok Hotel* and *Emerald City*. The latter was not a success, but it put Nicole in a modern romantic comedy, and the picture was later released in the United States (after other things had made her famous). But *Bangkok Hotel* was a popular hit, a six-hour miniseries, also written by Terry Hayes and based on real events. Nicole played Kat, a young woman who gets caught up in drug-running and ends up in the notorious Thailand prison. The series had many locations, including Goa, and it was written for her. Indeed, it was her starriest part so far. Her father was played by the very experienced English actor Denholm Elliott, and he said that he had never, ever met an actress with such ambition. The director Ken Cameron had this to say of her: "You are constantly surprised by the fact that one moment she seems to be a very young woman enjoying herself and being completely spontaneous. The next minute she is a serious actress, capable of a performance that can move you in a way that you don't expect from one so young. She looks wonderful, is enormously appealing on screen, and has something about her which belongs to the time. To have all those qualities is a rare thing."

In these very busy years, she had serious love affairs with two actors—Tom Burlinson and Marcus Graham. (As far as I can tell, every romantic relationship she had so far was with people in show business.) In addition, she helped nurse and sustain her mother through breast cancer. It was a family effort, but Nicole is truly close to her mother and an admirer of her humor and courage. As a result of her mother's experience, she became a serious campaigner against cancer.

People who knew Nicole in those days always liked her and her honesty. If she was in love, she was loyal. If she was working, she was dedicated. She did press interviews; she was fun on the set. She was modest, reasonable, and lively. But she was also cultivating an American career with the dedication of an Olympic athlete. In a way—odd in anyone her age—she believed in nothing but performing.

A young actor who worked with her, and who knew her a little socially, said in 2005, "It was often remarked, in Australia, how Nicole knew exactly what she wanted—to be a star—and knew exactly what she had to do to get it. Very focused and determined—but there was that old line being used: be careful what you wish for." Another friend said, "There was an ambition, deeply innate, and I thought that because she was so young it had to burn out. But it didn't. It became fiercer."

From about the age of twenty she had made exploratory trips to Los Angeles. She had managed to get the very respected agent Sam Cohn to take her on. Warren Beatty had met her and worked hard to woo her—with some film project being dangled. She turned him down and declined a Paramount picture. She was following the advice of the Australian Phillip Noyce, the director of *Dead Calm*, who gave her notes on being interviewed and doing photo shoots. But her work was being seen, and she did not quite come out of nowhere with *Dead Calm*. That was one of four films she made in 1989. And people like Cohn and Beatty were talking about her. Beatty was then on very good terms with the writer Robert Towne, and Towne had lately met Tom Cruise.

Dead Calm

You can think of *Dead Calm* as one of those things Nicole Kidman did on the way to becoming "Nicole Kidman." You can place it as a small, clever Australian thriller in which she looks hopelessly young—and you can argue that her being miscast damages the film's basis too much for comfort. On the other hand, *Dead Calm* is the best film she ever made until . . . well, until *To Die For*, in 1995. Which means to say that, if you were her supporter, you had to keep *Dead Calm* in mind during such things as *Days of Thunder, Far and Away*, and *Malice*, which were supposed to be bigger and more important.

Dead Calm is from a novel, by Charles Williams, published in 1963. The three-character film we possess is an abbreviation of a five-character novel that was the subject of another movie attempt, by Orson Welles, more faithful, but uncompleted. In the late 1960s, Welles shot it off the coast of Dalmatia. He cast Oja Kodar (his mistress) and the English actor Michael Bryant as the Ingrams, a couple who are on a yachting vacation when they are intruded on by Hughie, a psychotic. For Welles, Hughie was Laurence Harvey. But there are two other characters in the book and Welles cast those parts with Jeanne Moreau and himself. Which hardly leaves them feeling minor. Still, as happened so often, the Welles picture (called *The Deep*) was thwarted. Bryant had to fulfill a theatrical contract in London. Harvey died. And maybe the footage was less than terrific.

Still, *The Deep* was known of as an aborted venture when Phillip Noyce, who had already made *Newsfront* and *Heat Wave*, announced in

Dead Calm

1986 that he would do *Dead Calm*. He had Terry Hayes as his scriptwriter, and of course Hayes had been deeply impressed by Kidman's work on *Vietnam*. No one felt that Hayes and Nicole were romantically involved, but he was regarded as her mentor and champion. And so he strongly recommended Nicole (then nineteen) for the role of Rae Ingram, wife to the character played by Sam Neill (nineteen years older than Nicole) and mother to a three- or four-year-old son (who is killed in a car crash, with Rae driving, at the outset of *Dead Calm*). So it was a marriage that would seem to have occurred when Rae was fourteen!

There were suggestions that Hayes was smitten with Nicole, all of which he cheerfully denied. Nevertheless, in the event, Kidman won the part of Rae over competition that included Sigourney Weaver (forty in 1989) and Debra Winger (thirty-four). The two Americans were international stars with more box-office clout on a project that was budgeted at $10 million, a significant sum in Australian terms.

In tightening the cast from five to three, Noyce and Hayes did wonders for the tension of *Dead Calm*. There is a prologue to the film: John Ingram, a high-ranking naval officer (Neill), returns from a tour of duty expecting to be met by his wife and son. They are not there. In fact, the son is dead and the wife is seriously injured in the hospital as a result of a car crash. The couple take a voyage alone together on their fairly luxurious yacht to mend the wounds. Rae still has nightmares. She is on strong sedatives to sleep. But she wakes up screaming. The tender, older husband assures her that they can start again. The loss does seem reparable; we believe that they are in love and may have another child. There is no hint that the significant gap in age (he could be her father) has been stretched to the breaking point.

I say that because the screen cannot conceal the difference in age or erase the latent possibility that they might be divisible. One day, in a dead calm (and we have to wonder what dead calm means as a metaphor or a title), they see another sailing ship, apparently motionless and empty. Then they see a man coming across from that ship in a rowboat. When he (Billy Zane) arrives, he is exhausted and half crazy, but very handsome and much closer to Rae's age. His name is Hughie and he tells a story that the other ship is leaking, with five bodies on it, corpses, dead from botulism. The Ingrams are suspicious. While Hughie sleeps, John rows over to the other ship. He discovers the victims of evident murder, with signs of some kind of sexual orgy having taken place before the crime. He wants to hurry back to his own yacht, but Hughie has woken and seized control of it. So John is left on the ship of death, its motor broken, while Hughie sails away with Rae.

Phillip Noyce has settled for a film of action and suspense. Yet one only has to think of Roman Polanski's film with a similar setup, *Knife in the Water*, to see how there could be far more talk among the trio, with a threat of sexual betrayal as Rae becomes attracted to Hughie. By contrast, Noyce builds his picture around the modest but very resourceful heroism of John Ingram, and takes Rae's loyalty for granted.

The building tension—as John gets the engine going and pursues the other ship, and as Rae does all she can to lull and distract Hughie— is brilliantly managed. *Dead Calm* is a very compelling picture, but one absolutely content with surface action and overt hostilities. Whereas Nicole Kidman's performance—or is it more her presence?—does hint at what might have been more unsettling.

For here is a fascinating riddle in the study of acting: presence and performance are not always aligned. To give one classic example of this: in *Psycho*, Norman Bates is a demented killer, a very dangerous figure and the perpetrator of one of the screen's seminal murders. But the film is so constructed that his character comes to us through the unhappy, brooding, wistful, but very appealing presence of Anthony Perkins—I mean his hesitations, his quiet calm, his readiness to look deeply into people and their troubles, and the open wound of his shyness, his suppressions. Of course, all those things build a sinister force, too. But immediately prior to the motel shower murder, Norman and Marion Crane (Janet Leigh) have been engaged in the most thoughtful and humane conversation in the whole picture, and there is no doubt that Norman's sad insight has led Marion into what starts as a small confidence and becomes a full confession of her predicament. In a strange way, Norman has healed Marion before destroying her.

I do not want to suggest that *Dead Calm* is made with *Psycho*'s subtlety. I am not even sure that Phillip Noyce intended the disparity I see. Ostensibly, Rae is the bristling opponent to Hughie's wicked intent and the brave, ingenious enemy to his plans. She is the shattered kid ready to fire a harpoon gun at his sneering smile. She has come to hate him and to act on a desperate need to destroy him, for *Dead Calm* is finally an ordeal of survival.

And yet, Rae's decision to give herself in sex to Hughie is deeply ambivalent onscreen just because of the ways in which it yields to certain cinematic conventions. One of those is the fact that we never see a love scene between Rae and John. That's probably because he is still tender toward her traumatic loss, and so he feels sex might be an intrusion. But Rae—or Nicole—is plainly a very sexy kid. We watch her, and watch John watching her, luxuriating in the sea water as she swims. But she wears a black bathing suit, which, if you think about it, is a little odd or reserved for a fond married couple alone in the middle of the ocean. But it is enough, cinematically, to suggest the hint of a barrier in the marriage, and the most obvious causes of that are the loss of their child and the age difference.

As I said, Noyce does not pursue the potential misfit in the marriage. Just a little talk with the three characters might easily insinuate an element of sexual threat in which Rae is at least attracted to Hughie, leaving John a little jealous. That would help explain the oddly noncommittal way in which the eventual lovemaking between Hughie and Rae is filmed. In a way, she is letting herself be raped, but her actions are not quite that clear-cut. When Hughie sweeps off her sailing shorts, the exposure of Rae's bottom is arousing. And if Rae keeps her eyes open during the lovemaking, still she is not cold or numb to it. There is a sexual readiness in Kidman's presence—as well as the fact that she and Hughie seem alike in age and thus suited—that could make the psychological setup a good deal more engrossing.

It would be fair to argue that *Dead Calm* didn't need that extra innuendo—it was a hit, anyway, just as it is a very competent and compelling film. And you can argue, fairly, that it relies on three quite different personalities: the unstable, dangerous Hughie; the stalwart John; and the Rae who shrugs off mourning to defend her marriage. But that strength and valor would be a little more interesting if Rae had felt a twinge of sexual confusion and guilt. And I don't think it would be possible to think of that extra interest if Rae had been, say, a decent wife of the proper age. It is the fact that she is young, sexy, and unresolved that gives the film its secret spark. And that is why Nicole Kidman got "noticed" in *Dead Calm*, while the careers of Sam Neill and Billy Zane were hardly affected. There was a question mark in her needy eyes, and audiences as well as future filmmakers felt challenged to answer it.

Tom

A t first, everyone sees Nicole's love affair with Tom Cruise in terms of a big star picking up a newcomer—even if he is a few inches shorter than she is. What no one seems to notice is that the "kid," the girl, is not just taller than the guy. She is in so many ways more settled, more secure, stronger. The novice from Sydney has made eighteen pictures already, for film and television. He has done twelve. Of course, he has an Oscar nomination (for *Born on the Fourth of July*); he has generated huge sums at the box office; and he is internationally known. Still, no one really sees at first that maybe the guy, the star, needs rescuing.

But he has a terrific laugh that is made to signal his complete assurance, his absolute well-being, happiness, and rock-solid proficiency—whatever you want to call it. At forty-three, Tom Cruise still does this. On the *Tonight* show in the summer of 2004, promoting *Collateral*, where he is immaculate, lethally accomplished, and serenely alone (until he dies), Cruise still did that rocking act, leaning away as if some nearly uncontrollable mirth had overtaken him at whatever Jay Leno had said. Before he said it. You begin to see how compromising such an act can be. It's as if the Tom Cruise who goes on shows with his everything-is-perfect grin had never noticed or considered his own performance in Paul Thomas Anderson's *Magnolia*. That was a film where exultant laughter is at last stilled. He plays Frank Mackey, the powerhouse leader of a hysterical male cult, but a man who has avoided several large lies in his own life, and who comes to the point of being stripped bare by a quiet, calm, matter-of-fact interviewer, a black woman, who knows the facts and who is bound to apply them, like chemotherapy.

Thomas Cruise Mapother IV was born on July 3 (not the Fourth), 1962, in Syracuse, New York. He had a very hard time of it in life, so much so that a kind of power began to gather in him as being the only driving force that might overcome his difficulties. Long before he encountered Scientology, this air of attack in Tom Cruise was like a religion of achievement. And, of course, Tom's ascendancy was very American in the way it said, Look, anyone can make it to the top; and also deeply neurotic in suggesting that anyone who has ever failed has no option but to make it to the top. There is nowhere else to go. Moderate success will hardly count. There is no irony or gray in Tom Cruise. He believes in himself with an intensity that begins to get frightening the longer you think about it. Because you wonder if any actual man could live up to that belief.

His father, Thomas Cruise Mapother, was an electrical engineer, a tough man who sometimes hit the boy and left the young Tom bewildered as to why. Later, the grown Tom would admit to that emotional pain. He reasoned it out that the father had seen or felt a world of hurt and damage that he did not want for his son. But another view is that the father had all manner of reckless schemes to make them rich, and every time an idea failed the family had to move and start again, with punishment for the onlookers. They were all over the place: seven moves by the time Tom was eleven, he said, with places like Ottawa, Louisville, and Cincinnati figuring along the way.

So there were many different schools and a boy who was hardly ever in one of them long enough to find a teacher to trust, or to have a school take him seriously. So often the new boy, pretty and small, was bullied. He learned to fight back. "It's sink or swim," he says. "I chose to swim. It was about surviving, and going after what you want."

And so it was said about him at schools where he did poorly that he had dyslexia—a real condition, yet a regular excuse for academic problems of failure that the system cannot attend to. Though he was left-handed, the shuttle from one place to another had left him trying to be right-handed. There had even been a year—his freshman high school year—spent in a Franciscan seminary. The call of extreme solutions is there early.

Then, when he was eleven, his mother, Mary Lee, gave up on the father. She put Tom and his three sisters (Lee Anne, Marian, and Cass) in a car and drove away on a journey that ended in Glen Ridge, New Jersey. There was a divorce, even though the family was Catholic (with one Thomas Cruise Mapother being detached from another, why do sons and fathers have exactly the same name and just a number difference in a free and individualistic society?), and then the father fell short on child support. In his teenage years, Tom Cruise was poor and doing all he could with odd jobs to help his mother out. This is the testimony of pluck and ingenuity, if you like, yet it also stands for absence from school.

Cruise never likes to talk about how he has turned his life around. Later in life when he married the actress Mimi Rogers, she helped him discover Scientology. Whereupon interviewers ask him how that made a difference. How did a dyslexic learn lines? "I had to work at it with a lot of effort," he says. These answers are emphatic but vague. "It just took a hell of a lot longer for me. There's varying levels of what dyslexia is: reading things backwards, not knowing your right hand from your left. For me, it was skipping lines, letters backwards. . . . There was a study technology that L. Ron Hubbard had that I applied. In applying it, I had the ability to learn and read anything that I wanted to. Who knows whether I actually had dyslexia or not?"

At Glen Ridge High School, Tom was better known for track, ice hockey, and wrestling than for academic success. He was still said to be dyslexic, and then a knee injury incurred on the wrestling mat left him at a loose end. So he tried out for the role of Nathan Detroit in the school musical, *Guys and Dolls*. He came to life. His own mother was startled at the facility he had and the vividness of his playing. The audience liked him. Beyond his ability at sports, it may have been the first time in his life that outsiders had noticed and approved of what he did. He was only seventeen, and he had not graduated from high school, but on the spot he quit school and went to Manhattan.

His rise was famously fast. Working in construction and as a waiter, he got a role in *Godspell* on stage and that led to him being cast in a small but striking part in the movie *Endless Love* (1981). The same year he was cast in *Taps*, a film that starred Timothy Hutton and had Sean Penn above him in the cast list. The camera loved him—his dark hair, his deep brow, and his shining, intent eyes. Nineteen eighty-three was the year in which he arrived properly, no matter that he was only twenty-one. He had four films open that year: *Losin' It*, the least known now, about three kids who go to Tijuana; *The Outsiders*, Francis Ford Coppola's film from the Susie Hinton teen classic, in which Cruise was one of a cast of newcomers that included C. Thomas Howell, Matt Dillon, Rob Lowe, Ralph Macchio, Emilio Estevez, and Patrick Swayze (only one of that gang has really lasted as a star); *All the Right Moves*, in which he plays a high school football player; and *Risky Business*.

Risky Business, written and directed by Paul Brickman, is one of the seminal American teenage entertainments, a key movie of the 1980s, which is to say, an example of the merchandising commercial that turns into a full-scale movie, and of the new unironic fantasy that was let loose. It is about a teenager home alone (years ahead of that franchise) who calls in a prostitute. Put as baldly as that, you might say, Oh, don't be silly. But by the 1980s, the powers that gave movie ideas the go-ahead were undeterred by silliness or implausibility if they saw the guiding light of teenage wish fulfillment and box office. It's every boy's dream, was the justification that smothered "silliness." And the film was an amazing success. (Tom Cruise actually had a love affair with Rebecca De Mornay, the actress who played the prostitute.)

Taste and tact were always questionable matters in *Risky Business*—the film's title applied not just to its story but to the whole venture. No one doubted that it was the charm and energy of Tom Cruise that swept the problems away. He is adorable, cheeky, good-humored, decent, bold, shy, energetic, yet tender—indeed, compared with many of the other young actors around then (the Brat Pack), he is notably gentle and sympathetic. But the moment that clinches the film's impact comes when, alone in the house, in shorts and socks, he mimes to the song "Old Time Rock and Roll." That is a dream every kid has had, but easier than the actual lovemaking with De Mornay on a subway train. One hurdle trained the fantasists for the next. De Mornay can be seductive, sultry, and sophisticated, but still there is a fresh-washed Madonna's aura about her. She seems more than just a year older than Cruise. She can seem like a very smart, clean hooker—or a very pliant mother. Tom's ordinariness redeems her and us for watching such nonsense.

Risky Business was symptomatic in many ways of where film was going and of the leader Cruise might be. Paul Brickman had intended a bittersweet comedy, a coming-of-age film in which the Cruise character loses the hooker and fails to get into Princeton (like life). But as the movie was tested by the studio, its real owner, David Geffen, wondered about a happier ending. Much against Brickman's wishes the film was made more upbeat (or more like a movie). Its numbers soared. The positivism in Tom Cruise was extended to his audience, letting them feel as good as possible.

Cruise's stardom was certain now, and nothing really has shaken it since then. Perhaps age is the only threat it faces. Not that Tom Cruise has been uninteresting as an actor: he gave a stirring, heartfelt performance as Ron Kovic, the paraplegic, in Oliver Stone's *Born on the Fourth of July*, and he was brilliant, standing up to Dustin Hoffman's bravura self-indulgence, in *Rain Man*. At the same time, it is hard to know how to approach *Top Gun* or *The Color of Money* without getting into Hollywood's shameless catering to a young man's dreams of being cool in a world that is rapidly losing contact with adult sensibilities.

Top Gun seemed crass and adolescent even during the Cold War. The notion that war and fighter aircraft were playgrounds for boys was hideously in line with the attitudes of Reagan's America, an administration that was systematically lying to the public and to Congress, and endeavoring to set up a secret government. The film is shot through with clichés about teamwork, mavericks who learn to toe the line, and the fine place of women—Kelly McGillis is some kind of flight physicist so that Cruise can have a dream girl to lay. Moreover, that romance is exposed for its bogusness by the far rowdier and more credible relationship between Anthony Edwards and Meg Ryan, who for once stood for real life in a picture.

You can say that *Top Gun* was the dream of its producers Don Simpson and Jerry Bruckheimer (and their neofascist bombast goes on, long after Simpson's death). But there's every reason to think that Cruise swallowed the heroism whole. Apparently his political conservatism led him to relish *Top Gun* attitudes and to being the star and co-producer on three *Mission: Impossible* films, Cold War fantasies of a rare antique quality in which the hero, somehow, can fly! Nearly twenty years later, when a London *Observer* interviewer reminded Cruise that he had expressed a boyish enthusiasm for the Iraq war, his fumbling answer seemed to speak for a genuine naïveté and a certain awareness that young stars should not be ultraconservative: "You know what, that was out of context. I'm interested in helping people. I'm not interested in war in general. I love my country, and I'm glad to live in America, but also, I don't want war. It's not in my nature. It's just not who I am to see people dying."

Question: "Does he have any feelings about the next election?"

"I don't know what. . . . No, I kind of don't."

An actor does not have to be articulate about the real world and its complex problems, though maybe that responsibility hangs more heavily on a producer. Cruise sounds like a young man still so anxious not to offend he would sooner not think. But *Top Gun* and the *Mission: Impossible* films are addled celebrations of a kind of heroism that depends on the faith and hope of its heroes. And Tom Cruise is not suited to playing characters about whom he has mixed feelings. (That is what makes *Magnolia* so remarkable.) That is his limit as an actor, and let us propose for now that it must have been a limitation in the husband. So Tom was in all overt senses more potent than Nicole. Yet already, he was her junior as a performer. One question that hovered over the union was, How long could she ignore that?

Introducing Mrs. Preston

Men in Hollywood take it for granted with each other that they are all keeping their eyes open for the new girl. This need not mean anything in terms of their own marriages, or romantic stability. Rather, it is like following sports, demonstrating that you are awake or switched on in a business that would feel lost if it didn't have every year another dozen or so young women to "introduce." The screenwriter Robert Towne has grown up in the business with Jack Nicholson and Warren Beatty and made friends with them, which is to say that probably no more than half of his waking time is given over to consideration of these new young women.

Towne doctored the script of *Bonnie and Clyde* for Beatty. He wrote *The Last Detail* and *Chinatown* for Nicholson. He did *Shampoo* for and with Beatty, no matter that "for" and "with" are complicated prepositions in Hollywood and may have left Towne with the feeling of having been screwed. Writers take that status as a given, and that is one reason why Towne is looking to direct. He had a hard time in the 1980s, though. He lost a cherished project, *Greystoke*; he delivered *Personal Best* only after much controversy, more over-budget difficulties, and an affair with his star, Mariel Hemingway; he wrote and directed *Tequila Sunrise;* and he suffered an abortion with *The Two Jakes*. That sequel to *Chinatown* was something Towne was going to write and direct. The film started and then collapsed, for reasons never fully spelled out. A few years later the movie came back and now Nicholson was directing and having to send messages to his old chum for rewrites. The film was a flop. The friendship was over. Towne was in his fifties, with a second marriage, and not financially secure.

Which is one reason why he got attached to *Days of Thunder*, the sort of project that, in the 1970s, Towne might have disdained. He was a very good writer then, with high standards, and every hope of doing a lot of good work. Yet he had learned that writers do not wag the dog, and he had spent a lot of time with men far richer than he was or might dream of being. That atmosphere can change you, and so Towne was looking for a new patron. It would turn out that Tom Cruise filled the role in Towne's life once held by Beatty and Nicholson. So Towne came on board *Days of Thunder* to punch up the dialogue a little bit. A friendship developed quickly. Towne is cool, very smart, terrific company. When someone asked him how he handled Cruise's Scientology, Towne said, "I feel about it exactly the way Lincoln felt about Grant and booze: let's give it to my other generals." You can see Tom's grin and his fierce laugh at that remark. It lets Towne keep his independence, while showing Cruise knows his Civil War history.

On Beatty's recommendation, Towne had seen *Dead Calm* and been "very impressed." Robin Wright was up for the female role in *Days of Thunder*, but her availability was uncertain. So Towne proposed Kidman and very soon the three had lunch—at Toscana, on San Vicente. "It was clear," says Towne, "that Tom was smitten straightaway. It happens."

She says that from the moment they met they shared that feeling of having known each other already. They are left-handers, high school dropouts. And they started laughing: he likes to make people laugh, he loves to use his grin, and she is never happier than when laughing. Years later, Nicole admitted, "I was consumed by it, willingly. And I was desperate to have a baby with him. I didn't care if we were married. That's what I wish I'd done."

Another way of looking at *Days of Thunder* is to marvel at the way two children (looking just like adults) were able to turn their playtime into a big motion picture. Thus, he is Cole Trickle, the maverick Nascar driver who resents being controlled, but who has the nerves of steel to make a champion. She, at the age of twenty-two, is Dr. Claire Lewicki, apparently the best neurologist in the business, but ready to succumb to Cole's charm just like that. And Robert Duvall is the kidder, the teaser, the wise old team manager who can steal the picture from these babes. Robert Towne settles back in an imaginary driver's seat, touches up the dialogue, and with a straight face dresses up the role of the pretty neurologist to keep Nicole employed. And all of this happens because *Top Gun* grossed well over $400 million by running the same kind of boys-will-be-competitors routines in the air. Nicole gets $200,000—a very big increase from her Australian salaries—but Tom is on for $10 million.

Nicole has only a few scenes, while Tom is in everything—and anything he cares to throw in as an extra. She has moments when she realizes that she is just the obligatory girlfriend, and pretty fatuous at that. Claire Lewicki is a travesty next to the parts Nicole has been playing in Australia. But the break is too big to back away from and then it starts to get frightening, for she realizes she and Tom might be in love (as well as in a picture). That compensates for how badly *Days of Thunder* does: it grosses no more than $85 million, and loses money on its first run.

Their reactions to the love affair are intriguingly different. Nicole has lived a little and she adjusts to her devoted boyfriend, Marcus Graham, in Australia by missing many of his telephone calls. Nothing has happened yet with Tom beyond whatever embraces the script calls for. Tom is still married to Mimi Rogers. Some earnest honor compels him to move out of the Los Angeles house he shares with Mimi. Why? she asks. He can't say. Then he moves back. Mimi is smart enough to fly to the Daytona locations, to get a glimpse of Nicole and pick up the on-set talk about the two of them. She goes back to California, and in January 1990 Tom starts divorce proceedings. Not even a Scientologist marriage counselor can help. In February 1990, Tom sends his own plane to Australia to bring Nicole's mother to the United States so that she can inspect her daughter's new love. (If she doesn't like the guy—look at the plane.) Others in Australia, Nicole watchers, say, Fancy that.

Tom has told Mimi that he is "with Nicole" now, but he does not let this fact show in public. The divorce will go through: Mimi gets their house in Los Angeles and about $10 million. As for reasons, there is just a cryptic joint statement, "While there have been positive aspects to our marriage, there were some issues which could not be resolved, even after working on them for a period of time." There will be more to come—much more. But it is only at the Oscars of 1990—where Tom is up for *Born on the Fourth of July*—that he and Nicole appear in public together for the first time. They are side by side, next to Dustin Hoffman in the front row. Tom loses out to Daniel Day-Lewis in *My Left Foot*, but one mission has been accomplished. Presumably, it's around this time that he takes her skydiving, and puts his first kiss on her—in midair, in free fall—or was that a scene written by someone like Robert Towne?

In the fall of 1990, Tom and Nicole are more evidently a couple, she with a chunk of engagement ring on her hand. They watch some U.S. Open tennis in New York; they go to Australia, to visit her father; and she starts work as Mrs. Drew Preston in the film of *Billy Bathgate*.

This is the 1989 novel by E. L. Doctorow and a very hot property begging for screen adaptation and lucky enough to fall into the hands of Robert Benton as writer-director. It is the story of gangster Dutch Schultz as seen through the eyes of a kid, Billy Bathgate, who is hired to take care of Schultz's mistress, Mrs. Preston, while he is negotiating murder charges. Dustin Hoffman is to play Dutch Schultz and an appealing new kid, Loren Dean, is cast as Billy. There's a whole lot more to the film, including a flamboyant cameo performance by Bruce Willis as Bo Weinberg, who is tipped into the river with his feet in concrete, and a great performance from Steven Hill as Billy's gloomy mentor.

Drew Preston is a golden opportunity: she is a blasé, reckless society woman (married to a homosexual) who gets a thrill out of the underworld, and who finds a bigger excitement in seducing Billy Bathgate under Schultz's nose. Almost certainly, Doctorow intended Mrs. Preston to be a little older than Nicole Kidman, just as Billy was meant to be younger than Loren Dean. As it turns out (because Disney was unhappy with an affair between a boy and a woman), Nicole is only a year older than Loren Dean, and the film has a nice sense of two horny kids getting their hearts' desire together. But Mrs. Preston is worldly and classy and she needs to impress Billy with her refinement. Dustin Hoffman seems to have recommended Nicole for the part, but Benton was not initially won over. He gave Nicole two weeks to get rid of her thick Australian accent and sound like a New York socialite. She managed that, and needed only two seconds to be the dazzling, briefly naked flaunter of her own sexuality.

Mrs. Preston is described by Doctorow as a vision. First seen, she comes up out of a dark ship's hold: "And up she came, her marcelled blond head, and then her white neck and shoulders, as if she was rising from the ocean. I had not before in the darkness of the car gotten a really good look at her, she was very slender in her cream white evening gown hanging by two thin straps, and in this dark and oily boat, totally alarming, white with captivity. . . ." Benton saw the paleness in Nicole as no one had done before. In Australia, she had been tanned and freckled, but in *Billy Bathgate* she is as white as bone china, yet satin to the touch. It is plain enough that Benton adored her and Nicole made the most of every moment. A little later on, there is a casual nude scene—it is gratuitous, or would be if its nonchalance didn't say so much about her character, and the wonder that Billy feels at getting to see such a thing.

Benton was amazed that this apparent beginner had such "authority. It is not a thing you can teach. She had it. She is very matter-of-fact to work with. If she has a question, she's very direct. And she works! I mean it as a compliment, but she's a very simple machine. She does not need direction, especially from other actors."

Billy Bathgate has faded away as a movie—and that's not deserved. It is a lovely little picture and it has passages where Benton's eye, Kidman's presence, and Billy's feeling are quite perfectly filmed:

> She stood at the armoire and let the big towel fall, and she was altogether taller and longer-waisted and maybe her ass was a little softer and flatter, but there was the prominent spinal column of tender girl bones of my dirty little Rebecca, and all the parts were as Rebecca's parts and the sum was the familiar body of a woman, I don't know what I'd been expecting but she was a mortal being with flesh pinkened by the hot bathwater, she hooked on her garter belt and stood on each thin white leg while she gently but efficiently raised the other to receive its sheer stocking. . . .

You may say that getting dressed and undressed is hardly acting, yet I suspect that Nicole's Australian freedom came to her aid in portraying Mrs. Preston's brisk lack of shyness. So many American actresses might have been more coy. And quite plainly the public saw what Nicole was: a sexy beanpole, with gingery pubic hair, commas for breasts, and boyish hips. This was not a goddess. But she carries herself nude with an ease—more than that, a pleasure—that is so much more erotic than far greater bodies in erotic poses. Mrs. Preston was made for sex, and in that advertisement a similar claim was being slipped out to the world on behalf of the actress playing her. Glimpses from *Billy Bathgate* are still there on the Internet to be downloaded by a kind of voyeurism hardly current in 1990. Tom Cruise, apparently, came to the set for those scenes and many felt that he was guarding his treasure. Benton felt that Cruise was very discreet—anyway, he said, "They were just married. Wouldn't you want to be with her?" But maybe for movie people there is a literal truth in the way you may need a film to show you what you can see.

And so in Telluride, Colorado, on Christmas Eve 1990, with a modest crowd of the two families, and Dustin Hoffman and his wife, they are married, wearing blue jeans and in their bare feet. The music is Van Morrison singing "Someone Like You." Tom owns private planes, yet he is still living the emotional life of a boy. But anyone who understood Mrs. Preston's sophistication knows she is a good deal farther on in the world—far enough ahead to be alarming.

Not to Be Missed

(Or Believed?)

Synopsis: One day a young woman appears for a job interview at one of those mansions just down the coast from San Francisco. We never discover her name. She is in her twenties, tall, pretty, but crippled by shyness so that she worries always that she is too tall, and glaringly unattractive because of her wild red hair. She is interviewed by a handsome but distracted man (his name is Max Winter) who is absentminded, chilly, aloof, and seems hardly interested in her, yet he decides to hire her. Her job? To look after Max, his eight-year-old son. Max, the father, is a widower; his wife, Rebecca, has died recently in an unfortunate but mysterious accident.

Our heroine takes the job. It is residential, of course, and she soon finds that her position in the large household is very uneasy: Max barely speaks to her; Max the son is rude and aggressive and soon learns to mimic her stammer; and Mrs. Danvers, the housekeeper, treats her like an idiot. Indeed, things get so bad that our nameless heroine tries to run away, only to be captured and returned by the thuggish chauffeur, Walker.

A strange pressure builds up whereby the various people in the household begin to intimidate her. Why are they doing it? It seems that their common aim is for her to replace or play the part of the Rebecca they have lost. And slowly our heroine realizes that this is her only escape. She watches Mrs. Danvers dressing in Rebecca's clothes and admires her beauty. She learns to horsewhip Max as he instructs. She submits to Walker's sexual attentions. But most remarkable of all is the way she discovers of fitting in with young Max's needs . . . Let's just say that she concludes that it was Max the son who murdered his mother.

"I am Rebecca," she announces at last and the bizarre household comes to order. If only to save her own life, she has to kill young Max. And at that point, Max the father seems to wake from his deep sleep and becomes her devout lover. "Rebecca" decides she is happy.

Commentary: What can one say about this film *maudit* except that it still seems as unlikely as it did when only a rumor. The picture was shot in the early 1990s (maybe in 1991, between *Billy Bathgate* and *Far and Away*) at the lavish Malibu home of inventor and benefactor Max Palevsky. The script was worked up, sometimes only minutes ahead of shooting, by Robert Towne, and it seems quite clear now that it was directed by Roman Polanski, who had somehow entered the country illegally for a few days.

Needless to say, it is a savage pastiche of Hitchcock's *Rebecca*, yet one made with an unexpected feeling for the many psychic undertones in that classic. Thus, Tom Cruise's "Sleeping Beauty" Maximilian uncovers many of the things only hinted at in Olivier's Maxim. Anjelica Huston is magnificent as Mrs. Danvers, though some viewers may be disturbed by her inability (or refusal) to stop laughing in some scenes. Warren Beatty is strangely satisfactory as Walker, the unlikely brute force, and Christopher Walken (in short velvet pants) is so daring as Max Jr. as to make the film unviewable in any licensing system one can predict. Still, the picture was obviously made as a weird showcase for the new Mrs. Cruise, and Nicole Kidman moves in clear stages from a freckled Australian tomboy with a stammer to a lustrous blond icon, not just a femme fatale, but an actress likely to devour her competition. Kidman stands out in this wacky household as the one person taking everything seriously, and her sotto voce improvs as the plot thickens are priceless.

Public Property, Private Lives

The most thorough portrait of a marriage in the world of Tom Cruise and Nicole Kidman is . . . Well, no, it's not *Eyes Wide Shut*. On reflection, I'd say it's *The Hours*. Not that that union, between Leonard and Virginia, is blissful. They seem to have no substantial sex life—or children. Still, as she walks off to her death in the River Ouse, Virginia has just written a letter to Leonard and left it sealed in a blue envelope on the mantelpiece. In the letter she says she doubts that any two people could have been happier. It's just that so much of her being or her energy are caught up in the tormenting matter of being alone while working on a book like *Mrs. Dalloway*, or whatever. In that unremitting crisis, marriage may be incidental. There are people who, when asked what Tom and Nicole had or have in common, reply, Well, the same sort of driving ambition to do good work. All that that means is that the marriage is never the big thing, or the inner thing.

In January 1989, when *Vanity Fair* published a cover story on Tom Cruise, they mentioned his marriage to Mimi Rogers briefly. It was there in the same sentence that referred to his taking up race car driving. But there was a full-page color picture of Mimi, an Annie Leibovitz, in which she is wearing red, curled up in an armchair and gazing at some unseen thing in a mixture of fear, fury, and resentment. Her movie roles were already sliding by then, and it was as if Cruise, or his people, had asked the magazine to put in a plug for Mimi to keep her sweet. Such things happen. And the magazine, tongue in cheek, had gone for that baleful, seething woman, the older woman look. A few years later, Cruise would tell another magazine, "If the press gets things right ten percent of the time, I'm a happy guy," followed by that famous rock-cracking smile, and then the ecstatic dry laughter.

Of course, Nicole is the one with a chance to learn. She does not really know Hollywood, except by being introduced by Tom. There are so many people she has not met before. There will be so many accusations that scripts or projects would not come her way without him. And, naturally enough, she becomes very defensive over that. She can live with the financial gap between what they make, she says, and at first it is easier because she is making so much more than she ever managed before. But a moment comes when a legitimate magazine wonders about using them together: "They recently offered us the chance to be on the cover of *Vogue* together, saying, 'You'd be the first couple ever on our cover.' We've never even done a photo shoot together. The *Vogue* cover was not of interest, particularly for me because then it looks like I'm riding on his coattails."

But Nicole did appear inside *Vogue*, and thus she made a vital meeting, with another Australian, Baz Luhrmann, who was acting as a guest editor. It was their first meeting, and it was a turning point. As Luhrmann recalls, "She was doing these impersonations of golden age movie stars. And there was this 1930s cream suit with a beret. She put it on, she just walked onto the set, and there was a hush. I gave her a pinch of story and she became a character. Sort of Lauren Bacall. I saw that she loved to be photographed. She could inhabit the space by making a heightened image. But it was set in reality. She fills the set with emotional energy. And then I saw that she'd do more and more takes, and it got deeper all the time. She always wants more takes. She's exhaustive and exhausting!"

This difference in attitude to stills shows in other ways. In an eighteen-month period they both do covers for *Movieline* magazine, which means turning up for a photo shoot. This is a chore for most stars, part of the transaction. Cruise's picture is a straight-on head shot by Lance Staedler. There are three other Staedler shots inside, all expert, and all alike, because Tom is doing Tom and wearing appropriate Tom clothes. He is candid, male, handsome, secure—and just a little dull because he doesn't give them the killer grin once.

When Nicole is photographed, by Firooz Zahedi, the effect is utterly different. The editor from the magazine who oversees the shoot remarks even then on the enthusiasm with which Nicole does the job: "Most actresses in that position are professional and just a bit bored. They reckon to give you the minimum of what you want. It's a deal you make with them. Nicole is quite different. She wants to do it. She starts imagining roles to play. She is in love with the camera and its process and she is clearly thinking feverishly about what it will do for her. That sounds calculating and I suppose it is. But at the time what you feel is her fun, her delight, her getting off on it."

It shows. On the cover she has wild, untidy reddish hair. She is in a camisole and she wears black stockings and black suspenders. The copy line is "I would love to play a sex kitten." You look at the picture and you get something more than just a sultry pose. There's an edge of real wit, and it's supplied in the very first paragraph of the interview story (by Stephen Rebello), which takes off directly from the shoot:

" 'Do you think I should try and find a new Elvis and remake *Viva Las Vegas?'* Nicole Kidman wonders, pouting out her scarlet lips, tossing back her mane of red hair and looking, in a sinuous black number, like such a 60s sex kitten that I wonder why I hadn't detected that Ann-Margret itching to burst out of the Samantha Eggar all along. 'Immediately,' I answer, 'and if Tom won't be your Elvis, I will.' Kidman breaks up laughing, then, waving bye-bye for now, sidles, barefoot, back under the lights for a few more photos. I've been watching her work the camera like mad—acting buoyant and loose while cranking up her heat in a way that critics have rarely accused her of doing in such movies as *Days of Thunder, Far and Away, Billy Bathgate, Malice* and *My Life.*"

What Rebello is observing is not just a sexiness in Kidman that had still not broken out on the American screen by 1994, but a playfulness that might not be to Tom's liking. It's hard to believe that she would hit her Ann-Margret look with Tom standing beside her. Despite his set-piece in *Risky Business*, it's hard to think that Tom Cruise is really loose and limber enough, inwardly, to go with such games. In every interview he does, he's guarded, in a stronghold, resolved to give away as little as possible. But in her interviews, Nicole is flirty, provocative, always on the point of being a pal with the interviewer. One thing about Tom's extraordinary laugh is that it seems to indicate enthusiasm and involvement without ever really taking him out of his stride. It's a man thing, maybe, but he seems to need control. Whereas every dramatic instinct in Nicole feels set on risk. Despite her self-awareness about competing with Tom's status, she may have begun to take on the instinctive wariness, waiting to see where he is before she lets the kitten show. But she wants the world to feel the flame burning inside her.

She looks at the camera as if it might be her confidant or co-conspirator. It is a look that says, Anyone who sees deep inside me—well, there's a reward, know what I mean? It is the beginning of the relationship Suzanne Stone is eager to have with every camera in the world in *To Die For*. And whereas in marriage—especially young marriage—there is the look in both parties of being unaware of others in the world, of being rapt and locked together, Nicole's hungry gaze does not deny her curiosity. This is not to say that in the first few years of marriage they are anything but happy, very much in love with each other. But just as she is smart enough to look at him and see the closed-off young rock he wants to be, surely he can feel the flirt in her, the energy that is always ready to do one more setup on the stills shoot. Tom is tough on interviewers: he keeps stopwatch time and after sixty minutes he is out of there. Nicole sometimes goes on and on, no matter that it's become dark in the room. She likes talking about herself.

There are times when Nicole admits to being surprised at how drastically her life has changed. She says she swore she'd never "get married. Live with someone. Have kids. I considered getting married, but not living with the person. I actually posed that possibility to a guy who I was going to get engaged to, and he said, 'I'm not calling up my wife for a date.' I come from a family where my parents are together, but I really believed that marriage couldn't last. So, I thought, either don't do it or, if you do it for fun, make sure you don't get trapped. I was going to be like my idol Katharine Hepburn, who said you couldn't have a career and a marriage. Then, I thought, 'Fuck it, I'm going to be happy.' "

To be Nicole, and happy!

They go on television together to say how wonderful things are, and how happy they are. They buy a house in Pacific Palisades—actually Tom buys it but they choose it together. In New York, one night, they decide to go skating in Central Park, and they do it without being mobbed in the way, in Westwood, they can sometimes take in a movie without causing a traffic jam. They hear the Neville Brothers play at a club in New Orleans. They make a film together, *Far and Away*, and live in Ireland for a season while they are doing it.

There is a story of how once in Paris, after regular hours, Tom fixes his searchlight grin on the people responsible and says he was wondering.

"*Qu'est-ce que c'est*, Monsieur Cruise?"

"The Louvre."

"*Oui?*"

Is it ever possible to have private viewings where people, celebrities, let's say, can look at the pictures without being harassed?

He is talking about privileged access, and access is a kind of magic that works both ways. It is a charm to get it, of course, but it is a bonus in bureaucratic life to offer it. And don't think the thanks, the smiles, and the sense of understanding may not last a bureaucrat a lifetime. Tom doesn't have to tell Nicole, as they are let in, to give this official an Ann-Margret squeeze and that one a feathery kiss. She knows the act. She is a professional. And maybe the question of most interest is, in that forty minutes or whatever in the Louvre, with just the sound of their heels on the hard floors, is she looking at the pictures or looking at the Tom that can gain such access? And is he looking at the pictures, or is he intent on her watching him?

Did they do Scientology together? As soon as she could in interviews, Nicole began to say that any ideas of that philosophy being imposed on her were rubbish, or "absolute bullshit." Tom had wanted to share the discipline with her and he told her as he told everyone that it had allowed him to live more decisively, effectively, and positively. She promised to keep an open mind, and she certainly read some of the crucial texts. But as to the suggestion that Scientology had been required of her in the marriage—"No way! I would never have married him if that was it. That would have been forcing me to do something I didn't want to do. He and I allow ourselves to be who we are. Am I someone following one philosophy? No, but there's parts of Scientology that are great."

Nicole was twenty-five in 1992; she was plainly dedicated to her career and restless at being out of work for a long time. She had tossed off a few statements indicating that in an earlier life she had never really considered having children. On the other hand, Tom had often talked about how much he looked forward to that. The failure to generate children was one of the flaws in the Mimi Rogers marriage. So it was natural that the show business press and the tabloids should speculate about the Cruise-Kidman marriage. And now they began to discover that another of the shared things in their marriage would be publicity and the urge in part of the press to cast doubt on their perfection.

Of course, the career of a mother is put in much more jeopardy by pregnancy than that of a father. The mother takes a risk with her body, or with what is actually her professional equipment if she is an actress. She also puts the degree of her professional concentration in the balance. She is liable to become much more interested in someone other than herself. And so, in some cases, actresses delay having their children; they elect to adopt; or they do not have children at all. And Tom, it seems clear, was pressing for a decision, in part because he was older than Nicole, and in part because he was tired of waiting.

There was every sense that they were seeking to get pregnant in the ordinary way. It's most likely that they would have taken expert medical advice on fertility and so forth, as well as considering methods of artificial insemination. But they did not wait as long as some couples wait to give nature a chance at taking its course. Thus, late in 1992, the story broke that they were seeking to adopt. Nicole said it was "pretty spontaneous . . . the opportunity just came up." The couple registered to adopt in Florida, a state that does not allow the natural mother to change her mind after the birth. Tom especially was very angry when details got out in the press because he had insisted on a confidentiality agreement covering all parties. It seemed that the adoption might be held up. But in the event a child, Isabella Jane Kidman Cruise (born on December 22, 1992), was adopted in early January 1993. As if to adapt to reality, Nicole said then that she had always preferred the idea of adoption to getting pregnant. Tom was over the moon: "Being a father is the greatest thing that has ever happened to me," he told the press.

Indeed, it was noted that he was suddenly more generous with his words and time, and more open in his feelings.

But then in the March 1993 issue of *Playboy*, Mimi Rogers posed for nude pictures and delivered a sensational interview. She was thirty-seven and there were many who attributed the splash to the decline in her career. In the interview, she said that the essential reason for the end of their marriage had been Tom's thinking of becoming a monk. "At least for that period of time, it looked as though marriage wouldn't fit into his overall spiritual need. And he thought he had to be celibate to maintain the purity of his instrument."

In time, Rogers said she was only joking. Nicole did all she could to help blow away any rumors. She told *Movieline*, "He's the best lover I ever had," and when the insinuation was pursued she said, "That he's gay? Really? Well, ummm, he's not gay in my knowledge. You'll have to ask him that question."

Then *McCall's* magazine chipped in, with a piece that alleged the marriage between Tom and Nicole had been arranged by his people to help secure his romantic image and that her movie career (or a shot at one) was part of the deal. These allegations were without substance and *McCall's* quickly agreed to run an apology and a retraction after Cruise's protest. I don't think there's a word of truth in it, just as I don't think Kidman had the duplicity to accept such an arrangement any more than she would have been prepared to be ordered around by her husband's Scientologist advisers. Later, in 1998, Cruise and Kidman were paid substantial damages by the London *Express* for similar charges—damages passed on to charity. This is not the only instance in which Cruise has sued successfully for such allegations. And whenever he does, he exposes himself to discovery proceedings and possible cross-examination.

Still, I have known many people, ignorant of the facts, who say they have heard that there was a lengthy marriage contract—they know people who claim to have seen it. In 1994 Cruise had made his first big departure in choosing roles by playing the vampire Lestat in *Interview with a Vampire*. It was a brave performance as a bisexual character, even if not fully successful. But plainly it had encouraged rumor mongering.

We may settle for Nicole's conclusion, candidly given, that she felt she had been made love to by a champion, thank you very much. But, still, she said, if you wanted to know Tom's inner man you would have to ask him yourself.

Even after one adoption, Nicole held out the hope that she might have another child naturally. In February 1995, Tom and Nicole adopted a second child, Connor Antony Kidman Cruise, an African-American, born on February 6.

So now they had two children in common, and of course they were happy, though it was by now notable that Nicole had also begun to share Tom's taste for an entourage of assistants who could help look after the children and lighten her load so that she could continue her career. And that was not going too well. She had been impatient at unemployment and must have wondered whether the unkind rumors about them were helping matters. In Tom, she could observe (and learn from) an actor who set up his parts well in advance, with a lot of money coming his way and a lot of control. He did not read or audition: he slotted himself into big ventures like *A Few Good Men* and *The Firm* (both of them big hits). He had just formed his own production company (with Paula Wagner, his former agent, as his partner) and he was looking ahead to *Mission: Impossible*. To hear him talk about himself, his career was hitting every planned, positive target.

Meanwhile, Nicole could only list pictures that she wanted but never got: *Thelma & Louise* (1991), in the Geena Davis part; *The Silence of the Lambs* (1991), missing out to Jodie Foster; *Sleepless in Seattle* (1993)—the making of Meg Ryan; *Mary Reilly* (1996), for which Julia Roberts took a critical beating in maybe her best acting job; and *Ghost* (1990), which went to Demi Moore. Of course, every actress in town hungered for those parts, and it's notable how they all went to actresses who would be passed by Nicole in the next few years. But no one ever knows what the next few years will bring, unless their plan is on Cruise control.

"Tom's girl" had had to go elsewhere—to *Billy Bathgate*, a flop, even if she got some good notices; *Far and Away*, nearly an object of derision; *Malice*—the sort of picture that needs a pretty girl who will be cute and take off her clothes for about $200,000; *My Life*—a flop with Michael

Keaton; and *Batman Forever*, where she played a shrink, Dr. Chase Meridian, and did pretty well being cute and sly in a franchise film where the heavy lifting and the big money were kept for Val Kilmer, Tommy Lee Jones, and Jim Carrey. Once more for that picture Kidman got $250,000, bimbo money, and she knew as well as anyone that bimbos got four or five years in pictures before being replaced. Demi Moore was set to get $12 million for *Striptease* to be made in 1996, the best money an American actress had ever had in Hollywood. Yes, maybe the film was going to be awful, but Nicole was never considered for it because she didn't have the breasts.

Malice

Why is the picture called *Malice*? It's hardly adequate warning for a plot in which human action becomes so preposterous that the film might have been expected to rise to the audience's mounting need to laugh out loud. Nor does it really cover the ways in which the people in it behave so badly—that seems to come from authorial neglect or indifference as much as from any special insight into unkindness. The nastiness in the film is aimless, unorganized, and fanciful; it has nothing else to do but cling to the desperate melodrama. So we have to look farther afield, and eventually our search may bump up against the fact that *Malice* is the kind of "opportunity" designed to discourage and impede young actors and actresses, anyone else involved, and the whole enterprise of movie. It's the kind of picture that gets a bad name for the business and the art, in which each one shoots the other.

There are careers that have foundered on too many movies as cynical and contrived as *Malice*—take Alec Baldwin's, for example.

I suppose Baldwin was regarded as the star, or the chief thrust, of *Malice* when it was made. On the whole, he has the most vivid and unlikely scenes. He plays Jed, a surgeon recently arrived at the hospital in a small Massachusetts college town. Almost immediately he has to save the life of a student who has been raped and nearly killed by the kind of serial criminal that scriptwriters like to plant in the Berkshires. After this operation, Jed meets the concerned assistant dean of students, Andy (Bill Pullman), and then Andy's wife, Tracy. She wears

baggy jeans and flannel shirts. She has a job working with young children in a day care center. She is pretty, of course, and fond and decent,
but very dull—even in 1993 when the film was made, after the sparkle
of *Billy Bathgate*, you had to feel that Nicole Kidman was putting on her
own brakes, that she was even leaning toward ordinariness. There is a
love scene with Andy, but it's the kind of clinch that reminds you how
chilly Massachusetts interiors are at most times of the year. And while it
offers a very pretty bare bottom, enough to bring credit to any actress,
that bottom is so guarded by a separate close-up that we don't necessarily trust it to be Nicole's, and we certainly don't feel the merry lust
that belonged to her Mrs. Preston.

Andy and Tracy are college poor. They have bills; they can't afford
drapes or blinds—the child across the way watches them when they
make love. So they rent a flat in their large house to Jed. He moves in
and has a lot of wild sex upstairs with several different women. The
chandelier swings in Tracy's bedroom below as she gazes up at the ceil-
ing bitterly (after nearly a hundred years, this is the art of cinema!). Jed
is altogether full of himself, and such a star at the hospital that you have
to wonder why he is content to be there. Be patient, this cockamamie
plot has its reasons.

The serial killer continues, as steady as the cold air, and in the
process he offs Gwyneth Paltrow in one of her earliest films—but not
before she has one very nifty scene as a gorgeous, spoiled flirt. (In films
like *Malice*, the lucky or shrewd actors have just one scene.) Why is the
serial killer given screen time? So that the dour town detective, Dana
(Bebe Neuwirth), can feel compelled to ask Andy for a sperm sample—
he has come under circumstantial suspicion as the killer. He delivers,
and this leaves Tracy looking the more wan and wistful: Andy may not
have enough sperm to be giving it away. (I know, this is facetious, but
truly it is the type of response that *Malice* provokes and requires.)

Anyway, Tracy's troubles grow. She has internal pains. It is said that
she has a specialist in Boston. And she wants to be pregnant. She has a
crisis—we see Tracy/Nicole doubled over in pain, calling 911, being
whisked into the ER, with Jed dragged away from the town bar where
he has had several drinks so he can operate on her.

It proves a complicated procedure. One ovary has to be removed. An early fetus aborts. And then Dr. Jed notices that the other ovary is "necrotic," or might be. There is some dispute over the matter. But the reliable testing procedure is not available for this emergency. So Jed consults Andy—save Tracy, he is told. So he takes out the second ovary, too. Incidentally, Nicole seems to perk up a little from this point on, as if to suggest that the procedure has been therapeutic—or is it just that her part is coming to life?

Bingo, she is suddenly a furious and vengeful woman, scornful of Andy for permitting the operation and dead set on suing Jed and the hospital. For the second ovary was healthy. Jed had been drinking. Twenty million dollars is in the air in damages. Andy is discarded. There is a scene in a Boston law office where such smart players as George C. Scott, Peter Gallagher, and Josef Sommer appear, and it is clear that Tracy is going to be made for life—or at last able to get designer jeans and rather more impressive tops. She might even think of doing something with her long, Rapunzel-like ringleted hair.

I wish that I could set plot aside, but this one keeps coming—like hurricanes on the unlucky shores of Florida. Tracy disappears. Andy is down in the dumps. But then one night, he discovers the serial rapist/killer, and he feels a little better about himself. Then Dana, gloomy throughout, but still Bebe Neuwirth, tells him he couldn't have been the father of Tracy's fetus. How does she know? Because the sperm sample he gave her revealed him as sterile! (There's a hint that Dana's despond is deepened by this discovery. She has a kind of rural Massachusetts yen for Andy, which is another reason for being gloomy.)

So Andy starts thinking and he begins to realize that his Tracy has very neatly managed an enormous economic elevation while abandoning him. He discovers that she has a mother who is still alive. I don't remember how he discovers that—and I'm not inclined to watch the film again to find out. Suffice it to say that the mother is Anne Bancroft, who has one terrific scene in which she spills a lot of backstory over half a bottle of single malt whisky, and leaves two impressions: one, that Tracy is not nearly as nice a girl as we were led to believe; and two, that a Nicole Kidman with more awareness or clout would have demanded a scene or two with Bancroft. The mother has the same frizzy hair and I can easily see them snarling at each other. I could even understand the notion of having the mother and daughter in cahoots on the whole fraud.

But what do we do with Jed? One of Alec Baldwin's colorful scenes as Jed is in the lawyer's conference room where, taunted with the question "Do you have a God complex?," he launches into a quite insane harangue about being God. Of course, this helps secure the settlement against him, as his own lawyer might have guessed and forestalled by crying, Fire! But no. Jed is in the plot with Tracy. They are very hot for each other, it is said, though Baldwin especially seems varnished in self-love. But the God complex is intriguing, and it threatens to get in the way of everything.

We are now on the wilder shores of denouement where anything might happen. Andy goes on the trail of revenge, and he tells Tracy he will settle for half the money. Tracy wants to be fucked by Jed but then when Jed says he might testify against her she shoots and kills him. Why? Well, sit down: Cunning Andy has said that spying child next door saw Jed inject Tracy with enough of a drug to destroy her first ovary (you recall her first ovary?). So Tracy is set to kill that child, and that's how the showdown occurs. BUT THE BOY NEXT DOOR WAS BLIND! This is ironic, I think. But how Tracy lived next door to the boy without knowing he was blind is more than the film asks.

So Jed is dead, Tracy is on her way to prison, and a rueful Andy is left with the gloomy Dana. It's no advertisement for Massachusetts or college life. And it's no kindness to Nicole Kidman either. I'd have to say that she comes in fourth among the actresses, trailing Bancroft, Neuwirth, and Paltrow. Yet that's a little tough. From the moment Tracy is free from her setup softy role, she begins to be more interesting. When she rips off her shirt prior to sex with Jed there is a look of absolute need and authority. She flowers a little in nastiness, and in the very last shot of her there is a hint of loneliness and madness.

Malice was directed by Harold Becker, and its screenplay was by Aaron Sorkin and Scott Frank, both of whom were on their way to much bigger things. The implausibility of so much competes with the brazen inconsistencies in Jed and the masked nature of the early Tracy. Still, it's possible that someone suffered through *Malice* and noticed in the last half hour the sudden look of appetite on Kidman's face. Suppose the film had been done from Tracy's point of view: a truly wicked girl, but one inclined to defend herself in her own mind because, after all, she's not as awful as her mother. You could do everything from her point of view so that we feel and enjoy the deceit. You could even stay in New England. Not impossible.

So someone might see a bad film, and a flop, and realize that while Alec Baldwin was falling away, that girl might yet make something of her greedy eyes. If she could do something with her hair.

To Die For

"Suddenly I had something," says Nicole. "The earlier parts that I'd had in America, so many were lame. But now, I thought, 'I can say these words.' I didn't change a line. Buck Henry talked me through the dialogue, and *The Graduate* was one of my favorite films. The sexuality was something I had never had a chance to do. And I relished the darkness of it all. It felt like being set free to play. There was no feeling of a studio judging you. Gus Van Sant had a wicked sense of humor and didn't like regimentation. I just had so many beautiful scenes and they felt so easy to do. People said the character was me, but the lines were all written before I was thought of. It was just that they freed me."

To Die For altered most people's ideas of Nicole Kidman as an actress, and as a force that might generate and sustain whole movies. It isn't just that she's good in the film—wicked, naughty, sexy yet always wide-eyed—it's that the entire picture had a commercial panache that overcame its modest scale and its near-independent approach. Once *To Die For* was out there, picking up prizes for Kidman and generating exactly the right word of mouth—that she was a new Nicole, or herself at last—it was fairly clear that with the kind of advance planning on which such things rely, *To Die For* could have been a much bigger hit. In turn, that would have offered the highly dangerous possibility that satire, a comic character study, and authentic black humor could still be the stuff of hits in American film.

In fact, the powers that be (the "regimentation") do not incline to believe such a thing—for how can they maintain their upright posture

To Die For

and their forward momentum if they ever begin to think that the audience might be grown-up, smart, witty, and fatalistic? In other words, while it was terrific for Nicole to make this breakthrough, she could have realized from the outset that a change in terms of how the audience and the business regard you is a two-edged sword. You may win the Oscar being Virginia Woolf, you may confound many critics in seeming to be the hand and the mind from which *Mrs. Dalloway* might flow, but what then? Don't expect Miramax or Warner Brothers to be fighting over your hopes to do George Eliot or Emily Brontë. You are more likely to be asked to play an idiot in an idiotic venture, with $10–15 million as the new sweetener.

Put that way, it may be easier to focus on the critical intersection in the enjoyment of *To Die For*: the fertile gap between the dumb cunning of Suzanne Stone and the brilliant innocence of Nicole Kidman. For this is not simply a movie where we enjoy Suzanne's small-town Machiavellian urges. It is one in which we gain much more from seeing the sophistication of Nicole Kidman being put to these ends. Of course, the two personae fit together as tidily and as prettily as . . . well, as Kidman's breasts in the violet-colored underwear she sports in one scene. Nicole is law-abiding, to be sure, but those on the film saw why it was working—because the actress and the character had burning ambition in common.

The picture came from a successful novel of the same name by Joyce Maynard. Leslie Morgan, in producer Laura Ziskin's office, read the book and liked it. They bought the rights quite cheaply and offered it to Buck Henry as screenwriter. In turn that led to Gus Van Sant coming on board as director, just because he and Henry shared an agent. It was a small, offbeat venture, until Henry turned in sixty brilliant pages. "I had no actress in mind," says Henry. "But when it was done, I thought of Jennifer Jason Leigh. Gus wanted Meg Ryan and I think Laura was keen on Patricia Arquette." It's like watching chemistry being tried out. Everyone knew that Ryan was the best bet: she had the popular support to make a tricky project viable. People liked her.

Six years older than Nicole, Meg Ryan was at that time several lengths ahead of her in terms of career: she had had her strange mock orgasm in *When Harry Met Sally* (and mock orgasms satisfy some audiences far more than the real thing), and she'd had the big hit *Sleepless in Seattle*. Meg Ryan was worth the role of Suzanne, though a shrewd observer might have wondered if she had the naughtiness it required or the same need to be famous. Meg Ryan could have done it; she might have been grand; but it wasn't obvious that she had energies just waiting for Suzanne, let alone the propensity for mocking self-awareness. For what is striking about Nicole's Suzanne are the multiple levels, and the actress's own ironic stance. (Suzanne wants to be news, and to cover the story—isn't that fair?) Kidman is stepping in and out of this Little Hope, New Hampshire, sensation, and she's tickled enough by the resemblances not to insist on being holier than Suzanne. In Australia, Nicole observers were amused at the way Suzanne's extraordinary search for fame echoed with Nicole's single-minded drive to get to the top.

There was a deal: Ryan was to get $5 million on a budget of $20 million. But did the actress wonder if she could make fun of Suzanne? Irony had never seemed Ryan's forte. She was already aiming herself at what became *Courage Under Fire*, and that was far more in the line of *Sally* and *Seattle*—a woman alone, appealing, plucky, heroic, with integrity, someone the public could love and admire. And remember that all through the business or the art of movies nowadays sensible (or otherwise) people screw themselves up on the question, Will I be liked?, which is not always that far from the more personal worry, Would I like me like that? In the event, Meg Ryan turned it down, though she may have been affected by the failure of Gus Van Sant's latest film, *Even Cowgirls Get the Blues*.

At that point, Nicole's agent, Rick Nicita, called Laura Ziskin and said his client was perfect for Suzanne. "Nicole came in to talk to us," remembers Henry, "and was spot on from the first minute. She was also the loveliest thing I had ever laid eyes on. But what she understood was Suzanne's lack of humor—so she didn't need to be coy. This was the courage, being Suzanne and letting the joke work."

Laura Ziskin was more doubtful. *To Die For* was a film that men and women "got" in different ways. Ziskin hadn't liked Nicole's most recent work. "But when she came in I realized 'she knew something' about this part. It was in her. That's when I learned she's not an ingenue.

She's a character actress in an ingenue package. Cast her as 'the girl' and she's not right, not excited. We had a lot of tape of local weather girls and Nicole watched it and got it. But then it happened: We put a blonde wig on her curly red hair. It was a Eureka moment. I thought, Carole Lombard!"

Nicole jumped at Suzanne Stone, the way a cat might pounce on a wounded bird—with a view to sport as much as appetite. "Once we started," says Ziskin, "she slayed us. It was brilliant and people were laughing on set."

The story of *To Die For* could be played in many ways. In the town of Little Hope, New Hampshire (a world that Joyce Maynard had studied at first hand in the years when she was involved with J. D. Salinger), Suzanne Stone comes out of nowhere. She has parents and a sister; the sister has been politely crushed by Suzanne, the father may have been flirted with to a point of ordinary madness, and the mother is simply that excellent actress, Holland Taylor, doing nothing, miscast, I fear, or simply neglected in the writing. Suzanne deserves more backstory— unless your concept is that she is so thoroughly self-interested that she never noticed her own family.

She marries a doltish Italian restaurateur (Matt Dillon), but it's not clear why. She has no interest in him, and he has no understanding of her. He cannot really do anything to help her ambition, which is to get on television. So she approaches a local station (a two-man operation) and talks herself into the job of their weather reporter—she calls it the Weather Center. That leads to her wish to make a cinema verité documentary about local high school kids, and in time Suzanne will use three of these kids to murder her husband. Why kill him? There's no better answer than there is to the question, Why marry him? Unless you are prepared to go with an inner surreal wisdom—not cockeyed, at all—that Suzanne's best chance of *really* being on TV is to be up close and personal in a scandalous murder case (one that makes the Boston stations!). Like a suspect. Like all the time!

Good as the film is, the script impedes itself and takes away from the most interesting idea of all: Suzanne's consuming desire to be on television—a lust for fame and attention that is nearly content-free. Thus the documentary she makes is far too reasonable a project—it's as if she'd heard of Ricky Leacock and the verité school he inspired in Cambridge, Massachusetts. And the beauty of Kidman's performance is her tremendous emphasis on cuteness, camera presence, and "style" to the detriment of character or personality. The very best thing about the film is the direct-to-camera narration Suzanne gives—still uninfected by the immorality of what she has done—still spinning the story to her own best ends. There could not be a better model for the way in which vanity and self-love have obliterated critical thinking. The acidity of the satire also requires that she has got herself married only to kill her husband (or to be accused of it) because that is the best promotion for an on-camera career.

Nicole had difficulty with these scenes, and the difficulty is very close to her engine as an actress.

"I battle with being shy," she tells me. "I have lots of ideas—many more than I actually give in a film. And shyness embarrasses me. I've never given a performance I think is really good. It's why I can blush on camera—because I am embarrassed, because I've blown it. Perfection never comes. I like scenes I've done. I liked *Moulin Rouge*. Stuff in *The Others, The Hours*. Never the whole thing. I'm hopeless watching my films. I don't see them any more. I feel literally nauseous. I can never see a rough cut. Kubrick made me watch playbacks on set on *Eyes Wide Shut* on the monitor. But that's all."

To Die For could be rewritten so that the murder trial comes halfway through. Suzanne is freed, while everyone knows she is guilty, and this infamy launches her to New York and the network level. She becomes someone exactly like Katie Couric, Diane Sawyer, or Suzanne Stone. She becomes the face on television, her eyes so wide it takes a philosopher to see that they are also shut.

And there is another forsaken direction: her relationship with the boozy, lascivious TV veteran played by George Segal, the man she sets out to meet and win on her honeymoon while the idiot hubby is off fishing. Their meeting is one of the sharpest scenes in this movie, and it leaves one lamenting the departure of George Segal. He could be the Addison De Witt (George Sanders) so vital to the crooked education of Eve Harrington (Anne Baxter) in *All About Eve*. And inasmuch as he would know the truths about Suzanne, then at the end he would be the man she needed to murder, to keep her trail clear. In other words, *To Die For* should vault from a high-number New Hampshire station to Manhattan and single-digit network exposure. Why not have Suzanne interview the pope, the queen, O.J.? The deaths should gather pace, but they should all be bouquets laid at the nail-polished toes of Suzanne. Far from being dispatched in an indirect rebuke for wickedness, she should survive (as it is, her murder is rather trite, and ungenerous), and be a queen of our new world, vacuous yet lovely, inane yet eye-catching, at her most serene in her triumphant confessions. Deep down, you see, Suzanne is an organism that understands TV: and today there is no royalty to match that. This is the kind of movie that the pathetic *Up Close and Personal* might have been if its leads, Robert Redford and Michelle Pfeiffer, had not been so desperate to be liked. Or if *Up Close* had been tart enough to have Pfeiffer betraying her mentor, Redford.

Imagine Redford as a Charlie Rose type who is Suzanne's last coup (she takes over his show), and she so devours that rather self-regarding dolphin that he is left like a bare, intact skeleton ravished and stripped by her dentally perfect piranha.

This dream of a film is there in the present *To Die For*, even if it is half-hearted to have Suzanne screwing Joaquin Phoenix's forlorn teenager when she might be handling the president's cabinet. Yes, I know, that's in bad taste, but bad taste is exactly what this frigid nation and its anxiety-ridden cinema require. The great virtue of *To Die For* is that it comes close enough to let us realize that.

In Joyce Maynard's novel, the narrative point of view keeps switching: over twenty different people give their take on what happened, including an invented Phil Donahue. It's important to the film that much of that panorama has been reduced. We do hear the halting testimony of the teenagers, the bitter sideswiping of the sister-in-law and the snide primness of the TV station manager in Little Hope. But these voices now seem employed to justify the one central voice, that of Suzanne herself—large, head-on, in a dreamy abstraction from any clear reality, at her prettiest. It is a kind of idealized version of what being on TV might be like—a silly rapture. And whereas in the novel, Suzanne sounds stupid, raw, petty, and very much like a real provincial sociopath, the movie's narrator is a psychopath triumphant (a little like Norman Bates at the end of *Psycho*). And nothing underlines the triumph more clearly than the confidence that confides in us—it is a bravura display of nudging reminders that this lovely girl is a dark manipulator, an organizer of murder, with a rapacious ambition. All of which we are supposed to understand, to accept, and to swallow whole. Because she is a celebrity.

Nicole says that the sustained confessional close-ups unnerved her technically—until she realized that they were boasts, or if not quite as vulgar as that, serene, lyrical, intimate admissions, the real glue that bonds us to her. It raises a very intriguing possibility, that the best and most penetrating way to explore evil in films is to shine the radiance of self-love on it, to let it sunbathe in the light of wickedness. And there's a way in which the film's very bright lighting scheme, its day-glo colors and the fresh-as-paint look of Nicole are all part of this. All through the film she shows off a lot of skin, and there's a sense of her gradually edging toward nakedness—the ultimate reveling in her badness.

Her skirts are very short. When she visits the high school class to propose her documentary film, one kid tries to look all the way up it. There are those brief, odd-angled lovemaking scenes with Joaquin Phoenix, cut off before you can see anything, but in general Suzanne is photographed like an advertisement for ripe fruit. And there is always an excess of light (quite unlike New Hampshire) on her, the way carefully concealed banks of light fall on the produce in a supermarket. Indeed, the America of *To Die For* has the high-key gloss and burnish of a market, and the selling of the self is the fat skin lotion on Suzanne's voice. Nicole was no longer Australian for this film. She acquired an accent—far more Californian than New England—as soothing as the stringed orchestra music in a supermarket, and as knowing as a TV anchorwoman who has learned the listless flirtation that is possible with the camera.

The very clever texture of the performance, and the almost merry teasing it embodies, all point toward the begging opportunities in making a film about television. There's a sublime moment (in the dreamy, drugged mind of the Phoenix character) when Suzanne's bland weather commentary becomes a tumescent sexual reverie. Kidman's comic persona is perfect for that weird double entendre that underlies the most chaste and fearful of all our media. It is perfectly attuned to the way in which certain television performers by doing nothing (or close to it) do sex—I always had the thought that Nicole's interpretation owed a lot to the weird glory of Vanna White on *Wheel of Fortune*. For a season, Vanna was a goddess: turning the letters on the show; appearing in a multipage *Playboy* spread (with or without her permission); writing her memoirs; and being a household name and dream. I saw Vanna once at Burbank Airport waiting for a delayed plane with her manager. She sat there fretting, turning, adjusting her looks and her look (they are not the same), as if being filmed all the time. And the crowd that numbly circled her, attending yet not intruding—as if she were a praying pope or a dangerous tiger—could not stop looking at her, because she was at that moment the woman on TV. You could say it was her ordinariness, her drabness, that made her accessible, or human, just as it was her cosmetic prettiness that made her "cute"—I fear that is the word. There was actually never any sense of character. And that is a part of Kidman's savage, happy fun with Suzanne. There is a kind of glee in her face, prepared to slide off on the pretty nonentity that can get away with being photographed and celebrated, without ever opening her score. Thus, Suzanne is America's sexpot (or at least Little Hope's) who needs to have instruction in the blow job.

Just because the picture falls short in some ways, just because it doesn't ride on Suzanne's lovely back to prime time and magazine covers, is no reason to disparage its values. *To Die For* is funny, nasty, and utterly unimpressed by the general ranks of Americana and Americans. There is authentic satire here, a reluctance to fall for any sweet consoling white lies in the dark scene. I suspect a lot of the credit for that is owed to Buck Henry, one of the underused talents in American film. But just as much comes from Nicole, from the wicked, exercising energy and appetite of an actress smart enough to think a great deal about such things as performance, personality, and the presentation of self in everyday life. She could have done more, maybe. But that is not to be ungrateful for what she does, which is to taunt us with the mystery of her sexiness and her ordinariness; to poke fun at us for being suckers for creatures like Vanna White; and to flex her aching capacity for something really demanding.

There's something else in the wicked fun. Anyone who has been married a few years has at least contemplated (and begun to list) the possible ways of eliminating a spouse. Seriously? No, not seriously— but in the age in which we are used to wondering What if?, nothing has to be fatal, forever, or serious, does it? After all, we talk of being ready "to die for" without really meaning suicide, and maybe without even knowing that in the age of Shakespeare "to die" could mean to have an orgasm. The best thing to be said about the film of *To Die For* is the sweet, tender way in which it acknowledges our asking What if? as we look at movies or television, at this or that empty, pretty smile.

And, of course, once you get to that point, then there's no doubt about the very knowing, stealthily intimate smile Suzanne reserves for the camera, for she sees us thinking of coming. She knows she's not the only one there. She exults in being watched. And one might wonder whether the excitement in Suzanne is also Nicole Kidman asking us, Well, what if I was like that, too? Do you think I am? This is a movie in which an actress begins to see the chance that she might be a phenomenon. The film is buttery with its own power. Bite into it and the melting juice fills your mouth.

It was noticed. Grossing $10 million, the modest film easily earned its money back. (It had been considerably scaled down with Meg Ryan's departure—Nicole was paid $2 million, not $5 million.) And while the daring and the quality were there in the concept, the script, and the direction (not to mention a faultless supporting cast), nearly everyone recognized it as Nicole's triumph or emergence. She was not nominated for an Oscar—and that is a further support for Meg Ryan's judgment at the time. There were stories of elderly academicians walking out on the "tastelessness" of the whole venture (Susan Sarandon would win the Oscar that year for playing a nun in *Dead Man Walking*). But the emerging enterprise of the Golden Globes picked on Kidman and gave her the nod for Best Actress in a Comedy. In addition, the

Boston Film Critics named her Best Actress. Best of all, maybe, everyone knew about *To Die For*. In the *Film Comment* magazine roundup of the year, Richard Jameson treasured the moment of "Wide-eyed fizzy innocence going all flat as Suzanne Stone (Nicole Kidman) flips a cute little umbrella out of her drink, takes a hard suck on the straw, and calculates how much screentime might be bought by 'doing things ordinary people wouldn't do' to George Segal's cock."

Something else came with the success: the widespread feeling that when acting is so good the nature of the player is incriminated. Or, to be practical, if an actress had to be Suzanne from nine till five, sometimes the "magic" lasted until six or six-thirty. Word did get around that yes, of course, Kidman had been great in *To Die For* because, really, it was her. Acting is a kind of immersion, and sometimes those drenched are too wet or cold to handle. But the shift in response was also part of the first widespread longing—that that blond teacher with a dress swinging up to her waist so that her panties showed would dance in our headlights. Anyone that ravishing probably deserved to be punished. (The cinema at its best always knocks on the door of our hypocrisy.)

So a lot of new people liked Nicole, but the first word crept out that she could be chilly and self-concerned.

Laura Ziskin was inspired to think of Nicole—with Tom even!—in a remake of one of her favorite films, the Lubitsch comedy *Trouble in Paradise* (1932), about jewel thieves who fall in love. It was a film from the heady days when screen characters could be wicked and adorable. But the young actors couldn't see it, and it has not yet been made. For every equation written in stone, there are others that pass in the night. The lessons are intricate: *Trouble in Paradise* today sounds farfetched—until it happens (with Hugh Grant, say, and Angelina Jolie). Then naughtiness might be "in" for a season. Equally, Laura Ziskin recalls that handling *To Die For* was always a matter of easing the anxieties in changing powers at Columbia (its studio). She adds, in 2006, "It's something you could never make today!" And that is often true—until you make it.

The Portrait of a Lady

I daresay a mood or a sentiment exists in movie stars that if you do something that amounts to a hit then you have earned the right to do something esoteric, difficult, something for yourself. Maybe. There was a time when actors kept the stage for those tender plans.

The Portrait of a Lady is an odd title, so plain, yet full of warning notes, and the harder to be sure of in an age that has learned to think of women as opposed to ladies. By now, we wonder if "lady" signals effeteness, or a lack of vigor. In her regular life, does Nicole Kidman want to be regarded as a lady or a woman?

A portrait is generally supposed to be complete. If we look at a great face by Rembrandt or Lucian Freud we expect to feel the wholeness of a life—its entirety—even if the picture in question fixes on a moment and a glance. One gesture or attitude speaks for fifty or eighty years. We know this person. Yet Henry James's *The Portrait of a Lady* is a long book that ends so strangely, or abruptly, with such a sense of drama or action still to be worked out, that completeness hardly seems applicable. Unless being a lady is what can get someone like Isabel Archer into the predicament she faces at the end of her book—an odious, merciless husband and a stepdaughter who may be fatally damaged by her father. Is it even possible that being what James calls "a lady" is loaded with irony and a recipe for disaster in the new times of 1881? Was Henry James asking whether being a lady is enough?

Imagine a portrait by Titian, *A Portrait of a Gentleman,* a person of about forty, mature, confident without being arrogant, plainly with

The Portrait of a Lady

means (we see it in his clothes). It is a portrait not just of the man, but of the times in which he registers as a gentleman, a knight, an aristocrat, a man of importance, a man who could get his picture painted. We feel a harmony in the view through the window—a garden, tidy, with sweet country, the vined terraces of Tuscany beyond. But now suppose that the window has been changed. Suppose, instead, we see ruined buildings, the smoke of battlefield fires and two dreadfully wounded men supporting each other as they hobble away. Yet the assurance in the man's gaze has not altered. I don't think Titian did such pictures, but irony was not in vogue in his day. Goya could have managed such a contrast. Henry James might have meant for irony to grow as a book is read—after all, when he called another novel *The Golden Bowl*, he was not offering us a perfect object, but something deeply flawed.

I begin this way because it is no ordinary show business task to take on *The Portrait of a Lady*. The depth of the writing (which is not the same as narrative depth, or content begging to be dramatized) almost requires what Nicole will say as the film reaches theaters, "This film means more to me than any film I've made. And I know it does to Jane [Campion], too. Some films you make which you can walk away from. This is one we're very protective of. We're out there feeling that we have to shield the baby. Protect the baby!" And there is the earlier promise, from Nicole's childhood, that they would work together one day. Both women feel that *The Portrait of a Lady* is the fulfillment of the gentle contract implicit in that attention. And the metaphor of "the baby" hardly comes by chance.

Nicole Kidman will say later that the first time she read James's novel, at fourteen or so, she did not altogether understand it. Nevertheless, to attempt the book at that age, and to come away impressed, suggests a rigorous approach to education in her home and precociousness in the child. She reads it again in her late teens, and it means more. That may be the right time to stop reading James's great book, for very soon her sense of it may deepen so far as to make it clear that a movie of *The Portrait of a Lady* is not possible. That would be a sensible, respectful decision—and one borne out in many ways by the film to come—but think what we would lose from it. And when, within the space of a few years, an actress can go from playing Dr. Claire Lewicki, a doll neurosurgeon, to Miss Isabel Archer in a version of *The Portrait of a Lady*, directed by Jane Campion—well, who is going to have any doubts about what that represents?

Campion has just made *The Piano*, a remarkable film about sexuality, marriage, and escape set on a wild Pacific shore. It is a film in which Holly Hunter and Anna Paquin win the two female acting Oscars—not that anyone regards the men in the film, Sam Neill and Harvey Keitel, as less than brilliant. It is a great film, and although no one remarks on this at the time, it is like an astonishingly bold, free adaptation of Jamesian themes and problems whose creator had the wit to employ an un-Jamesian setting (one of melodrama, action, and acting out). It may even be an advantage of such an approach that the character of the woman in *The Piano* is speechless—what bolder way is there of defying the intense inward articulation of a heroine in James, that feeling that it is the need to puzzle over feeling so much that prevents or does away with the habit of doing things?

I don't mean to say that Jane Campion went through the process of thinking out how to do James on film by ignoring every one of his outward rules. But the ideas in an artist's mind will prevail—and, like Isabel Archer (as Gilbert Osmond sees it), Jane Campion is the kind of person who always has too many ideas. But in her next step—as she comes to do Henry James "properly"—the advantage of reckless liberty becomes more apparent. Not that that is any reason to do without her film of *The Portrait of a Lady*—just a way of suggesting the blunt truth, that it cannot work.

There are very interesting preludes to the James film, not least the apparent agreement between Campion and Kidman that Kidman will have the part—that of a young American lady, an orphan, who comes first to England and then to Italy; who is loved and courted by most men she meets; but who elects to marry not just the worst of them all, but someone who embodies the network of wickedness, moral indifference, and imprisonment that will sharpen Isabel and bring her of age until, like an archer, she might reach for a fatal arrow.

Director and actress meet in Sydney, and Campion remembers the impact: "She came into the flat, and we couldn't take our eyes off her. She was very bold with us, and very sweet, wanting to discuss with us the whole book and at the same time blushing and feeling a little awkward. She was bold and unsure at the same time."

But then, as the plans advance (despite the report that Ivory-Merchant may intend to do the same book), Jane Campion loses a child very shortly after his birth. (You may remember that Isabel Osmond will suffer the same fate herself—and it is left unexplained by the Henry James who does rather flinch from matter-of-fact events in life.)

So there is a delay in the project and in that time Jane Campion takes the trouble to see a few things—*Days of Thunder, Billy Bathgate, Far and Away, Malice, My Life*, and *Batman Forever*—and feels that the fourteen-year-old may not have done the best job at looking after her talent. Aren't these pretty mediocre pictures in which she is the girlfriend, the wicked woman, the sex thing, and so on? So Campion wavers, and Kidman is angry. Perhaps it has all been a test; perhaps fierceness, as opposed to obedience, was what Campion was looking for. At any event, Kidman consents to some "auditions"—two days' work in Los Angeles, readings with Campion herself, working from the novel. After that, Campion calls her and says Nicole is her Isabel.

It is in the gap caused by the death in Campion's family that Nicole films *To Die For*, and if that is her best work yet, still it is a long way from the code or mood of Henry James. But it is a strengthening of her confidence.

It would be hard to fault the preparations for *The Portrait of a Lady*. Jane Campion is very "hot" at this moment, and the James book is the kind of famous classic no one has read. A great deal of filming will be done in Italy, in September 1995, after a start in England. Gardencourt, the Touchett country house, is beautifully established—though lovers of the book may still hunger for a little more attention to the nourishing tranquillity of its garden and "the perfect middle of a splendid summer afternoon." The places in Tuscany and Rome are as faded and noble as old ruins; a kind of gloomy, half-subterranean chapel (or tomb) is an inspired choice for a key scene between Osmond and Isabel. And the cast is illustrious: it takes real wit to have Shelley Winters married to John Gielgud, yet it is right for a marriage where the partners are never together; it would be hard to improve on Martin Donovan as Ralph Touchett, Richard E. Grant as Lord Warburton, Viggo Mortensen as

Caspar Goodwood, or Mary-Louise Parker as Henrietta Stackpole. I will come to the glory of Barbara Hershey as Madame Merle—Serena Merle, the name is made clear in the film.

The problem centers on John Malkovich as Osmond. Consider the situation. Isabel Archer is plainly our heroine—not just because Nicole is in the part, or even because the title of the book would seem to direct us toward her, but because the action is directed by her character and by her determination: "I think I have to begin by getting a general impression of life, do you see?" she tells Mr. Touchett after she has turned down Lord Warburton's proposal. "And there's a light that has to dawn. I can't explain it, but I know it's there. I know I can't give up. I'm not afraid, you know."

That is very good scriptwriting in what is a brilliant adaptation (by Laura Jones). Not only does it sound like talk, as well as talk that helps us understand action, but the stress on "knowing" alerts us to Isabel's vulnerability, the arrogance of intelligence. And Kidman is quite marvelous in these assertive moments: she sounds American (most of the time); her red-brown hair piles up on her head in a credible yet unsophisticated way; and her brave blue eyes stare out of a very pale skin and slightly red-rimmed eyes. She is as pretty as Isabel needs to be, but there is an authentic rawness, a feeling of the person not being fully fashioned yet.

And this Isabel rejects Caspar Goodwood, declines Lord Warburton, and elects not to consider her cousin Ralph. He loves her, it is evident; she is at ease with him—the book establishes that more fully than the film. But he is sick, and she has written him off because of it. Of course, it has to be said that James's inability or reluctance to pursue what is the most natural and appealing bond in view is very much his own and rather more a part of his oddity than true to Isabel's nature. After repeated readings of the book, I still believe she might have chosen Ralph—and who knows what that would have done for his constitution?

But James undermines Isabel's real spirit and intelligence as he explores it layer by layer—this is the thing that is so hostile to film in his writing. And what does he do? He has her fall for Gilbert Osmond.

This is a little easier to manage in the book, where we do not have to see Osmond. So we hear his lizardlike eloquence; you see, I cannot even account for his talk without being frightened by him. And not even James can plot the thing out without the earlier scene in which Madame Merle presents Isabel to Osmond as a target or a goal. In other words, their planning precedes the meeting. We fear the worst. Not that Osmond succeeds by any kind of charm or lightness. He does not put on an act to win Isabel. In the end, James is mystified—we have to recognize that he does not grasp how it is that women or men succumb, how they fall in love. In the book, there is a conversation that ends with this quite magnificent prevarication:

> On this he took a rapid, respectful leave. When he had gone she stood a moment looking about her and seated herself slowly and with an air of deliberation. She sat there till her companions came back, with folded hands, gazing at the ugly carpet. Her agitation— for it had not diminished—was very still, very deep. What had happened was something that for a week past her imagination had been going forward to meet; but here, when it came, she stopped—that sublime principle somehow broke down. The working of this young lady's spirit was strange, and I can only give it to you as I see it, not hoping to make it seem altogether natural. Her imagination, as I say, now hung back; there was a last vague space it couldn't cross—a dusky, uncertain tract which looked ambiguous and even slightly treacherous, like a moorland seen in the winter twilight. But she was to cross it yet.

Even in the novel, it comes to be accepted that Isabel will marry Osmond. Ralph predicts that the union will be a prison and she tells him she's thought about it and is content. Yet Jane Campion seems to know that this resignation will not pass in a modern movie—and despite the studious period costumes, this is a picture coming at the close of the twentieth century. Later on she will use titles—A Year Later . . . A Few More Years Later—and in that passage Isabel's face becomes beautiful and tragic, her hair goes from ginger to a drab brown, and she is in agony over Gilbert. But Campion knows that movie audiences expect a big scene—indeed, she has signaled how well she knows this by that crass and quite awful "dream" sequence in which an earlier Isabel is lying on her bed, being kissed and touched in turn by Warburton, Goodwood, and Touchett (they might be undertakers, assessing her body for their rites). This is a risible moment, but it speaks to a director's knowing that audiences will think, This girl, Isabel, she does want to get laid, doesn't she?

So Campion arranges (this business is not in the script) a magnificent scene in a half-lit chapel or grotto (the one alluded to earlier) where Osmond comes upon Isabel with the parasol she has lost. As they talk, he does a good deal of choreographic magic with the open sunshade, and Campion lets its shadow play on the shadows of the two figures. There is something vampiric in his wooing of her. Finally, using it as a circle to enclose them, Osmond kisses Isabel.

This is not possible onscreen without actually asking Malkovich to kiss Kidman. And this is not pretty, not enticing, and not remotely credible as a prelude to marriage. And it is Henry James's failing, which is why he never wrote such a scene himself, and might have fainted if anyone had ordered him to.

I do not think there has ever been a person in the audience seeing that kiss who has not cried out, "No!" It is a moment where we want to get at the screen, and it speaks terribly to Isabel's vaunted spirit and intelligence that she yields to this snake's second-rate parasol routine.

I used to take it for granted that the fault was simply Malkovich's, that that icy, sinister voice and those staring, hard-bead eyes were unmistakable (Kidman admits to feeling humiliated by him sometimes). Let me add that as *The Portrait of a Lady* opened, Malkovich had just made *In the Line of Fire* (where his assassin actually stuck a gun in Clint Eastwood's gaping mouth), *Heart of Darkness* (where he is Kurtz), *Mary Reilly* (where his Dr. Jekyll is so chilling you don't even think about Hyde), and *Mulholland Falls* (where he is the venereally degenerate monster who runs the atomic energy program and flattens Jennifer Connelly's great breasts by having her tipped out of a plane).

You can say that that history is irrelevant. But if it's hardly possible to watch *The Portrait of a Lady* without marveling at the journey Nicole

Kidman has made, then it's impossible not to wonder whether she didn't see a Malkovich film along the way. And one would have been enough.

Yet it's not quite right or fair to say he was wrong for the part. As Osmond becomes the tyrant (and he gets there very fast in screen time), as we see him lolling on his quattrocento bed, wearing a fez, scolding servants for putting the wrong cushion on a sofa, and generally behaving like a shit, John Malkovich is perfect, entrancing, and actually very restrained. As well he might be, granted the impenetrable roguery in which Osmond is protected against any sympathy. Gilbert Osmond is a man to murder, and if James had been writing forty years later (at the dawn of the careers of Faulkner and Hemingway), then murder it might have been. Better that as a departure than the silly dream scene. But Malkovich seems to understand how this man is a monster of "taste," yet dead to flavor. He is matchless in the majority of the picture and really very frightening in the world where a slap in the face is the extent of visible violence.

But in being cast, he breaks the bowl of the movie in two pieces that no glue can mend. I have wondered whether other actors could have done better—William Hurt could have played the part, for sure. Kevin Spacey? Too young then. Warren Beatty? Too old, perhaps, but if Beatty could have been persuaded to try it, let alone to be unlikable, he has the charm and the sexuality as well as the awareness of taste, the selfishness, and all the armored nothing in Gilbert Osmond. He might have been marvelous. He could, I think, have made it credible that Isabel falls for him. He could even have been an Osmond at the end who thought he was right. And it is the final failure of Osmond as a character that he is locked in the worst confines of melodrama—he is a villain fit to be hissed. Suppose he had his reasons—an attribute or an opening neither James nor this movie bothers with.

But this is where we confront Jane Campion's most nagging worries over the novel she supposedly admires. What is her attitude to her own title? As I said already, the Laura Jones script is a masterpiece of fidelity: a remarkable quantity of Jamesian nuance or hesitation is included in this draft. Time and again, the characters speak James's words—they seldom seem to be using a language from another period. But Campion cannot settle for James's use of the word "lady."

I have mentioned one bold addition—the "dream" of sexual possibility that overtakes Isabel (though its sensuality is very modest). Another, far more crushing, comes at the outset. For the film begins with the murmured voices of young women, and the image then becomes a montage of young women today, a montage that goes to color and then finally arrives at Kidman's Isabel, on the edge of the woods near Gardencourt where Lord Warburton has just proposed to her. She is clearly agitated by this proposal—the close-up of shocked eyes might go more easily with the first twinge of cancer in a young woman.

But what is this gallery of young women (chosen, it would seem, almost at random—they are not striking or memorable women) but a feeble, vulgar concession to making this movie "relevant" in 1996, in an age of "feminism"? In the published screenplay, Laura Jones calls these people "women." If an assistant director had called out to them, "Now, come along, ladies," he would have been practicing irony, or mockery—at the recent shift in relative status. You do hear the word "ladies" used like that, and you can usually hear within it the subtext that makes clear "women" is the more correct term. Jones says of her women: "Independent, impatient, unacquainted with pain, a confidence at once innocent and dogmatic, spontaneous, full of theories, with delicate, desultory, flamelike spirits, facing their destinies."

That is valiant nonsense, just as Campion's parade of females is a disaster coming at the start of this film, and a horrible admission of uneasiness—not least the knowledge that James strictly, almost religiously, neglects something that Campion would now think essential: in a nutshell, she will not be showing Gilbert in bed with Isabel.

It is vital to both the greatness of James and his limits that he would not have dreamed of such a scene. And he, or defending scholars, could easily argue that for 1881 that sort of intimacy would have been intensely anachronistic. Yet people had sex in 1881: Isabel has been made pregnant by Osmond. In a film in only a few years' time, *Cold Mountain*, in what is a far less socially sophisticated 1864–65, Inman and Ada have rather lush, picturesque sex in a photographic tone that adopts the idiom of lovemaking from modern cinema. Moreover, it might be possible to show the horror of the marriage to Osmond, the cruelty or perversity in Gilbert, very quickly.

A quick glimpse of that violation would seem to me a more reasonable addition than either the introductory women or Isabel's dream of lovemaking. But show a modern audience that kind of curb to liberty (let alone fondness) and you can hardly rein in their energies or their lust for vengeance. They are going to want the very thing that James knew he had avoided. That thing is some kind of moral and active response to the thrall of Gilbert Osmond; it is something equivalent to Nora walking out of the house at the end of A Doll's House—and really, Osmond's fastidious gathering of precious things in his interiors does furnish a kind of doll's house.

But the modern viewer expects more than Isabel quitting Osmond by means of divorce. There needs to be a financial settlement that exposes Osmond, and in some way he needs to lose his Pansy—so that she might be a stronger bloom in the world. We can forgive James for not taking those steps, but Jane Campion knows how much a "modern" movie needs some version of them. To say nothing of the energies of Kidman's performance or the competitiveness in her eyes. She is very good in the film, and she is only seriously held back by James's reservations. But in an odd way, as the film advances Isabel becomes less than a central figure. It is at exactly that moment that Madame Merle becomes so impressive.

Serena Merle is a riper part. She is a mature woman; her grave face speaks to pain and pleasures known as a younger woman. But now, at the end of this story, she is devastated. Her plot is known, yet her place is fragile. Barbara Hershey's great performance feeds on Merle's secret knowledge and waits to be damned by it. She is the most modern person in the film because her guilt and her cleverness are inseparable, and because her position in the story is so perilous and illicit. As Isabel discovers that secret, Merle loses any support from Osmond and she risks losing the respect of her daughter. If only because there is so much more that is dramatically graspable, Serena Merle becomes the most felt person at the end of the film—and maybe she becomes the lady whose terrible portrait has been painted.

Barbara Hershey is nominated for Best Supporting Actress (she loses to Juliette Binoche in *The English Patient*). No one else is noticed, and the film does poor business. It's hard to wonder why anyone thought it might work out differently. There is an audience for this kind of material in BBC television serials (a fine version of *The Portrait of a Lady* was done in 1966), but it's hard to stretch beyond that unless there is a much bolder attempt at "modernization" and clarification.

Still, for the first time in her life Nicole Kidman has been in a major film, directed by a considerable artist. Jane Campion makes grotesque errors along the way, yet they hardly matter or disturb the movie eloquence of so much of the rest. In the playing, in the settings, in the use of darkness and light, so much of this film is engrossing and satisfying. Kidman has shown herself full of understanding and dramatic energy, and willing to be part of an ensemble. What she means, I think, by seeing the film as a baby to be looked after is that it has been a more challenging experience than any she has had before. But there is a consequence to that: once you have gone so far to inhabit a character like Isabel Archer, the harder it is—not just technically, but in your own spirit—to go back to anything trivial, cute, and seductive again. An actress can alter the way in which we see her in one show. But she has to realize that that changes our future expectations, too. If you touch an author like Henry James, or a husband like Gilbert Osmond, you are changed for life, and pretending to be sunshine will convince no one.

The teaming with Jane Campion becomes more than a friendship. Susanna Moore's extraordinary novel *In the Cut* was published in 1995, the year before *The Portrait of a Lady* opened. "It never occurred to me that it could be a film," says Moore. The agent, Bob Bookman, reckons the book is disgusting—it is the story of an intellectual woman, Fran, living in New York who becomes involved sexually with a cop looking into some serial killings. It is the more candid, erotic, and sordid in that it is written from the point of view of a Fran who is low on self-esteem.

But then Moore gets a message that Nicole Kidman wants to option the novel. She is interested in playing Fran. Is the author interested in doing the screenplay? Jane Campion is involved, too, as the potential director. The three of them meet.

"Nicole was completely delightful," remembers Moore, "intelligent, smart, she had freshness, a slight naïveté. She was an exhaustingly quick study and she was putting it all together. I could see her learning on the job, with great charm and fun. She had what I call an 'island girl' recklessness—tomboyish, outspoken, fearless. I think it comes from growing up amid nature."

The meetings on the script take place at Nicole's house on the bay at Sydney. Moore remembers it as "impeccable, very organized and clean. Jane and I dressed in a very ordinary way but Nicole did her workout, running on the beach, and appeared with her hair washed, fully made up and in exquisite clothes every day!

"We had many humorous and amusing talks," she continues. Jane was adamant—Nicole could not look too beautiful as Fran. She has eyeglasses, brownish hair, no designer clothes. "Nicole was amused. She said Fran was a design failure. But she wasn't in the least deterred. She wanted to do it."

Moore does two versions of the script. And then Jane Campion was to do a final version. It is sold to Miramax, though Moore felt that Harvey Weinstein was more interested in Kidman than in the book.

Time passes and Nicole's life goes into crisis. Moore says, "I think she began to lose interest. Maybe she felt the subject matter was too emotional, too sexually fraught. She was feeling very vulnerable." It is something we can return to later.

The Peacemaker

Toward the end of the twentieth century, when the Cold War could be said to be over, surely the free and the less free worlds alike have every reason to think that, in the event of some rogue escapade with a lost, stolen, or strayed nuclear warhead—and by 1997, we have realized that not every megaton of death and destruction can be accounted for, let alone found—there exists a security system based in vast surveillance technologies, infinite military delicacy, the intelligence of several thousand like-minded people (many of them in Intelligence itself; this was a time when that capital *I* meant something), and unsleeping leaders with more contingency plans than any team in a Super Bowl. Or is it all going to come down to the desperate and old-fashioned antics of Dr. Julia Kelly and Col. Thomas Devoe?

God help us—you know the answer.

In an age of relative peace and security (despite the ghastly cruelty being practiced in the Balkans), *The Peacemaker* (from DreamWorks) could be regarded as a Hollywood "entertainment." Nearly ten years later, as Hollywood's grasp on action entertainment is so plainly slipping away, it's easier to see the film as typical of a kind of insane detachment from anything that might be called politics, and at least one item in the gradual and inadvertent campaign by which the public has lost all faith or patience with entertainment films. The question was asked even at the time (after the bold moves of *To Die For* and *The Portrait of a Lady*): What is Nicole Kidman, or anyone, doing in this stupid picture? It seems even more glaring and incriminating now.

The most available answer is that she was being more or less cute and thirty and a "nuclear scientist" and the head of the White House Nuclear Smuggling Group. I suppose you can argue that all of this was in line with her Dr. Claire Lewicki of *Days of Thunder*. I think I prefer such surrealism taken to an extreme. Why not entrust Drs. Kelly and Lewicki to Hilary Duff, Shirley Temple, or Dakota Fanning? Why bother with stuffy notions that this kind of eminence requires time, maturity, years of research, the wrinkled forehead that comes from much study— and even spectacles! Dr. Lewicki does have a pair of those, but Dr. Kelly is wide-eyed, and very nice, and probably capable of doing a modest job with the filing.

I am not being facetious, or even disdainful of women in high office. It's just that like any hopeful member of a democracy I am against children and idiots in positions of responsibility. As will be clear by now, I like looking at Nicole; I love her hide-and-seek eyes, and I am grateful for the way she is introduced in *The Peacemaker* by an underwater shot of her, swimming—doing what was once called the Australian crawl— in a decent but arresting black bathing suit. (In passing, it is an interesting question why the introduction is shot underwater, and why it is given several seconds more than are strictly necessary in a race-against-time picture. I'd guess that someone at DreamWorks liked the idea of getting Nicole visible in a swimsuit. Better that than show her lecturing on the half-life of various isotopes, which might be more to the point.)

For the rest, Nicole does a rather stagy version of the comic-book frame, "Gulp! What, me?" (when she realizes that she's the one who has to save the world); offers herself as a somewhat piqued and hassled distraction when George Clooney's Tom Devoe behaves like a country boy James Bond; and thereafter, more or less, finds a fetching way of striking poses of alarm, action, and alacrity in a white suit. All of this before her climax and crisis, when she is able—with all she's learned at the Lawrence Livermore laboratory—to dismantle a nuclear warhead that has wormed its way into New York City. That action saves the city, but its more telling effect in this film is to make Julia OK in Tom's manly gaze. They don't have a romance (there isn't decent time in this humorless film—it would take a Hitchcock to appreciate his respect for her thighs as she is unscrewing the big one). Clooney plays the entire film like a fellow who has never gotten over being pissed off by Pearl Harbor, and the film does nothing at all to remark on his steadfast notion that shooting first (someone, anyone) is the best way in an international crisis.

As you can see, it is all very silly, and I am not above a scathing, light touch with such solemnity. Once upon a time, a Hawks or a Hitchcock could have shown us how in a crisis the flaring chemistry between man and woman might be the most promising explosion in the offing. It would need tact and a witty script, but the shock of having NUCLEAR THREAT put in its place by wordplay and kissing strategies could be more satirically useful than this mad rush for NOT HAVING A BLOWUP.

As it is, the chemistry between Kidman and Clooney (or what the script allows them) is at the level of damp indoor fireworks—a sour smoldering is all we get. On the other hand, in the very opening sequence of the film, before the swimming pool, we hear the collision of two trains in the old Soviet Union. This leads to the detonation of a nuclear warhead and a quite extraordinary moment—beautiful and terrifying—in which two Russian peasants, aroused by the noise of the crash, get up, walk forward to offer help, but are caught up in the nearly liquid advance of the explosion. It's easy to think that people at Dream-Works put more thought, magic, and sheer moviemaking into this scene than into anything involving Nicole and George.

And there is the death knell for such trite schemes as *The Peacemaker*. As some critics noted at the time, it is a picture that has wandered absentmindedly close to real things. The initial theft of warheads by a rogue Russian general leads (by plot devices measureless to man) to a very sad Bosnian politician who gets hold of one warhead and sets out with it for New York, there to rebuke the West for their casual attitude to the tragedy of the Balkans. This man, named Dusan Gavrich, is played by Marcel Iures and he is quite unlike anyone else in the film—he is late-middle-aged and not good-looking; but he is deeply sad and thoughtful; and he listens intently to classical music; he is the soul of a wounded Europe, and even if he is a little dotty he has a gravity and integrity that could only lead an audience—even a Dr. Julia Kelly—to ask, Excuse me, why does this gentle man want to blow up New York?

In 1997, more or less no one in Hollywood reckoned that such a question needed answering, but that was largely by looking away from what was going on in the old Balkans. Today, such a film could not be made with the same light heart, though one can easily imagine a few digital picture makers at DreamWorks itching for the chance to show liquid fire and blast rippling across Manhattan. There are technicians who never see or feel the light of day or life: some work in the Pentagon and some in Hollywood.

Don't be misled, I am not suggesting that the Balkan situation of the 1990s was beyond filming. I think a healthy cinema would have taken it on, and I can only hope that the system's ability to do massacres efficiently might have affected some viewers. I can even see Nicole Kidman—the actress of *Birthday Girl*, say—taking part honorably in such a film, delivering the accent of Serbia as well as the haunted look of a refugee. Actresses can do that. They often say they hunger for such chances and such harsh realities.

So one has to stress that *The Peacemaker* is something far sillier and more shameful than a drama set in the Balkans. And it may be halfway legitimate in 1997 for Nicole to say—and think to herself—that she didn't really have the choice, granted her status, and granted the way she believed she owed the world and Tom a mainstream picture. So she did it. She was Dr. Julia Kelly, in white, and in comic-book images. But then you'd have to remind yourself that in 2005—another time—she gave herself in the same way to another piece of political nonsense called *The Interpreter*. By 2005 she had far more power, and a much better salary. But again she was lending herself to the disastrous wisdom and to the feeble tradition that no one can expect entertainment movies to notice the real world. Whereas once choice has won one battle for itself, it has only won the privilege of further struggles.

It is a fit subject for one of Virginia Woolf's most stringent analyses on modern folly, and a degree or two crazier than my remake of *Rebecca*.

Eyes Wide Shut

On March 1, 1999, Tom and Nicole see *Eyes Wide Shut* for the first time, in a Manhattan screening room, with just a few Warner Brothers people. Warners has paid for the film, so their people can hardly be prevented from being there. But Stanley Kubrick, who is still desperately anxious and protective over his picture, sends orders that the projectionist is not to watch it. But since a projectionist has to see, to maintain focus and framing, perhaps he is to follow the film's title and keep his eyes open and shut. Is this the dictate of genius or neurosis? Nobody can be sure, but in the film business few have experience of one without the other. Power is to be exercised, or it will be lost. Kubrick, long ago, learned to exercise his unique status. But Stanley Kubrick will die five days later.

Still, on March 1, the couple watch the film through twice, no matter that they are being observed (studied for reaction), scribbling notes to each other. "It was my obsession," says Nicole later, "our obsession, for two or three years." But obsessions are hard to share, and even if Tom and Nicole were making the same film, they were instruments in Kubrick's vision. Nicole (who has lost her voice temporarily) never actually speaks to Kubrick about the film. She faxes him. He calls back with a message—he wants to talk to her. But he is dead before she can return that call. So whatever private relationship there has been between actress and director—and there is, always—there is no resolution in this case, no thank you, let alone an attempt to discuss what the

Eyes Wide Shut

film means. For Tom and Nicole, it is simply dropped in their lap. Less than a year later they will be in the process of divorcing.

In 1995, as Kubrick and the writer Frederic Raphael worked on the script together, they had sometimes discussed Tom and Nicole as casting. This reminded Raphael that his intense and seemingly private quest with Kubrick might one day become a public spectacle, a movie— but, working with Stanley, Freddie had often had to cling tight to the sheer mountain face, hoping the mountain liked and needed him, but sometimes feeling he had been left dangling. He heard a story late in 1995 from his agent that Tom and Nicole had actually passed on the project. But Raphael wondered; he had himself been ready to drop any project to work with Kubrick.

Kubrick had told him how Tom and Nicole had come to his secluded house, near St. Albans, in Hertfordshire, in a helicopter, landing on the lawn. They had sat on the sofa holding hands while he told them about the picture. "He'd look at her," said Kubrick, "she'd look at him and he'd say, 'Okay, Nic?' and she'd say, 'If it is with you.' They're a truly married couple. It was kinda touching." Later, when the marriage is over, Nicole will say they lived in a bubble.

But Kubrick does not say whether they understand that it is to be a film about a couple split apart by suspicion, jealousy, and the power of fantasy. He tells them he imagines they can shoot it all in twelve weeks, though he has not been that brisk since the 1950s. He does not say he may be wrong in his estimate of the schedule; he does not give any hint of his own cunning, or of what may be a trap for them.

He tells Raphael, however, that Nicole has agreed to do two days' nude shooting for the picture. He probably grins when he tells Raphael that that might be a good time for him to visit the set. He may not know yet that the nude shooting will take six days.

Stanley Kubrick is sixty-seven in 1995, and he has made two films in twenty years, *The Shining* and *Full Metal Jacket*. In an odd way, that restraint has added to his reputation for genius, though neither film did especially well. No one has thought to wonder whether Stanley might have gone "rusty," doing so little and living in his English seclusion. He does not fly or travel; he has not been in the United States since the early 1960s. Somehow his reputation is sustained—by films like *Barry Lyndon, A Clockwork Orange, 2001: A Space Odyssey, Lolita,* and *Spartacus*—so that, when it comes to *Eyes Wide Shut,* Warner Brothers will advance the money he requires, without much dispute or questioning. But the absence of unequivocal hits in that list does mean that Tom and Nicole in the deal will add to Warners' optimism.

This new project is a little unusual for Kubrick. It is not only a film about men—if you consider his earlier work, it is fair to say that they are pictures about men and their philosophies, men and their systems: Can Jack Torrance write his novel at the Overlook Hotel? Can men rob a racetrack and get away with it? Can the grunts make the army work and survive war? Is Barry Lyndon's cynical ambition enough in life? Can man stay man in space? Can boys love violence and Beethoven? Will Spartacus defeat the Roman Empire? There are women in these pictures—though not really in *Paths of Glory, Full Metal Jacket,* or *2001*—but they are perfunctory, obligatory, or entirely wicked. These are not films about love or sex (except for *Lolita*—and some say that its love is for language). What matters in men for Kubrick are other things. Has he ever worked with a great actress or a beautiful woman?

But what Kubrick has offered to Raphael at the outset is a novella by Arthur Schnitzler—*Traumnovelle,* published in 1926—that will be adapted with surprising fidelity in the finished film, even if turn-of-the-century Vienna has given way to modern New York. It concerns a young couple, a doctor and his wife, with a daughter and a nice apartment and a happy marriage, apparently, but with dreams . . . dreams in which each one is unfaithful to the other. Raphael is drawn to the situation and its eroticism. He does remind Kubrick that this is a departure in the director's work. He does say, "It's cute, but it turns all that happens into a dark tale that gets tied up with a flourish like a pat little bow. There's not much progression, is there?"

This is an early warning, and it comes when remedies might still have been sought. But *Eyes Wide Shut* ends with massive uncertainty, and the feeling of a psychic load not quite delivered. It's as if the divorce between the leading players is the ending it needs.

Cruise and Kidman move to England with their children; they doubt the three-month estimate, and they want to indicate their commitment. Neither one of them has acted in so prestigious a project before, or for a director so secure in the pantheon. They may even think of Oscars coming their way eventually, though they could check it out for themselves that only two players have ever been nominated for acting in a Kubrick picture—Peter Sellers for *Dr. Strangelove* and Peter Ustinov for *Spartacus* (he won), both of them over the top, or floating. By contrast, Tom and Nicole would seem to be getting ready to play the two human axes in a triangle completed by desire. They have to be good, yet nominal.

They will rent a house in Regent's Park, as well as a smaller house in Hertfordshire. They have their children with them, and there are vacations to the Lake District. It is during their London residence, on September 6, 1997, that they both attend the funeral of Princess Diana. It is a mark of the curious way in which celebrities have only themselves to talk to. Nicole has had an odd rapport with Diana. A friend observes, "If Diana had had as much instinct for power as Nicole has in her little finger, she'd have been Queen of England."

Shooting begins at Pinewood studios in November 1996, with a careful re-creation of some New York streets and the apartment where their characters, Bill and Alice, live. But by the standards of most Kubrick films, these sets are modest. There are a couple of party scenes, but the majority of material in the film is intimate, with just a few characters involved. It does not seem in outline to be too demanding a picture. Yet the shooting will be drawn out over a period of two years, and the budget will reach $65 million. Kubrick has said in advance that he plans an extensive rehearsal period. But he will film many of the rehearsals (which demand full costume and sets) so as not to miss special moments.

He spends an unusual amount of time getting to know Tom and Nicole—he says he needs to have this insight to draw out their best performances. Many scenes are shot over and over again—a method Kubrick has often employed before, but which dismays and exhausts Cruise and Kidman, especially when they have no clear instruction on what to change in their performance. Moreover, as the work goes on, Kubrick's development of a paternal role with his two stars turns on talk about their own lives. Nicole says he gets to know her better than even her parents do. Together, the extended schedule and the natural bloodlust of the British press toward celebrities promote rumors that Cruise and Kidman require some psychological and sexual education to do their work. (Later on, they will successfully sue to have such suggestions withdrawn.)

At this point, the intricacy with which real intimacy is being manipulated or exploited becomes very complex. Kubrick has always felt that he needed a married couple—he had thought of Alec Baldwin and Kim Basinger—but is that because a real couple would find it easier to play those parts, or because a shiver of possibility would add to the box-office sensation of the film? Of course, you can say that Kubrick is above such thoughts—that he is an artist, a genius—but then recollect his hint to Frederic Raphael about the best day to visit the set. Was he promising the body of Raphael's character or of the actress playing the part?

In the press, above all, this "revelation" is tied to the old allegation that Tom Cruise may be bisexual or gay—an allegation Cruise has always vehemently denied. No one could propose that Kubrick (an inveterate gossip) was unaware of that talk. Which makes it more notable that he has a scene on his New York streets at night where Cruise's character is buffeted and harassed by a gang of young toughs who call him "Faggot!" A filmmaker can hardly work without digging into the real personality of his players—but doesn't that make it kinder or more prudent in the case of *Eyes Wide Shut* to hire players who are not married? Cruise and Kidman will speak later of their intense experience with Kubrick, but many people on the set note the director's special attachment to Kidman. He likes to have her around all the time, even though in the final film she is onscreen only a third of the time given to Cruise.

A director is an interloper in any marriage, if he is male and his actress is married. I do not mean he has intercourse with the woman. That is a blunt transaction compared with his demands. He says, I have to talk to you privately, intimately, because I have to talk to you about the way your desires—your desires, Nicole—may merge with and give body to your character. Alas, this has to be done away from your husband. It must be just the two of us. And in the case of *Eyes Wide Shut* there is this extra twist—Oh, Tom, I must take Nicole away to somewhere private. This afternoon. We may stroll in the garden, or in the lanes of Hertfordshire. We have to talk. You understand. For you and I talk in the same way, when she is not there. Cell phones were created to mark and define this torture.

Kubrick is devoted to secrecy. He does not like people on the picture to know that it comes from Arthur Schnitzler. He requires that no one involved make any statements about the work to the press. Now, of course, it is easier for a novelist alone with his work-in-progress to establish that confidentiality than the leader of a venture costing $65 million—and not even his own $65 million. But it is a further reach of this need for privacy that a film is a collection of private deals or undisclosed intimacies. And not just on this film. Famously, on *East of Eden,* Elia Kazan whispered something in the ears of James Dean and Raymond Massey before shooting key scenes. It need only be "He doesn't really like you, so challenge him"—the same words to both men—for insecurity in life to come to the aid of the characters.

Such ploys work. And many directors take advantage of them. So it is no wonder here if Stanley sometimes says, Tom, I have to talk to Nic. Can you play Ping-Pong for a half-hour, or a day? Or look at the chess problem I've left on the board? There will be little things he has confided in each one of them, swearing them to secrecy. And they honor the pledge. He encourages them to make the set for Bill and Alice's apartment feel like their own home. He lets Nicole make some changes in the decor. She brings in some of their books and she piles Tom's loose change on the bedside table. He lets them spend occasional nights together on the set, sleeping in Bill and Alice's bed. Then he decides that a time has come when they should live separately for the film.

They may joke about these moves together, when they are alone and when they are Tom and Nic. But they are too much in awe of Stanley to challenge him, or to say, Don't be silly, let's just shoot the film. When it comes down to it, they are both young and earnest about acting, and inexperienced. Neither has done very much on the stage, and stage is a valuable corrective to the conspiracies of film. It is not that intimacies cannot occur in making a play, but the performance is real, public, and continuous. It is like running a race. It depends on the courage, the strength, the insight, and the being of the player. Whereas in film—so fragmented, so disconnected—actors sometimes wonder what the film is going to be. This is a mysterious authority for directors, and a large extra demand on trust from the players.

Nicole will say that she was afraid at first, literally afraid that she would not be good enough to handle some of Alice's long speeches. But then, "At certain times he was very controlling but at other times not, he allowed me to just get lost in Alice and after a year and a half I just became that woman, in a weird way. I know that sounds ridiculous, but as an actor there is reality and there is pretend and those lines get crossed and you're working with a director who allows that to happen; it's exciting and dangerous—that's when the work becomes so much more than just making a film."

That is credible and touching, and very interesting—except that it leaves one wondering when you are making a film what more is there, or ought there to be, than making the film?

Not everyone yields. Harvey Keitel has been cast as Victor Ziegler, the friend to the couple. But there is some disagreement—Keitel will not speak about it—and he is replaced by Sydney Pollack, the director. Very soon, there is a rumor in London—unfounded—that Keitel had a love scene with Kidman that became overheated, so that she requested his removal. Nicole denies this. The young woman whose father has just died, and who calls in Dr. Bill, was originally cast as Jennifer Jason Leigh. Those scenes were shot. When, months later, Kubrick told Leigh that he needed her for more scenes, the actress was committed to another picture. So she was dropped from the film. Her part was recast and all the existing scenes had to be reshot.

Eyes Wide Shut has a schedule with long periods when Nicole is not on call. Another film could be fitted in. Stephen Frears has a modern Western in preparation, *The Hi-Lo Country*, in which two cowboys fall in love with the same married woman. He asks Nicole. She wants to do it. But Kubrick is too insistent on his own vagueness to let her go. He needs to feel she is at hand. So Frears casts Patricia Arquette.

Robert Benton has another project: *Lovesick Blues*. "It's two brothers and a woman they both love, set in Texas in 1947—it's based on my family background. And I talked to Nicole and she agreed to do it. This was during *Eyes Wide Shut*. But I could never lick the script, and there was trouble getting the money."

Then there is the naval officer in *Eyes Wide Shut*. In the aftermath of the first party they attend together, where both Bill and Alice have flirted lightly, there is a long conversation about flirtation and fantasy. It is one of the scenes Kidman was alarmed about, and it is the first sign of Alice's innate hostility to Bill. They are smoking pot together, shortly after the scene where they confront a mirror, with Bill caressing her from behind in a kind of striving for satisfaction. And this is shortly after Alice has looked at herself in the mirror to the music of Chris Isaak's "Baby Did a Bad Bad Thing"—a tune that Stanley let Nicole bring to the picture.

Alice admits to Bill—though it is done in the manner of a tormenting boast—that once in a hotel lobby she had a brief glimpse of a naval officer, and would have given herself to him then and there, on the spot. In the script for *Eyes Wide Shut,* this is the nude scene that has been part of Kidman's contract for the film. Not every actress is prepared to do nude scenes, and so they are often stipulated in the contract, even though if the actress asks, Well, what will it involve?, she is told, I really don't know yet. Don't worry. We'll come to it.

Stanley Kubrick's organization has found a young Canadian actor and model living in London. His name is Gary Goba. He is twenty-nine, and he does an audition in which he is asked to take off his shirt. This was in the summer of 1997. Nothing happens. Goba decides that he hasn't got the part—whatever it was. Then in December, he gets a call: Would he do a sex scene with Nicole Kidman?

Goba never sees a script. He is told he will have nothing to say. He should simply do as he is told. It will take a few days. He agrees.

He is driven to Pinewood and there are Tom and Nicole to meet him. "She was introduced to me and I guess she knew she was going to be meeting me. She stood there and chatted with me there on the stairs, heading up to makeup, for maybe two minutes or so. She was super sweet, really, really nice and relaxed, and said, 'Hi, pleasure to meet you and I'm looking forward to working with you.' "

The scene Goba was hired for is the black-and-white fantasy that Bill sees, in his car, driving to the woman whose father has died, and thereafter, after Alice has told him about the naval officer, it is a scene of Alice and the officer having sex.

Their set is a hotel room. Kubrick tells Goba that Nicole will be lying on her back and he is to come in on top of her. "Let's get right to it," he says. The two players take off their robes. They are stark naked. Goba notices how beautiful she is. And then Nicole asks for a closed set. The lighting is fixed. There is no need of sound. Stanley Kubrick—he was a photographer for *Look* magazine as a kid in New York—will operate the camera himself. It is just the three of them.

It lasts six days.

Many situations are shot that do not figure in the film. There is a scene in a bath, for instance. There is also a scene in which Goba administers cunnilingus to Nicole, in some detail, for which she wore a pubic wig—just so any indelicacy might be avoided. The restraint of the filmmaking process, its etiquette, is wondrous. At what point is Nicole protected by being Alice?

You can see the edited result yourself in *Eyes Wide Shut.* I do not mean to suggest that the scene is gratuitous or unnecessary. It is an important part of the arc of the film—as Kubrick had admitted at first. Not that it had to be as graphic as it is. Not that it is easy to see why six days were needed to get it all done. Not that the situation—with the man hired and paid to pretend to make love to her—is not unsettling. Of course, she was paid too—and paid more. Not that Goba ever denied his helpless falling for Nicole during the work. Not that anything ever came of that.

But isn't it possible that the element of fantasy, or imagining, in sex is being driven close to madness by a culture in which it is cold-bloodedly duplicated—even with the addition of a wig for m'lady's pubic hair?

Then consider the end product in this strange case—look at *Eyes Wide Shut.* The black-and-white scenes are erotic, I suppose, but it is notable how far they are to be read as Alice's dream or rapture. It's not just that the naval officer has nothing to say; his face hardly shows. He is a body, a mouth, hands; he is a hired tool. Alice is in sprawling delight, lending herself to every silent ingredient of the acts that equals pleasure. Her hair is thrown back, her mouth is open, she is uninhibited—I do not think there is a moment at which any viewer would conclude that Kidman's professional or personal shyness has impeded her ability to portray Alice. She is, once again, the person who loves to be photographed, who loves to pretend. Work consumes her; she admits to wanting to give over everything to it, to being "skinless" as an actress.

But Bill has no such scene in the film, even though he carries the great load of the story. He is the one who goes off, out into the world. He attends the woman whose father has died, he receives her passionate kiss, and can go no further because the boyfriend arrives; he is picked up by the whore (who seems disinclined to charge him), and yet he cannot quite do it; he meets his old friend Nightingale, who tells him about the mysterious but plainly sexual party; he gets the necessary costume for that party, and encounters the libidinous daughter of the costume keeper; he goes to the party and is rescued by one of the virtually naked women, who is ready to sacrifice herself for him. And then he tries to work out the intrigue behind the orgy and whether a death has occurred. There are long passages of the film where it is all Tom, and Nicole is nowhere to be seen.

And yet in all his adventures, Bill is belittled. Nearly every woman he meets is taller than he is. At the orgy, the women seem to have been selected for their perfect, elongated figures. And Tom is for much of the time dressed in a dark overcoat that falls below his knees, which has the effect of making him seem more diminutive than normal. If that sounds a little unfair, consider how far Bill is steadily tempted without being satisfied, how often he is humiliated, how often he fails to have the kind of sexual vitality that he imagines Alice enjoying. It's not just that there is no scene in which Alice dreams of Bill as a sexual animal. He is called "faggot" on the street; he is clearly perceived as gay by the clerk at Nightingale's hotel; he cannot come with the whore; others are enjoying the costume maker's daughter; he is told to take off his clothes at the orgy—but never gains that liberty or splendor (and Alice has both). He is intimidated, menaced, and denied, and he takes it all while looking—I have to say this—as resolutely boyish as Tom Cruise.

Notice the anxiety attached to Bill and the ease that belongs to Alice. And realize, please, that if Stanley Kubrick is a genius—or even just a very skilled filmmaker—it is in part because of his ability to make us feel those things about his character.

In describing the film, I may also have begun to expose one of its most serious limitations—a lack of plausibility so great that its atmosphere seems like old paint. As I take it, in both the Schnitzler original and Kubrick's film, the mood or thrall of a dream must be maintained.

That difficulty is one of the things that had always troubled Raphael. And it is a further strain on Cruise that as he strides deeper into the dream plot, so his obstinate reality works against him. There are actors who can seem to be caught in a trance or a dream, and then there are those who are so downright solid or filled with common sense. It is the difference between Johnny Depp and Tom Cruise, between James Stewart and Gregory Peck. And that difference leaves Cruise as someone who always seems ready to flash his cocky and appealing grin at the camera, whereas a Depp doesn't believe in the camera or the grin.

We are talking about something that distinguishes great film stars from the common, about the ability to carry a film into fantasy or legend, past absurdity. And it is a problem that damages *Eyes Wide Shut* fatally. In contrast, just think of the way in which Jack Nicholson's comfort as a ghost aids and abets the mounting dread of *The Shining*. It's as if, playing in that film, Tom Cruise might have shaken his head, grinned, and said, This is crazy, whereas Nicholson would smile and say, But isn't everything?

The orgy and the intrigue in *Eyes Wide Shut* are so close to collapse. And the notion of this country estate of debauchery on Long Island is too stagy to pass muster. The orgy and its iniquity lead nowhere, in great part because they take us away from the marriage between Bill and Alice, and the question of whether it can survive. Somehow, Alice needs to be at the orgy for Bill to be trapped.

It has always seemed to me that the most fruitful way to proceed with *Eyes Wide Shut* would have been to have every major woman Bill encounters be a version of Alice—and be played by Nicole: the cold, repressed, and dissatisfied daughter; the lovely and pliant whore; the child wanton; the mysterious rescuer at the orgy. After all, Nicole can create so many different looks—so many partners. These could be the aspects of Alice that Bill needs to sustain his relationship. And then it could be that the looks, the touching, and the love that these other women have received from Bill have magically healed Alice in his absence.

Of course, it is only playful or whimsical to remake a film that has been finished—yet it can amount to useful criticism, too. I think Cruise would always be miscast in that construct—it needs Depp or another sleepwalker; it needs a pliant imagination. But done that way, as a series of scenes for two, in very strange, distorted settings—where the decor was far more suggestive than accurate—then *Eyes Wide Shut* might be a masterpiece. But it needs a sensibility—like that of Renoir or Ophüls or Hitchcock—that knows woman can be magic.

As it is, I think Kubrick makes a film that whispers to Nicole, You are a real actor, a sexual phenomenon—and he is not. No one can see the film without inhabiting that dismay. So why should the two central players not feel it themselves?

Everyone wants to see *Eyes Wide Shut*; until they see it. Every rumor of the movie's sexual content, every malicious story about its shooting, are sharpened by Kubrick's death, and then by Warner Brothers' decision to open the film by giving all reviewers a flat two-day notice of the film itself. One preview screening (the one I see) is at the new Metreon complex in San Francisco on the morning of Wednesday, July 14 (opening day is Friday the sixteenth). There are over two hundred critics from the Bay Area at the Metreon, and their expectations combat the slow portentousness of the film.

About an hour into the showing at the Metreon, just as the orgy is about to begin, a fire alarm goes off in the building. By the building's laws, the film has to be stopped and the critics ushered out. The film is interrupted by as much as half an hour. In that time, there is talk that the screening may have to start from the beginning again: these seem to be the Warner Brothers instructions, or the orders of Stanley himself. When this is spoken aloud, the critics respond with one low bellow of protest and horror. They have been cut off on the brink of orgy. It should be the most tempting moment. But they have had enough of this congealed tempo and the film's emotional deadness to insist on saving time. A call is put through to Burbank. The situation is conveyed to the authorities. In the event, the screening resumes where it left off. And you know that most people are counting the minutes, aggrieved and unforgiving.

For a moment, the film has a chance. In *Variety*, Todd McCarthy reckons it is "a riveting, thematically probing, richly atmospheric and just occasionally troublesome work, a deeply inquisitive consideration of the extent of trust and mutual knowledge possible between a man and a woman."

On opening day Janet Maslin in the *New York Times* finds "a spell-binding addition to the Kubrick canon. . . . A dead-serious film about sexual yearnings, one that flirts with ridicule yet sustains its fundamental eeriness and gravity throughout." Then something strange happens at the *Times* itself. Other people there have seen a different film. That Sunday, book critic Michiko Kakutani calls it "a lugubrious, strangely static work" and an "unfortunate misstep." Quite quickly, Ms. Maslin steps down as the paper's film critic, to be replaced eventually by A. O. Scott and Elvis Mitchell (in time, Mitchell gives way to Manohla Dargis). But the *Times* rewrite is on the public pulse. Most reviews are dismayed or horrified. The public turns up on the first weekend: the picture does $21 million. But it falls off by over 50 percent in the second week and by more than another 50 percent in the third. Eventually, the movie that cost about $65 million will bring in $55 million at the domestic box office. That is the equation of failure. The worldwide box office is $160 million, but only a portion of that is real income counting against the costs of manufacture and promotion. Like many other Kubrick films, *Eyes Wide Shut* is a loser on its first run.

And Cruise and Kidman are exposed as the targets of recrimination. There is no doubt but that they entered the project with earnest, idealistic hopes. But the audience is not there and their own work is treated in a divisive way. In the *New York Review of Books*, Louis Menand dislikes the film and he fires off at the actors: "It was therefore a mistake to have given Cruise and Kidman a lot of acting to do. Cruise is a star; the camera loves him. But he is not an actor with a lot of range. Kidman is an actress, but she is not a star. She is a pretty and somewhat pinched woman, with a flat voice, who gives the impression of working very hard."

In the *London Review of Books*, Michael Wood is more penetrating. He calls Kidman "a talented actress doing what she can with a numbed partner." And without Kubrick there, this all too easily feels like a film about them.

The Blue Room

A s Stanley Kubrick is shooting and cutting his movie adaptation of Arthur Schnitzler's *Traumnovelle*, the idea arises in London for a new stage version of a Schnitzler play, *Der Reigen*. This was adapted once before, for the 1950 movie *La Ronde*, by Max Ophüls, a very great film, in which we see a single action—physical love—being passed around a circle of Viennese characters in 1900, as if it were a snuff box or an infection. The film stars Anton Walbrook, Simone Signoret, Serge Reggiani, Simone Simon, Daniel Gelin, Danielle Darrieux, Fernand Gravey, Odette Joyeux, Jean-Louis Barrault, Isa Miranda, and Gérard Philipe. And, of course, the little tic, the idea of love, passes full circle.

This is a time when Tom and Nicole are mixing in London's creative circles. They become friendly with the playwright and actor Patrick Marber, and are interested—the two of them—in doing his play *Closer* on stage (years later it becomes a movie, with Julia Roberts, Clive Owen, Jude Law, and Natalie Portman). Nothing comes of it. But Marber passes the word on to his pal, stage director Sam Mendes, that "Nicole is looking to do a play."

"I met her," says Mendes, "because I had loved *To Die For*—it seemed to me that she had played a level of cool manipulativeness that she really understood. It was a mixture of poise and wannabe. But I was taken aback by her physical beauty. She was giggly and exuberant and like a young deer learning to walk. And she said, 'I think Tom is going to let me do something.' "

Mendes mentioned *La Ronde*, done by just two people; he'd seen it like that at the Edinburgh Festival. And Nicole said, that's funny, because *Eyes Wide Shut* is Schnitzler, too. "She lit up," says Mendes. "She said, 'Do you think I could do it?' I said, 'I think you could.' "

Very quickly, Mendes asked David Hare to make a play text for Nicole. Hare was unsure. He had heard that Nicole said she was going to do Ibsen's *The Lady from the Sea* on Broadway, but then backed out. "She'll never turn up," warned Hare, but just in case, he wrote the play. They were uncertain until the contracts were signed, says Mendes, but just as swiftly, "Nicole would call and say, 'Are we really going to do this?' and I realized, yes, we were."

David Hare acknowledges that the Schnitzler is not the greatest of plays, but he sees some fun or spark in making it modern and setting it in the bleakly amoral London that has barely survived AIDS. It is a play intended for the Donmar Warehouse, a converted theater with only 250 seats, essentially bare and intimate, which has just had a sensational revival of Eugene O'Neill's *The Iceman Cometh*, with Kevin Spacey as Hickey. He sees that Nicole Kidman could be the women in the play— a teenage prostitute, a French *au pair*, a politician's wife, a model on cocaine, and finally a star of the stage. As in so many things about London at this time, there is a sexy mix of high-mindedness and exploitation at work. Indeed, that is the real British fuck of the era, a swift card trick of lust, art, and nihilism. It works.

Sam Mendes will direct (he has just had a hit with *Cabaret*, but this is in advance of his movie debut, *American Beauty*), and Iain Glen will play the male roles. It happens that at almost the same time David Hare will make his own stage debut as an actor, in *Via Dolorosa*, a one-part play he has written about Israel and Palestine. Stephen Daldry is directing *Via Dolorosa*, or trying to advise the uneasy novice actor who is also a distinguished playwright. And as early as August 1998, Hare notices that there is an odd initial aversion to Kidman in *The Blue Room*. Referring to the London theatrical community, he says, "They resent the idea of Nicole swanning in from Hollywood and taking a job from our local actors. It is very rare to feel you are working on a project that everyone wants to fail."

It is easy to imagine her own adrenaline at work in that field of barely masked hostility. And it is clear in advance that *The Blue Room* is fairly explicit sexually, which means that she will not always have too many clothes to wear in a theater where the audience is close to the actors. There will be five weeks of rehearsal, and then eight performances a week, and Nicole and Iain Glen will be paid the Equity scale of £250 a week. At some point she is going to have to say to Tom that she is taking off her clothes in public for less than $500 a week. What is not clear is how much Kubrick knows about this venture, or may have encouraged it—having Nicole scandalous in a Schnitzler play cannot hurt his film. But perhaps Nicole will only expose her own limits as an actress. Her last stage experience was ten years earlier in Sydney in *Steel Magnolias*. She says she would far rather do this stage work than a mediocre film, and some reckon that the risk is the chief spur.

Unhappy with his own rehearsals, Hare is amazed at the family feeling that develops on *The Blue Room*. The play is prepared in a small, hot room in Brixton. Mendes recalls that Nicole arrives, looking perfect, every day, wearing a new outfit and bringing lunch for other people in Tupperware. Sam Mendes says how good the text is. On the contrary, Hare insists that his version of Schnitzler will need to be reworked during the rehearsal, and he flinches at the rather violently Brechtian way Mendes is doing the sex acts in blackouts with a voiceover recounting the transaction in very dry terms. Need it be that cold or grim? Hare wonders. One day Nicole brings in Japanese take-out lunch from Nobu—that could be £250 gone in one fragrant gulp.

There are some hesitations over *The Blue Room*. In the first weeks of rehearsal, Nicole feels technically restricted. Glen notes the delicacy they had to find for so much public intimacy. He is much relieved when Tom Cruise comes to a rehearsal and gives a terrific strong handshake and the assurance of friendship. The story gets about that Tom and Nicole, and Glen and his wife, Susannah Harker, are fast friends who will do Christmas together. Hare notices how very quickly Nicole learns things. "You don't see that richness of physical texture in British acting, that incredible amount of brush strokes." He thinks that in performance Nicole is giving Glen sexiness while he gives her wit. He doesn't like the way *The Blue Room* is shaping, yet he knows that is probably because of anxiety over his own acting in *Via Dolorosa*.

Mendes and Hare are both amazed at the way Nicole learns. For

Mendes, "She was always game, but for a few weeks she was scared of the stage. She kept everything small-scale and cinematic. And then we were doing the scene where she is the actress and she has to come on, full of herself, but really wanting sex. I said, 'Stop—do the entrance again. You've got to establish this woman in ten seconds, and you're whispering.' We did it twenty times, just her entering. And suddenly she got it, and she said, 'Can I really be this big?' You could see her becoming empowered!" As Hare put it, "She's the fastest learner of all time. Give her a practical task and she'll do it."

Shortly before the real opening, Nicole has a panic attack. She is worried about the different English accents—the degrees of class—required of her. And she is aghast at the huge, sheer fact of an opening, of having to do the whole thing, ninety minutes without an intermission, instead of just a minute today and then thirty seconds tomorrow, working every word and action until they feel right. She telephones her father and he does his best to reassure her—he gets her to start deep breathing. She talks to Tom and he says there is no way out—you signed on, you have to do it. None of these aids is novel or unexpected, but she needs to be told. And it is part of a strange affliction in acting—that in the end, walking out of the dark into the light, or just doing twenty seconds sixty times in a row, you can say you are powerless, like a slave, under orders. It is the thing you wanted to do, but at the last moment you seem to have forfeited your own liberty.

Is that what you always wanted?

Previews for *The Blue Room* open at the Donmar on September 10, 1998. There are awkward nights, but the house is packed from the start. No one is exactly there to maintain the traditions of theater. This is a sensational event—it is seeing Nicole Kidman in and out of her underwear, and naked for a moment. They say it is fifteen seconds—and surely many are counting—as Nicole turns her bare bottom to the audience so that Iain Glen can see and describe what he sees. On the official opening night—as they can be reviewed—Nicole sends David Hare six bottles of Petrus: that could be her money for the show. She gives Iain Glen a racing bike.

The reviews are helpless. They know the show is review-proof, and every bit as sensational as it promised to be. In the *Guardian*, Michael

Billington says that David Hare has spoiled a masterpiece, but everyone raves about Kidman and Glen. And everyone concentrates on Nicole. In the *Daily Telegraph*, Charles Spencer says she is "pure theatrical Viagra," the kind of remark that could do wonders for a drug. But Spencer adds, "The vision of her wandering around the stage with a fag in one hand and her knickers in the other as a delicious French *au pair* will haunt my fantasies for months."

Most of her reviews are anywhere between enthusiastic and besotted, and clearly there is a kind of wonder in London in the way a celebrity has come down to present herself to a mere handful of people. She has borne witness to herself, or her potential. In the *Independent on Sunday*, Robert Butler does say that "100 minutes is a long time to gawp even at Nicole Kidman." He also raises the intriguing point that, for 1998, this *ronde* is very heterosexual: "But then, you can hardly expect Nicole Kidman to jump into bed with herself."

On film would be another matter.

In the upcoming *Evening Standard* theater awards, she wins not Best Actress but a special award—as if to say it is for people who do not normally do theater. At the same time, there are some who see that the play is a sketch that responds to her presence, not a profound work that needs a deep performance. Which is not to say that she would be incapable of that at another time. If she chose to do it.

This is the biggest sensation she has caused—only *To Die For* comes close to it—and that other city that reckons it deserves every sensation clamors about the unfairness of life. Mendes noticed that there were people in the theater who were not regular theatergoers. The tickets became prizes. But late in the run one was found for Stanley Kubrick.

So *The Blue Room* had to go to New York—Nicole has not quite gone naked in public until she has done it in New York as well. So the show moves to the Cort Theater and opens there on December 13, 1998. It will run until mid-April, presented by the Donmar Warehouse and the Shuberts, with Roger Berlind, Robert Fox, and Scott Rudin. Advance ticket sales are over $4 million.

The critical reaction in New York is more measured. In the *New York Times*, Ben Brantley says, "A distinct chill emanates from the hottest show on Broadway." The house is larger. The audience is farther away.

It is a bit of an anticlimax. London was helplessly agog for the sex, but New York keeps its cool.

Brantley sees the show as grimy antiromantic and not much more than maneuvers. But Nicole does very well: "Ms. Kidman gives a winningly accomplished performance, shifting accents and personae with an assured agility that never stoops to showing off or grandstanding. It is also a performance that obviates prurience, despite the fact that she often wears very little and at one point, only briefly, nothing."

This is not just kindness, and it is not mistaken: Nicole Kidman does a very solid, thoughtful acting job, but she is smart enough to know that she barely needs to sigh or slur a word to keep the prurience there, like moonlight. Since this run she has not been back onstage despite every assurance of competence, agility, et cetera. Was she finding out about theater—or gaining access to her own daring? As Brantley concludes, making the best he can of a thin play: "The entire evening is not unlike Ms. Kidman's much-discussed body: smooth, pale and slender."

But the onset of power and opportunity are revealed in the facts of the future. Both Hare and Mendes believe they had seen her through a turning point. Now, anything could happen—and it does. Two people at the play are Stephen Daldry and Baz Luhrmann, and within weeks they are proposing the great battles of her career, *The Hours* and *Moulin Rouge*—and it's worth stressing that range, from a bluestocking to a red-light girl.

Birthday Girl

*T*he *Blue Room* is over in the early spring of 1999. That is how Nicole
Kidman is in New York to see that early screening of *Eyes Wide
Shut*. She is exuberant; she feels her power—quickly, in the act of leaving London, she has promised Sam Mendes that when he comes to do
his farewell show at the Donmar (for he is headed for Hollywood and
American Beauty) she will appear for him in two plays—Olivia in *Twelfth
Night* and Yelena in Chekhov's *Uncle Vanya*. In the event, he will let her
off: her friends know you can't trust her promises. As Mendes puts it:
"Her agent Rick Nicita once said, 'There are two words you will never
hear from Nicole's lips—"yes" and "no." ' "

The time spent in England for Nicole was like a rain that nourishes
the plant. By contrast, Tom goes back to America with little sign of
alteration. He is still set on being a superb hero whenever possible. But
Nicole is no longer quite "the girl," or a regulation female lead. She is
suddenly shopping for character parts, varying her voice, her hair, her
look, in the absolute confidence that knows who she is. Deprived for so
long, she is greedy for work and ready for a burst of activity never far
from danger. But she seems touched, too, by England's reminder of
what Australia stands for.

There are observers who have been troubled by the life the Cruises
lead. One writer working with Nicole recalls Tom's fear of stalkers.
"Wherever we went, cars pulled out behind us. If anything happened it
had to be reported. It was such an unreal life. And then they'd go off to

the art treasures of Italy and they'd take their own art history professor with them to explain it all. A lot of the time Tom was not there—he was so busy. But then he'd arrive at dinner, charming and very winning. Almost too perfect, deflecting attention away from himself, making it all about you. He's good at it—but was it sincere?"

But you cannot work in the London theater without being touched by the regular risk—of having work or not having it, by the dirt and problems of the city (they did rehearse in Brixton, and the limo can hide only so much from you). Nicole is surely observant enough to see that as her clothes change, Iain Glen, say, comes in the same outfit. It may be that his wardrobe is not that large. Five hundred pounds a week for her is peanuts; for him, it is a job. In London, you see, people may do great and dangerous work in pinched circumstances without thinking about it. But the observer—if she is as smart as Nicole—cannot help thinking that in America, actresses are often surrounded and soothed by the flattery of those they work with. But in London, with Sam Mendes and David Hare, you are going to be teased and needled as much as you are loved and written for. And an actress had better learn to know who are the right people to be around—the ones who rain on your ground.

The one time she can get away from *Eyes Wide Shut*, Nicole goes back to Hollywood to make *Practical Magic*—directed by Griffin Dunne, with Sandra Bullock as her co-star. They play sisters into witchcraft, and Kidman is the one who falls in love so regularly she kills one of her guys. It's a comedy, and the role is offbeat enough to be promising. But the results leave Nicole very disappointed—it will be another five years before she makes what you might call another American film in America (*The Human Stain*). Does it ever occur to her that she has not made a better American film than *To Die For*—the film that Laura Ziskin has said is what they don't make there any more?

Then she accepts a very small film, out of England, *Birthday Girl*, which is made by Film Four and Miramax, with some assistance from Mirage. The real filmmakers are the Butterworth brothers—Steve, the director, Tom, the writer, and Jez, the writer-director. It is set in the general area of St. Albans in England, and may be said to be the dream of a shy English provincial boy who might have heard that Nicole is up at the manor house with Squire Kubrick doing something grand.

John (Ben Chaplin) is a bank clerk in that town. Using the Internet, he finds himself a mail-order bride from Russia, Nadia (Kidman). It's only when he meets her at Heathrow that he realizes she can't speak English. He is about to send her back with a buyer's complaint when he seems to realize that his "bad luck" is Nicole, a huge, sexy Russian girl, dressed in varieties of pink, red, and brown, in boots and leather, with long red hair and the kind of devouring attitude for him that another young Russian phenom, Maria Sharapova, will manifest in a few years for every tennis ball.

Of course, Nadia falls for Ben: he teaches her English; she helps him see that sex need not stay a dream. Nicole has to work very hard on the language, in particular on a Moscow suburban accent. The rest comes naturally in a small romantic comedy that takes on greater scope as Nadia's two pals, Alexei (Vincent Cassel) and Yuri (Mathieu Kassovitz), arrive from Russia to help her compel John to rob the bank in St. Albans.

It is shot in England and Australia, which allows the family to be together as Tom shoots *Mission: Impossible II*. It is not much more than a B picture, ninety-three minutes long, but there is enough to invoke comparisons with Preston Sturges. In the end it settles for sentimentality, and I think it can be argued that the whole thing would have been funnier and more painful if John had been ten or fifteen years older, the bank manager more mature and thus more innocent (Ralph Fiennes, say). Never mind. It is an authentic entertainment in which Nicole flounces and flirts her way through a foreign language and a garish wardrobe and is seldom less than adorable. Without effort, she commands the film and leaves the world clear—with Nicole in that mood, you could make nearly anything. The film is held up, mysteriously, for it seems fluent and natural when it is released. But even in 2002 when it opens (after *Moulin Rouge, The Others,* and *The Hours*), it seems plain that her time in *The Blue Room* has unleashed an unmistakable sexuality and humor within Nicole. The comparison with Carole Lombard grows in strength, and there are references now to Barbara Stanwyck and Jean Arthur. It is a minor film, but in the great days of Lombard and Stanwyck it was often the comfort with which they did small things that proclaimed their genius. Alas, no one, not even Nicole, seems to learn the lesson—that this is a way to go.

To this day, *Birthday Girl* is not well known. It is a film people have heard of vaguely, and so it is easily confused with films not actually made, but so credible as to be nearly visible—like this:

There is an island named Réunion, just east of Madagascar in the Indian Ocean. It belongs to France, and I suppose that is one reason why François Truffaut set the start of his film *La Sirène du Mississippi* (1969) there. It is a film made just a year after Nicole was born on another island, Oahu, and maybe there is some hint of the sea breeze in her hair that keeps me seeing Kidman in the part played by Catherine Deneuve. Deneuve—so intense a presence onscreen that acting hardly shows—is a force any actress needs to study. Deneuve is more beautiful than Nicole. No, don't be foolish, don't argue it. And she is all the more phlegmatic in the way—especially when young—she ignores her own radiance. She has the spirit of a nun, or a slut—and the implicit denial only makes her more arousing. You never see Deneuve giggle or pout or flirt. That is the lesson.

Anyway, Jean-Paul Belmondo plays Louis Mahe, a prosperous tobacco grower on the island. But he is alone, and so he has sought a mail-order wife in the correspondence columns of a newspaper. And he is at the dock as the boat bearing her arrives. But he does not recognize her. No wonder, for she does not resemble the photograph that "Julie Roussel" sent to him. Moreover, it is revealed gradually that in several small habits and bits of behavior, this woman who has come to Réunion for Louis is not the woman who answered his advertisement.

On the other hand, she is Catherine Deneuve, who, despite a natural reticence, seems ready to fall in with the narrative scheme of arranged marriages by being his lover. So Louis does not protest the difference too much. A movie has entered his life.

There is a brief idyll on the tropical island. They fall for each other. They are married in every sense of the word. And then the thing that we have dreaded happens: Julie disappears with most of Louis's money. Louis sighs. Another woman arrives, sister to the real Julie Roussel, complaining that Julie is nowhere to be found. Louis hires a detective to track down the woman who made a fool of him. He wonders if he is really angry and vengeful, or in love.

Despairing of his rather dry and formal detective, Louis himself returns to France, where one day by chance he happens to see his Julie in the background on a television show. He is able to pursue her. He confronts her. For an instant, she is the trapped animal, defiant and dangerous. But then she launches into a lengthy life story about the terrible times she has had and the degrading lengths to which she has been driven to survive. Louis falls more deeply in love with her. But then his detective arrives, in triumph, having tracked down the false Julie—her real name, by the way, is Marion. To save Marion, Louis himself kills the detective.

They are on the run, pursued by the law. They go to the remote countryside. It is winter and they hide out in a small cabin in the deep snow. Then gradually Louis comes to believe that Marion is poisoning him. He accuses her and he asks why. She breaks down. She had not believed he truly loved her. But Louis was ready to die for her. She is persuaded. She is? And so the two disappear into the snowstorm.

The film—known as *Mississippi Mermaid* in Britain and America—was not a great success, perhaps because its spectacular titles promise so much more or less than this intense love story against all odds. It is *l'amour fou*, I suppose, and I would not mind any more than Louis, I think, if finally, to save herself, Marion cut the ailing Louis adrift. Still, it is a story I could see with Nicole in it; it would be a vehicle for her and Russell Crowe, with her surveying his pained earnestness without a flicker of expression. You see, if the situation is right we only need the actors' presence.

What Are You Looking At?

She is pursuing a very delicate line—that of being a free agent, a wild woman, responsible for herself, while being obedient to us and our fantasies. Her signal is, Like me!, and that can mean a challenge or a warning. Be like me, or You are like me. But before that bravery takes over, it is beseeching. It says, Please, like me.

This daunting boundary is like being a whore or a goddess, knowing that the allure of one relies on the leverage of the other; and knowing that, without those two contradictory models to offer us, Nicole might fall apart, or be reduced to nothing. So she builds up two warring archetypes in herself—that saucy girl who dangles what we want in front of us, and that licensed wanton, the purveyor of dreams. And the way she resolves the clash or the puzzle is to perfect that look, over the shoulder, or with the chin dipping down into the shoulder, so naughty, so provocative, and so full of understanding, the regard that says, What are you looking at? And, remarkably, there is such a momentary, spurious sexual tension to the whole act that we are transfixed and stammer over the words to describe what we are looking at—instead of attempting to understand the great mess that has been made of seeing. For the thing that once was a synonym for understanding—seeing—has now become a drug or an enchantment.

Let us try to track the process that occurs. Somehow or other, in the spring of 1999, it becomes known to the magazine *Esquire* that Nicole Kidman is "available for a cover." This is shortly after the New York run of *The Blue Room*, and at a time when Kidman and Cruise and their children have gone to Australia. Tom is working there on *Mission: Impossible II*, while she is shooting *Birthday Girl*. But it has helped set that film up that the couple can be in Australia together, and that the supposed English locations for *Birthday Girl* can be found comfortably in and around Sydney.

What does "available for a cover" mean? It is a career move, a step taken in the marketing campaigns for one or more projects, adjusted to the needs of a magazine. Everyone has to get something out of it. And at this point, the most pressing occasion in Nicole's career is the opening of *Eyes Wide Shut*, scheduled for July 16, 1999. That is just about when the August issue of *Esquire* will hit the stands. So Warner Brothers and PMK, the publicity firm handling Nicole and the film, have been sounding out magazines for their interest. Decisions will have been taken by those parties over the best way to sell *Eyes Wide Shut*. Is it the last movie by Stanley Kubrick? Is it a Tom Cruise sell? After all, he dominates the film in terms of onscreen time. Is it Nicole? Or could it be the two of them?

What do I mean the two of them? Well, a married couple at work, on a film about whether they can trust each other. This against a rising tide of unsubstantiated folklore regarding their apartness on the picture, and their need for sexual counseling during the production. There is no truth or foundation to these stories and several publications are successfully sued for airing them. Yet more or less "everyone" has heard them—which means there is something in us that wants to believe in them. We have to take some responsibility here, for our desires are being played upon by the marketing process as much as by the casting shrewdness in Kubrick. For now that these two magnificent forces are together, we are ready for them to part. Put it down to our seething need for agitation and action, as opposed to stability.

So, *Esquire* is pitched about Nicole: she will give access if the cover is guaranteed. Because, at this stage, putting Nicole inside the magazine, tucking that chin-and-shoulder act inside, is like a putdown. It would be like saying to the public, Look, we sort of know that *Eyes Wide Shut* is not very good. Whereas no one at *Esquire* has yet been allowed to see *Eyes Wide Shut*; after his death, Kubrick's authority will be sufficient to have the film withheld. But there are bits that can be seen, and there has been a trailer in theaters, with the shot of Nicole looking in the mirror and Chris Isaak growling, "Baby Did a Bad Bad Thing."

Esquire will say it cannot guarantee the cover; it will probably say even now that it didn't, because editorial independence does not allow such guarantees. But in fact a deal is made that says Nicole will give the writer of a piece on her so many hours (types of activity may be defined) in return for a guaranteed cover. That shoot is in the magazine's control, though there will be agency people there and the photographer (Peggy Sirota) will need to be approved, along with the writer (Tom Junod). The August issue is laid out well in advance and the cover "art" is scripted and directed with a copy line that will be "Eyes Wide Open: Nicole Kidman Does a Bad, Bad Thing."

The piece in *Esquire* and the shoot are like a small movie. They are not reportage. They are not an occasion for a journalist to go to Australia as open-minded as his tape recorder to find out what Nicole thinks about Kubrick, the picture, Tom. Instead, the *Esquire* piece will be a self-sufficient event, with its own storyline and production values— its looks and its lines. More than that, Nicole and her people know that any magazine will refuse to show her what is written, though they will have veto power over the art. In other words, Nicole is at a level in the business where she can kill a picture of herself that she doesn't like. But the thrust of what is written is outside her power. And *Esquire* is not alone among magazines in its recent history (and the editorship of David Granger) in treating celebrities roughly. Not long ago, it had Kevin Spacey on the cover in a piece that speculated on his sexual leaning—albeit in a jokey way that could be used as cover (as in cover your ass). Spacey denied being gay and attacked the piece.

The Nicole cover is in a burnt summer light, worthy of the last August of the century. There she is in profile, her right shoulder raised, her chin lowered, three-quarters on, in the long brown hair she will have in *Birthday Girl*, with just a flap of brown cloth covering her breasts and a considerable expanse of white skin—exactly the white that will be talked about in Tom Junod's text, a white that has a streak of icy blue in it, a rare milky hue at odds with an age of suntan and the bronze mahogany of Australia. It is the quality of flesh you find in Ireland still, and in religious paintings of the Renaissance, and it is a mysterious fusion of the spiritual and the erotic—as pale as Cranach. It leaves you realizing that Nicole has or has had the equipment to play a saint. But the scanty dress, the seductive glance, and the copy line are much closer to the image of a fallen saint—the female model most cherished by the media at the end of the millennium.

Then there is the text. This begins in Junod's Sydney hotel room, with Nicole in his bed. She is fully clothed, but how aware is she of her dangerous game? The piece starts out by plunging us into the action (just like movies), where a somewhat befuddled Junod is having some swift moves put upon him—no matter that it might be said that Nicole has upstaged the rather guarded *Esquire* libido by coming on a whole lot more accessible than they foresaw. Whatever the answer, Junod gets it down on paper in his titillating style. "She gasps," he notes observantly, "for she's a girl of very vivid breath."

Junod has picked up on the way Nicole can accent herself in a very flirty manner. She draws attention to herself—not just to her self, but to the lines and length of her body, to her way of looking, deciding, and breathing. It is something film people do all the time—on camera and off: "She moves a lot, Nicole does. She's twisty. She scoots along until she is sitting at the foot of the bed, with her feet on the floor and her hands capping her knees. . . . It reveals the stripe of her belly which is so pale it's almost blue, the color of ice milk."

Everything she does, or everything Junod has her doing, is like a hectic nonstop show, punctuated by the way her strong blue eyes stop and stare at him and ask, What are you looking at? What are you staring at? She knows, from moment to moment, that it is her belly, her breasts, or her ass that he has noticed. She knows what men are noticing, and she can walk around a room, "doing nothing," but ticking off the sights and sounds of that country, that continent, Kidmania or Nicholy or Nicholia (this is the sadness, the melancholy, that falls on guys who are looking at her for too long).

Junod sees her "doll's face pulsing with mischief and the possibility of intrigue." She is by now in his bed—it's somewhere to be in the ramble around his room—when the phone rings. This is the phone in Tom Junod's hotel room. Or is it the phone in the movie she's playing? All I'm wondering is, which one is surprised? (Remember the scene in

Scarface where Pacino tells one of his men to call Robert Loggia at 3 p.m. and just say the plan to kill Al—Tony Montana—didn't work.)

Junod picks up the phone, and it's Tom, as in Tom Cruise. Who says, "Listen, man—is my wife there?"

"Yeah, Tom," says Junod—he says he says. "She's right here. In my hotel room. In my bed."

"Yeah, in your dreams, buddy," says Tom—which is where a lot of movies and magazine pieces take place and is rather what you might expect as a Tom Cruise line if the Junod (Do you know what he said next?) idiot had actually added on, In my hotel room. In my bed.

But Junod passes the phone to Nicole and she explains. "I'm afraid so, darling. I'm afraid I'm in his bed at this very moment."

Of course, later on in the same piece, the two Toms are on the phone again and it's rather more as it might be in life, with Tom telling Tom to ask Nicole to hurry up because he and the kids are starving—in that open-air Australian way. Along that way, they've climbed a tower on the bridge in Sydney Harbor, they've gone to a bar for beers, with the subsequent air of tipsiness. And all along the line, Junod, the magazine writer looking for a sexy, scandalous piece, has been fed Nicole-isms, just like a lion tamer passing gobbets of raw filet mignon to a lion.

"This was the first time she'd asked me 'What should we do?' but it wouldn't be the last, because even when she's seemingly asking for guidance, for direction, she's looking to top you—to show that whatever you decide she'll agree to and wherever you go, she'll not only follow, she'll pass you. As such, there's a coyness, a flirtiness, an undercurrent of twisty emotions to her question, reminiscent of that tingly moment at the end of a date when the ante is either upped or it is not."

All of which indicates what very good magazine she gives.

The piece in *Esquire* is fallen upon with glee and envy by the rest of the media. It can so easily be read as a sign of Nicole's recklessness, her deliberately provocative behavior at Tom's expense—or of her wit and our foolishness. It's up to us, how it's all read. Junod is interviewed and he is incoherent with the press, as if compelled at last to reveal himself as an accomplice in a fiction which he had hoped was his—not hers. "The story is and was a flirtation. I was flirting with her, not only when reporting, but when writing. It's that genre of celebrity journalism. And she flirted back. I just think we kind of liked each other. Of course, it was professional."

But it is a story too good to be untold, or to be put back into its shell. Stories never go back in the bottle. Tom Cruise may never have picked up a phone, may never have existed in the story's world, but he is a reader and an onlooker, too. And it is very hard to imagine Tom Cruise doing a magazine piece of his own getting into, or giving rise to that predicament of being in, a woman writer's bed. You can easily enough imagine him reading the piece and saying to Nicole—it is not so far from the plight of Bill in *Eyes Wide Shut* being left to wonder what Alice did—What were you thinking? And that is enough to make Nicole Kidman herself realize that she had been there in this little *Esquire* movie, playing herself—and what had she been thinking?

Rouge

I t is not common for actors and actresses to devise in their own minds, ahead of time, the kinds of parts, or entire stories, in which they might be seen to the best advantage. If they are inclined to that vision, they are on their way to being writers or directors, or to being, as they could put it, so calculating, so cold-blooded, such hams, that they will hate themselves. Actors usually cling to spontaneity. Nicole is one who does. There are other actors in our history who have been very comfortable, and cynically assured, doing just "their thing." Especially in the movies, where the range of parts was often rationalized according to the dictates of a factory system, there were players who found that they were forever remaking their old hits, playing themselves, and fit to scream. But most actors love surprise.

I think it's fair to say that two of the great stars of the studio system, Joan Crawford and Bette Davis, went a little mad as they were asked to do ever more exaggerated versions of things at which they excelled. In hindsight, it's easy to see that their nature—a rare level of emotional energy, inhibited by social pressures and various male estimates of what a woman might be—drove them from romance and drama to the heightened absurdity of the horror film. They met, or collided, in *What Ever Happened to Baby Jane?*, a picture that still jumps from romance all the way to horror, and which cruelly exploited the public notion that the two ladies had become grotesque showoffs or uncontrollable prima donnas. What else had the system ever intended, except that their real quality and their eminence would destroy them? Few were left by 1960

Moulin Rouge

to recall the delicacy they had both offered once as actresses or as desirable women.

I don't want to spend too much time on this sidebar, no matter how tempting. Except to say that in Davis and Crawford in the 1930s, onscreen, you can see a struggle going on between toughness (or strength) and the feminine. Crawford was flat-out beautiful once. Davis may have been no more than very pretty, but she was alluring, rather like the sister who knows that her wit, her quickness, and her sexy mind are going to have to make up for other things. They both found success, but they took different paths. For Bette Davis, it was fulfilling: she was East Coast, a WASP, of fairly good family and education. She was stepping down from her class one or two levels to be a sensation in movies (as opposed to the stage).

"Joan Crawford" was not her real name. She was Lucille Le Sueur, and that was dumped for a name arrived at in an MGM contest. She was from San Antonio, which in the early twentieth century was a Hot, Mex place. And there were stories that Crawford had been a dancing girl, wide-eyed and loose. Her own studio helped put out the story that she might have appeared naked in a blue movie. This set her up at MGM (the home of Garbo, Norma Shearer, Jeanette MacDonald, Greer Garson, and Margaret Sullavan) as the tramp trying to hold her own with ladies. As the beauty in Joan's face became fierce and then frozen, don't doubt the pressure of that paranoia. In maybe her greatest film, *Mildred Pierce*, she is a divorced mother trying to make a living, desperate to be respectable and horrified that her child, Vida, has become a monster. Every now and then, as sad as a moviegoer, Mildred still dreams of being made love to.

I don't mean that crudely—it is the essential look in young actresses (and many much older) and it has always been there in Nicole Kidman. Bette Davis was respectable and elitist: she would play Queen Elizabeth, the regal Margo Channing. She spoke very well. She had old-fashioned style. But she longed to be desired, too, and her best work is summed up, I think, by *The Letter*, where admitting that overpowering need is what drives her through the mounting intrigue into a trap made by her own lust and passion. We know this all along, when she puts all those bullets into her feeble lover in the first scene—fuck you, every shot says, but fuck me, too.

Both women fought their studios. (They had studios to fight!) There was a great crisis in Crawford's life when Metro declined to renew her contract—*Mildred Pierce*, made two years later at Warners, was vindication and revenge, but it was also a shift toward *noir* violence or melodrama that would consume Crawford as she grew older (she was forty-one the year *Mildred Pierce* opened). Davis was at Warners far earlier and angered that the studio favored its male stars and gave her a lot of trash to play. As if to prove her independence, she went away, to London, broke her contract, fought a court case there, lost, and was humbled—yet won the ultimate victory. She came back, contrite and smoldering (her ideal state), and Warners relented. They found better roles for her. And she was a star until at least 1950.

Yet we all know (indeed, it may be the best-known thing about these raddled broads) that they ended up gaunt, scary, drunk, and worse, monsters of ego and role-playing, terribly betrayed by their disaffected children, real or adopted—the pattern of adopted children for the great stars is not new.

What has this got to do with Nicole Kidman? Just that while the studio system has fallen away—so that she has no proprietor to look after her, or to feel constrained by—still there is no way for her to be in movies but to hover between the two implicit messages to the camera: Wouldn't you like to fuck me? and You know, I'm a nice girl. Until you've tried it, don't minimize how far that inward conflict can take hold of you, like a mood that can be treated but never dismissed. And Nicole Kidman the nice girl, the good girl, the one who might be desired by everybody, wants better parts, more interesting, brave, wondrous creatures set in their eternal stories. If she is like most actresses, as I said, she does not always know how to contrive those things. She cannot summon an everyday Joan of Arc for herself, not without her smooth forehead becoming the furrowed brow of Virginia Woolf. You see, whereas writers take immense pride in working at the dull stone of a language for years, trying to free the unique words of a story, actresses—players—believe they must be taken with another persona, that it must ravish them and occupy them so that the shock comes close to stopping them from breathing. It needs to be sudden, barbarous, elemental—like life, like lovemaking.

And if you spend time with actresses, you will soon enough notice a kind of fresh emptiness, a shining vacancy, a need, waiting to be filled. You can see and feel it before the word "action," in that inhalation that means to summon up another life. You may say that sounds like some great athlete preparing for a stroke—it might be Maria Sharapova, drawing back her forehand and sucking in the breath for the orgasmic cry that will go with the shot. But Sharapova's forehand and her "unconscious" sound-making are her. With an actress there is something different, stranger, and more alarming. For the actress—the one whose outer skin is so famous and beautiful—tells herself that she has, as it were, vacated the premises so that this other being can come in. (It's like renting: you want an empty apartment, don't you?) Of course, the actress knows that once this habitation occurs then something akin to marriage follows—it's as if the newcomer picks up the landlady's old clothes, her favorite perfume, her handkerchief, and says, "I could use that." But actresses want to be invaded by strangers. It is wanton, reckless, absolutely unrespectable, and it's one reason why some feminist theory regards acting as a metaphor for prostitution. But actresses need to be rescued from their void—at least for a moment. Nicole Kidman is unusually smart among actresses, but still she clings to instinct and from time to time is heard to say things like, "I don't quite know who I am, or what I am, or where I'm headed." That uncertainty, by a great paradox, is vital to our sense of knowing her.

And whereas Nicole Kidman can reckon that she was blessed by being recognized for *Dead Calm*, hugely lucky for getting the nod on *To Die For*, still there has never in her life so far been anything like the gesture that starts *Moulin Rouge*. Those who have cast her have their fingers crossed. She has been lucky or unlucky. She has been the beneficiary (or not) of being her husband's wife. But one day as she is doing *The Blue Room*, a bouquet of long-stemmed red roses arrives at her dressing room with a note—"I have this great character. She sings. She dances. And then she dies." You notice, a film is not mentioned: the gift, foreshadowed by red roses, is no more or less than ectoplasm, sweet jelly, the queen's nectar to fill her up. And it is rescue, so sudden and unexpected that in an instant the actress realizes something she had never quite grasped before—that she has been in prison.

Rouge II

T here are people who do not like *Moulin Rouge*, and they are going to have to be patient. But maybe, even for them, I can find a compelling way of presenting this unexpected piece of theater, or of explaining the radical shifts in our heroine. Think of it as a response to the "imprisonment" of *Eyes Wide Shut*. No, I do not mean that word literally; nevertheless, that film was a prolonged submission to the will and vision of one man. Nicole was not taken into the confidence of that visionary. She cannot be sure what the film will do when at last she sees it—and I do not mean "do" as a business venture; I mean "do" as in whether it will be tragic or crushing; comic or hopeful; erotic or depressing. The actors cannot be quite sure of the story, let alone whether their characters are happy or not. And they accept that in making this mystery they will give of themselves forever, or for as long as it takes.

There are stories out of *Eyes Wide Shut* of the visionary's perfectionism leading to many takes—are they not much short of a kind of ordeal, a form of extortion, a measure of power? There can come a time, after so many takes, that the players begin to believe that some vitality is being drained from them, until they hear the rattle of their own emptiness. There is something sterile or deadening in the process, something that may seem to threaten the self, its gaiety or life. Stanley Kubrick is paternal, charming, considerate, superior—is he our best Gilbert Osmond? Put it another way: Is the end product—the visionary's film—a justification for the cold grilling that went on, or for the gradually applied enervation? Or could it be that the energetic, risky girl, the Australian, the island woman, has a tremendous itch to do something very physical, something crazy or out of control, something filled with the passion of a group, something as far removed as possible from the stealth with which Stanley makes his quiet, private deals—his secrets— with everyone on his films?

How about an emotional triathlon—beach, ocean, and mountains— after a claustrophobic game of chess? How about a movie with all the seemingly unorganized energy and fun of the commedia dell'arte, or of an Indian movie musical? You see, the first defense or explanation of the furious busyness of *Moulin Rouge*—a thing that some people claim to be fatigued by—is that it has the motility and the passionate vibrations of primitive cell forms. It is bursting, the one cell, itching to become two.

The Australian director Baz Luhrmann has an idea to reinvent or reinvigorate the musical. He means the American musical, such as Metro-Goldwyn-Mayer made in the forties and fifties. But he brings many different provocations to his cause: the films of Michael Powell and Emeric Pressburger, films like *The Red Shoes*, where music and drama were so blended that no one can pick them apart; he is affected by *Lola Montes*, the Max Ophüls film that showed the famous courtesan reliving the tableaux of her life as a circus entertainment; he is thinking of *One from the Heart*, that Francis Coppola "failure" where Las Vegas was rebuilt in studios, and songs filled the characters' heads as much as dialogue—rather in the way of those Jacques Demy musicals, *Les Parapluies de Cherbourg* and *Les Demoiselles de Rochefort*, where all the chat is sung. And he recalls the experience of watching an Indian musical being made—a piece of Bollywood—where songs, dance, drama, romance, tragedy, and farce were as pleasingly intertwined as limbs in pictures from Indian erotic art.

After the red roses, Nicole requests a script. But there isn't one yet. Instead, Luhrmann tells her that he will want her to sing and dance, as well as everything else, and that he will need her for a lengthy, unpaid rehearsal period in Australia where her competence (at musicals) will be assessed and where both the screenplay and the effervescence of the film will be prepared.

She jumps at the chance. She may or may not know that in casting Luhrmann has considered Catherine Zeta-Jones (who has sung and danced on the London stage) for her part. But Luhrmann is Australian, and he has seen and felt the engine in Nicole. He can also guess that on a movie that will eventually cost over $50 million, Nicole is the bigger box-office attraction. But he says that it is seeing her sexual bravery in *The Blue Room* that persuaded him. In a very romantic way—à la Paris 1899, or according to everyone's fond estimate of that time and place— it is a story about doing what you do for love. He is looking for some hint of repressed abandon, of an energy waiting and needing to break out. He will admit later that he is surprised by the intensity of what he gets. But Baz believes in luck.

Musicals famously have simple texts or stories. That is not always true: *Meet Me in St. Louis*, *The Red Shoes*, and *Lola Montes* are really films with music. They have substance, character, and a complicated situation. *Moulin Rouge* is simpler than that, but not simple-minded: it believes in play (and putting on a play), in love (and making love), in art (and above all the making of art) being transcendent. In essence, this code is *la vie bohème*, a realm where artists starve in garrets, courtesans perish from consumption, and impresarios will sacrifice anything and anyone to put on a show.

And keep the lease on their theater. A rather tougher view of this warm family ambience is to be seen in Jean Renoir's great film, *French Can-Can*, where the theater owner is a serial romancer (and user) of his own stars, none of whom ever disturbs or rivals his love affair with performance. By contrast, *Moulin Rouge* is a remake of *French Can-Can* such as would enthrall the undergraduates in a good university theater department. It is full of an innocent adoration of theater that does not reflect much experience of that tricky world.

But innocence and talent, with unstoppable energy, hardly need to be excused. And if the concept of Paris is shamelessly naive and fairy-like, that serene romanticism is offset by two things: the very modern, cute knowingness that makes the songs not original so much as an endless dipping in the great songbook of love; and the fail-safe curb on sentimentality, built in from the outset, the fact that our gorgeous heroine will die. Her paleness is starry, but it is bloodless, too. For she leaves a little of her blood on every pillow and handkerchief, as tidily as Keats does in every schoolgirl poet's ledger of glory and sacrifice. Hadn't Luhrmann told her early that she dies, and isn't Nicole's rapture kept from girlishness by the shadow of death that keeps looming up on the bright moon of her brow?

Of course, Ms. Kidman does not have to die, and she is not exactly underpaid in this giddy tribute to theatrical communism. But if she was seeking rebirth, there can hardly have been a more encouraging venture—to say nothing of the eager, exuberant company of so many Australians, and the certainty that Australia could make an American musical in ways that no longer obtained in America. This is, finally, a film in love with show business, theater, film, and the sudden ability of Australia to dispel the cool, tasteful colors of modern cinematography with a version of the old Technicolor where every hue seems painted, still wet, like blood or any other bodily fluid. You can smell and taste human heat in the color scheme, along with the implicit cry of woe that America has managed to industrialize and neutralize color on film.

Just as Luhrmann assembles and rehearses his show in what is an abandoned lunatic asylum—a great shell of a place—so this is a movie placed nearly entirely within Harold Zidler's Moulin Rouge. Yes, the action does go outside the theater. There are exquisite views of an entire Paris, as if seen through a Méliès viewfinder. But the other places (Christian's garret, the rooftops of Paris, the Duke's house) are all so theatrical that they seem nothing but enclaves within Zidler's great palace. For the exuberant confidence of Zidler is that he can put anything and anywhere on his stage—so long as we the audience are prepared to believe.

And so Christian (Ewan McGregor) comes to Montmartre in 1899 to write. He is a poor boy with nothing but talent to keep him alive, and bring on maturity. He meets such emblematic figures as Toulouse-Lautrec (John Leguizamo) and Erik Satie (Matthew Whittet). And as Christian meets Zidler (Jim Broadbent), so he becomes the lever of mistaken identity in Zidler's attempt to use Satine (Nicole), his star, to entice the Duke of Worcester (Richard Roxburgh) to put up more money for his theater. Thus the fatal intrigue is set up: Christian and Satine are the lovers challenging gravity; the Duke is the hapless lecher, waiting to be humiliated; but Satine has the power in her body to fund the theater, if Christian can endure her betrayal.

Don't be alarmed. Everything works out. Christian and Satine enjoy one another like soft young rabbits. The awful Duke is booed and ridiculed. Christian acts out the entire spirit of Zidler's theater and Satine's romanticism by departing from the set text (the Duke's version), blurting out the songs of true love. And the audience goes wild. Zidler is in heaven—or, rather, he has brought heaven to Montmartre. Satine meets her appointed death, just as nicely as Juliet dying every night in some giddy run of her play. And Christian is going to turn the whole story into a great novel or screenplay. Of course, he is writing *Moulin Rouge*, having lived it out to the full, and so the closed circle of the work typifies Luhrmann's ecstatic notion about the radiant harmony between life and art.

It would be pretty to think that such an elegant balance existed, and the only words to describe the film adequately are in the range from "pretty" to "ravishing." That kind of praise tends to be barbed now, and it often went with complaints that *Moulin Rouge* was far too busy, exhausting but empty, too desperate to cut and keep cutting—too swift, perhaps, to allow an audience the time to see through its clichés, its tricks, its frenzy for the sake of frenzy.

From time to time in this book I have employed the analogy that acting is like prostitution. It is an analogy, not a diagnosis, and I am far from the first person to have noticed it. That supreme exponent and critic of cinema, Jean-Luc Godard (who was once married to his actress, Anna Karina), was haunted by the thought that in paying our ticket price we buy a portion of erotic fantasy personalized by this or that actress. It was the cheapness of that trick (a nickel a look) that made the movies such a sensation in the first half of the twentieth century. And *Moulin Rouge*, while it is insistently cinematic, is also deeply pledged to the vitality and inspiration of that older idea, of theatrical teamwork, of the ragtag of beauties and gypsies who gather together to put on a show. To that extent, it is a picture for those of us who love collaborative art and its highest rapture, playing for an audience. And *Moulin Rouge* the film is busy with audience and the warm noise and anticipation that one can find still at the circus or in live theater.

But *Moulin Rouge* is a movie, too, in which the circumstance of audience (for us, in our dark) is less warm, less noisy, and so much more intent on voyeurism. And Nicole's Satine is both the girl tossed in the circus air and the idea fixed in film's amber. For the overall experience of *Moulin Rouge* is of this beauty whispering to you, I'm yours, darling, while saying that to every man in creation. And while every actress and every Nicole may enjoy the notion or even the practice of being well loved by just one fellow, still an actress and a whore floats on other wings—the ones that say she belongs to everyone. And Satine is a heady part, one that helped alter the course of its actress's life.

If you had to fall in love with a courtesan, or a whore, Satine is just what nice little boys would hope for. There is nothing rough or abrasive about her; you know that from her name, and her utter compliance. And if ever you wondered about whether she might be tainted with infection, you had only to feel the unique brightness of Nicole. Satine may have a fertile, dirty mind (and every little boy hopes for that), but she seems to have a lucky purity. It's not just that she's a tart with a heart; she's a whore who doesn't know how to bore. (She will die rather than go stale, or old.)

You could marry this girl, if she wasn't going to die. Or if she wasn't so hell-bent on being Satine, on singing, dancing, and descending on the manly throng at the Moulin Rouge on a strawberry red umbilical cord, and strutting her long white thighs as if they were the hands on life's clock, whirling onward—if she wasn't such a performer. If she wasn't Satine, the most famous whore in the world, instead of just your girl.

And that's where her death is so poetic, for death is the gentle escape she has, the way of saying, Oh, why do I have wings if not to fly away and find some other man, darling, his face upturned like a flower full of sweetness. Men are so sweet! That is what a whore says, but it is what an actress does as she flits from Lady Macbeth to Tracy Lord to Hedda Gabler to Eve herself. She leaves dead roles behind like folded wings. Some of her characters may actually die onstage or onscreen, but moving on is always a small death. I remember once, long ago, directing a play on a fine set, and the cast and the crew that had enjoyed the show sat up half the night on the set reluctant to let it die. But the dawn came. Actors move on. And is it any wonder that they begin to acquire an unusual passion for death? Do you remember Nicole talking about that? And do you see how in what may be her three great or most personal roles—*To Die For, Moulin Rouge,* and *The Hours*—she does perish (to live another day). Granted that pattern, maybe it would have been better for *Birth* (her other great challenge) if that story had found her ending, instead of just her astonishing image of a person breaking down in her own wedding dress, in a seething ocean.

Moulin Rouge finishes shooting in the fall of 2000. Nicole is injured near the close and she says she is more exhausted than she has ever been. But "working with Baz was like holding hands and jumping off the cliff together." Did something happen during *Moulin Rouge*? Something large and unruly? Yes, of course, but the details must rest a while, and the personal adventure is smaller, I think, than the creative one. No one appreciated that more than Baz Luhrmann, whose trust in Nicole was exceeded by far by the performance. Let him describe it: "I felt a change happening to her. You see, she needs to get high emotionally. It's something that puts her at peace. It allows her to find something like flying in her work. And once she had got that, it was a release. We made the film at the Millennium and we had an extraordinary party. It was ecstatic. And she could have done the high-wire without a safety net. And, of course, I'd known some people would hate the film and some love it. And some people told her to hide when they saw the film. But she went out and fought for it, even though it was a hard time for her. She took flight!"

Separation

When the fateful day comes, the press release talk will be of "divergent careers which constantly kept them apart." It sounds like the mismatch between a woman who likes to sail around the world on cruise liners practicing card tricks and a fellow who is forever going up the Amazon on journeys of botanical or zoological research.

In other words, as the intelligent and benevolent outsider studies the romantic affairs of actors and actresses, he could be forgiven for saying, Well, really, why don't they just stick with their own sort? Who else is going to have as full an understanding of locations at opposite ends of the earth, good reviews for one overlapping with bad notices for the other, to say nothing of the relative coolness that may emerge in a couple when they are both of them walking around their mansion (or the realm of hotels in the mansion style) summoning up the nervous energy, the vision, and the escapism to pretend to be someone else? More or less, love and marriage still have the ribbons waiting to be tied up in pretty bows: the one that says to thine own self be true, and the other that says to your lover be faithful—or don't let the discrepancies show.

Every day all over the world marriages are entered into with a degree of amatory devoutness that easily transcends agnosticism or atheism in the parties. We are raised to believe in love, still; and the movies are only one of the strands of popular culture that have sung the loyalist song. On the other hand, for the drab masses—slow, timid, and relatively unfunded—show business people have also pioneered the social process known as divorce, making it more accessible and less shameful, as well as a prelude to that stranger pastime, serial marriage.

To look at the generality of film stars could easily lead you to wonder whether what they need in marriage is not someone steady, consistent, professional, caring, understanding, patient, and long-suffering—something between a dogged parent and a very efficient housekeeper, and someone who can accommodate the star's necessary flights of fancy (being someone else) without alarm, incredulity, or mirth. Of course, stars do equip themselves with such people. Sometimes, indeed, they are parents and/or housekeepers. Whether hired in or pledged to family allegiance, these people are the entourage. They may be agents, publicists, lawyers, personal trainers, purveyors of the aid, intuition, and assistance that come from doctors, drivers, bodyguards, or game players (that is, people skilled at playing games with the stars). Quite often, they have to bring many of those professional skills to bear, and so it is preferable that they never entertain romantic thoughts toward the star. Granted, if the star is very attractive, this may be difficult. Still, the effort should be made. It is hard enough for an actress to stay married to an actor—far harder to persist with a gardener or an aerobics instructor. So it is, in many show business careers, that stalwart cooks, mechanics, and fencing masters watch a great line of fresh lovers come and go. It follows, of course, that the observers must be discreet, never giving any lover a hint that he is not unique, and never thinking of securing a pension by taking the accredited list to the *National Enquirer*.

For the stars, the actors, there is something durable and reliable in these professional relationships that is always at risk with the "special" and perilous ties—I mean lovers, spouses, and, above all, children. Children are especially awkward in that they cannot—yet—be divorced. A time for that may come, no matter the huge sentimental resistance, but children only grow older, more knowing and sarcastic and vocal, less loyal but more attached (or more of a monetary drain and liability). This is a helpless training for answering back, when the professionals employed know that every fresh display of creative ego in the great ones is to be greeted with straight-faced awe and respect.

(This can be especially hard on those medical practitioners whose area of expertise is less the health of the body than the stability of the mind.)

This preamble shows how easily a topic ostensibly regarded as tragic or unfortunate can slip over into satire. For while there are thousands happy to read every detail in the reports of weddings, millions wait for the acrimony of divorce for their entertainment. The stars may deplore this intrusion on their privacy, but do they really know how to inhabit that domain? So much of the mythic structure of their screen lives is destined for that horizon called "happily ever after," and so few retain the pre-Columbian terror that beyond that line they may fall off the table called Earth. Consider this: either Tom Cruise and Nicole Kidman came together believing in the perpetual union of Cole Trickle and Dr. Claire Lewicki, and thinking to share in it, or they were both of them without the imaginative conviction acting requires. I doubt that. When actors fall in love on camera, I think they reveal a sentimental rawness that some sophisticated laws may yet learn to guard against (even if the lovers have all the screen wit and aplomb of Bogart and Bacall). It is easy for actors to kiss and feel excited, and it is quite natural for them to find a bed. But to marry is a real misfortune and a sign of minds desperate for belief when other parts of the body speak to them of mere lust.

In any event, it is a retainer Nicole and Tom have in common, Pat Kingsley, head of the publicity firm PMK, who delivers the flat announcement: dated February 5, 2001, "To Whom It May Concern":

> Tom Cruise and Nicole Kidman announced today that they have regretfully decided to separate. The couple who married in 1990 stressed their great respect for each other both personally and professionally. Citing the difficulties inherent in divergent careers which constantly keep them apart, they concluded that an amicable separation seemed best for both of them at this time.

It was an interesting unison that omitted the point of view of their children. As late as December 24, 2000, apparently, there had been a Christmas party for friends with affection on view. I put it that way not because the affection was necessarily an act; rather because it is what others saw. Only a few years earlier, Tom had been telling anyone that

their marriage was "for keeps." In the summer of 1998, Kidman told
Movieline, "Our relationship is a great one. We work really hard at it. It
isn't perfect by any stretch. We're brutally honest with each other at
times. I get worried when Tom goes up in a plane because it makes me
think, God, I don't know what I would do if he wasn't in this world." In
1997, for her thirtieth birthday, Tom simply hires a chateau in the south
of France, with staff, and flies in all the friends Nicole would want.

That was when the couple had just emerged from the prolonged test
of *Eyes Wide Shut*. Nicole, incidentally, wouldn't talk about the movie,
though she indicated that that was more because of Kubrick's plea for
secrecy than because of any confusion on her part. That film had been a
new kind of enterprise, and I don't think we can underestimate the way
its failure may have answered many of the questions it raised in the
players' minds. They had lived with dark jokes—that the sexual candor
might be beyond one or the other of them. They had been subjected,
both during filming and after, to false rumors concerning their marriage, including the idea that Kubrick may even have chosen them as
sacrificial victims. And Stanley was not there to explain himself, or
defend them, when the film came out. It was as if their risky volunteer-
ing for *Eyes Wide Shut* required success and prizes. It won neither; on
the contrary, in some quarters the film was ridiculed for its stilted plot
and archaic attitudes. And consider that for actresses, a great failure in
work may mean more than a loss in life—because it may last longer and
bite more deeply. David Hare, who met them right after the filming,
believed that they had established a deeper and more dependent relationship with Kubrick than was usual for actors with a director. And
now they were in mourning.

Even if one elects to regard Cruise as an earnest boy, his reaction is
intriguing. All his working life he had taken on parts that shone with
charm, heroism, or dramatic valor. He had been humbled and crippled
in *Born on the Fourth of July* (the one film he made Nicole see after they
met) and he was plainly moved by the ordeal and extremism of Ron
Kovic's life. But he had also been Top Gun and Cole Trickle and he was
the hero in *Mission: Impossible* as well as in *Jerry Maguire*, the jerk who
is taught to live a more honest and caring life. The apparent urge
toward the positive was as powerful and as quick as his grin, and

together the two could make light of reality. This was still a man who, on *Inside the Actors Studio*, responded to James Lipton's questionnaire by saying that his favorite word was "Yes!" and his least favorite "yes" (when the speaker didn't really mean it).

Still, as if some powerful doubt had come over Cruise during *Eyes Wide Shut*, he took on the part of Frank Mackey in *Magnolia* (1999). Paul Thomas Anderson's film, I would suggest, was everything that *Eyes Wide Shut* would have liked to be, except that it was made quicker, with far less fuss and at much less cost. It is a great American movie and by far the best work Cruise has ever done—indeed, it is so good that it alters one's entire view of his potential.

Mackey is the inspiration and the onstage front man for a male movement called Seduce and Destroy, a savage repudiation of feminism and the weaknesses in men that it may have exposed. Cruise does not have a great deal to do in the film; it is likely that he filmed it in less than two weeks and for a far more modest salary than he can command. He is seen onstage, in full rant, leading a meeting in what might be regarded as a satire on some of Cruise's own characters, or of his blazingly shallow self-confidence. And then he is shown in an extended interview with Gwenovier (April Grace), who has discovered falsehoods in Frank's famous biography and gently, apologetically, insists on putting them to him until a terrible cold wrath wipes away his smile.

This is extraordinary acting, in part because Cruise had never before (or since) exposed himself to so challenging a project, but also because he had never entered with such will into being unlikable. Cruise might have said, Well, this is for fun, for kicks, for exercise, or to show anyone who doubts me that I can do it. But it is a part of himself to which he has not yet returned. And it is so vivid a portrait of fraud, violence, and emotional dishonesty as to leave one wondering how he reconciled it with his Scientologist beliefs and his very positive career. He was nominated for a supporting actor Oscar; in the event, he lost, as he had done for *Born on the Fourth of July* and *Jerry Maguire*. But Cruise's Frank Mackey is one of the best performances I have to consider in this book. How far Anderson's cult leader was intended as a mirror of Cruise's own status—or how far Cruise read it that way—I cannot say. But here is something more, and more distraught, than a boy.

Cruise went back to being Cruise. He was doing *Vanilla Sky* as his separation came into force, and in the future lay a second *Mission: Impossible*, as well as *Minority Report, The Last Samurai, Collateral*, and *War of the Worlds*. Those were four more big films, whereas *Magnolia* had been small in everything except its impact. Of those four, none I fear was completely successful. Yet there is a darker side to the man that is evident in them, a feeling of carefree youth being over. He makes his money in the way an industry does, and nothing seems likely to deter that—at least nothing but real age and the cracks it leaves in his grin— but you don't have to be too ingenious to see signs of Cruise's narrowed confidence in recent years. In the terrible certainty that told the *Today* show's Matt Lauer that the host didn't know about psychiatry, there was a glimpse of soul, turmoil, a real actor, and a stranded person. Perhaps he was an idiot to believe in his Nicole; but perhaps he was the person most troubled by their failure together.

If we allow that the person most moved by a performance is the actor in question (I say this without sarcasm or offense—I think it is a given if the thing is going to work for others), then attend to Frank Mackey, who is stripped bare in an interview and then compelled to meet the father—the dying Jason Robards—that he has tried to forget or deny.

In a way, this book has to be about Tom Cruise, too. For just as I take the breakup with Cruise as the liberating and altering experience in Kidman's life, so we have to see that Tom was changed, too. That change is not over. He seems less secure. He has behaved in ways troubling to some and ridiculous to others. But they only follow a path he pioneered with Frank Mackey.

Divorce

The announcement of separation by Pat Kingsley was made to fore-stall tabloid press stories, but it could do nothing to still the public discussion over why "for keeps" had come to a close. In the first instance, Tom Cruise moved out of the family house in Pacific Palisades and lived at the Beverly Hills Hotel only a short distance away. Then very quickly he came to the house with a truck, loaded it with personal possessions, and shifted his base to New York, where he was filming *Vanilla Sky*. The press could act as if doom had always waited on the couple, but someone like Sam Mendes, a friend to both, was genuinely amazed at the split. Robert Benton was surprised, too, but he says, "The intense pressure to sustain Tom as a star is very different from that with ordinary actors. And Tom is a very decent man."

People break up because of other people, sometimes, or because of what is called infidelity or being in love with too many people at the same time. There was press speculation that Cruise was involved with Penélope Cruz, his co-star in *Vanilla Sky*, and later on they did make a show of acting as if they were together or in love. But they vigorously denied any involvement before the split. That thought was eclipsed when it became clear that Tom was suing Nicole for divorce.

That made it easier to believe that he saw himself as the wronged party. Quickly, therefore, the press calculated that perhaps she had had an affair with Ewan McGregor during the intense shooting of *Moulin Rouge*. It was not hard to find substantiation that they had been very close at that time—and it had been in Australia. Yet Nicole and

McGregor issued statements of denial, and he was married himself. There were stories that Nicole had been "wild" for a few years—but there was no proof offered for any of that speculation. Indeed, it was quite easy to treat such rumors as part of a vague trend of feeling against Tom. After all, he was older, more powerful in the business, and he was a Scientologist. Had he become a stern keeper of his own wife?

On the other hand, Nicole would not be the first actress who felt the need for an adventure at some point on a picture. The frequency of "location romances" might shock many people outside the film business, and I am talking about affairs involving all levels of worker. Not just stars or supporting players, not just directors and producers, but grips, script girls, gaffers, and hair stylists sometimes get involved in trysts that have a fixed termination date, whereupon the lovers go back happily enough to families, spouses, and children. The departures from fidelity are so taken for granted that sometimes they are discounted, and there are wise, patient spouses (of both sexes) who have learned to overlook such dalliances. The degree to which such loves are connected to or influenced by the practice of fiction, or escapism, is intriguing. But anyone in pictures has known at least some actresses who can hardly summon up a role without feeling they are in love. There are actresses who "know" they look their best when someone loves them, and is making love to them. I put "know" in quotes not just because this is beyond science or optics, but because the ladies' conviction is all-important in the transaction. Equally, directors and cameramen would say that actresses look their best when in love but not satisfied—after all, that is the essential romantic condition of the audience, to be desirous but to be apart.

That behavior can get talked about if someone works a lot and if their status is high enough. It can grow to such a point that the "innocent" party will no longer tolerate it, because their own love is being betrayed, damaged, or mocked. The more deeply anyone believes in love, or depends on it, the greater this pain is likely to be.

Tom will say later in the cover of confidentiality that settles on the case that Nicole knows what the grievance and the divorce are about. That is a shrewd tactic if there is a power struggle at hand, for it could imply that the fault or the departure is hers—her decision, her responsibility. It also leaves us wondering if the man is too much of a gentle-man to spell it out. As such, it is the kind of one-upmanship that men have employed over the ages. And its effectiveness is there in the lame result: Nicole can do little more than say, no, she does not know the reason. She with her knowing look. Some friends to both of them also note that when the break came Nicole went public—talking to the press, to Oprah—making her scenario, while Tom stayed silent and let the world think what it might. Some of those friends are proud of him for that.

I doubt that a ten-year marriage found only one reason for its rup-ture. The given grounds for divorce vary according to fashion and local-ity. In much of America, and certainly in southern California, divorce has given way to "irreconcilable differences" (the claim Tom makes). What that usually boils down to is that the people do not like each other any more. That seems obvious, maybe, yet onlookers can over-look the loss of trust and sympathy—the withering of respect—when much more overtly melodramatic incidents are given pride of place as marital troubles. If you think of it in terms of *Eyes Wide Shut*, the thing that troubles Bill is not so much that Alice might have screwed with the naval officer, but that she tells him she might have done it. That seems unnecessary, unless cruelty has become a need.

Then another matter breaks in on the divorce, in many ways the most curious. Early in 2001, Kidman admits that she is pregnant. Gos-sips are ready to seize on this information, without ever saying whose child it might be. But Nicole says that the child is Tom's. She says that she and her husband were intimate during December and even into the new year. Later on, she will say that the fetus has aborted. She will indi-cate that her unhappiness is ample reason for that. And if she still loves Tom and is at last pregnant by him then it's hard not to imagine her dis-tress. She will later say that she is prepared to have an independent examination of the fetus to establish that Tom is its father.

In the area of powerful tactics, this would be a trump card, for it speaks to the innermost feminine being as well as the heart and soul of family instinct. Moreover, until that point, this seems to be the first child Tom Cruise has been able to beget. Nothing is ever stated in pub-lic about why he might have such a difficulty. Yet it's easy to imagine

that impotence—or some word like that—would strike hard at so positive and youthful a personality. He has adopted children. Reasons for
the adoption are never given, though it is not uncommon in stars—they
may not want to give the time that pregnancy involves; women may not
elect to subject their figures to the risk. Yet Nicole has said on and off
over the years how she would like to have a baby, and somehow she
leaves no doubt about how she envisages that happening. Of course,
the pregnancy proves that Tom can be a father (just like his later con-
ceiving with Katie Holmes).

The miscarriage in question occurs on March 15, 2001, just weeks
after the divorce announcement. Yet neither it nor Nicole's public urg-
ing that the two of them seek counseling changes his mind. Did he turn
his back on his own child? Would he have certain knowledge that he
could not have been the father? Anything less than that would surely
have made him a wreck, yet Tom appears to conduct himself at this
time with assurance. As if he disliked Nicole. She is in the hospital
briefly at UCLA and Tom does not visit her.

The meanest thing that Tom does (and meanness is a measure of
dislike, as a rule) is to claim that their marriage has broken down within
ten years. Nicole disputes that, and her point seems clear. But Tom may
have sought to get within ten years for legal reasons, with a view to
making a better settlement for himself. Lawyers advise such things, and
businesses as large as that of Tom Cruise seek counsel early.

The case never comes to court, and both sides have reasons of broad
public relations for being glad about that. But it does involve detailed
negotiation, inasmuch as Tom and Nicole seem not to have had a full
prenuptial agreement when they married. For a star of his scale and a
relative novice, that says a good deal about their early love and trust. It
further refutes the story sometimes put about that she was a wife taken
on—and paid a large sum—so as to clarify his sexual ambivalence.
There are other reasons for doubting that—above all, that a youthful
earnestness seems to live in both Tom and Nicole that would be horrified by such a compromise.

Still, there is a story to be told about the money. When they made *Far
and Away* together, Tom was paid $13 million and Nicole was paid
$250,000. When Tom did *Mission: Impossible* in 1996, as star and

co–executive producer, he walked away with something close to $70 million, which included gross points on the box office—a percentage of the revenue from every ticket sold. In the previous year, on her break-through film (the first for which she was paid in seven figures), *To Die For*, Nicole got $2 million, and no points.

On *Jerry Maguire*, Cruise received $20 million against 15 percent of the profits. In the same year, for her lead role in *The Portrait of a Lady*, Kidman was paid $2.5 million. And, of course, the Jane Campion film was a disaster, whereas *Jerry Maguire* was one of the great hits of the nineties. Even at the point of *Eyes Wide Shut*, which turned out to deprive them of other paydays, Cruise was paid $20 million while Kidman got $6.5 million. It may have been said, in the negotiations, that Cruise would be onscreen much more of the time than Kidman. So it proved, though others could argue that Kidman's reduced minutes are more vivid and did more for an ailing picture.

It is not that Kidman had done badly on her money. By the time of the separation, her earning power was up in the area of $6–7 million a picture, and that is a level enjoyed by only a handful of other actresses. But Cruise was a powerhouse, and plainly the driving force on films where in theory they were sharing. Nicole hardly lacked for material things. The couple had several houses, ample staff; they had their own aircraft. But those things belonged to Tom. Then grant that on *Eyes Wide Shut*, they faced a kind of crisis not just in the matter of marriage but in their versions of ambition. Was the sexual inquiry disarming for Tom? Was the gap in salaries shocking to Nicole? Could those two grievances run together? And wasn't the film, in some ways, a signal failure in Cruise's career?

Magnolia then could stand as Tom's bitter retort—see, I can do that sort of thing, too, but maybe I don't choose to. His Frank Mackey was as great a departure as Suzanne Stone had been for Nicole in *To Die For*. With this difference: whereas Cruise was genuinely appalled by Frank, Nicole was transported by Suzanne's instability—it seemed to be a symbol of how much acting might mean for her, and it was something at which she was a natural—putting on a naughty, seductive act, while Tom was always earnestly trying to be this very positive version of himself.

It may have been a small thing at first, but then a more important thing as their children grew older, that Nicole had never thrown in her lot intellectually with Scientology, and had never bought into the notion of a kind of fierce, committed ardor in life. She preferred pretending, while Cruise was not the first great star in American film who may have been a little disturbed by acting because it seemed close to being gay.

And the thing that is left is a mounting dislike, a difference, and a drastic distinction in what acting may be. There are those who believe that it was a clash between career and family. Was Tom upset that Nicole saw too little of the children and sometimes became impatient with them, as if there was something else on which she needed to concentrate?

As it happened, Nicole had a project that put her with children: David Fincher's *Panic Room*, about a divorced mother and two children seeking refuge in a high-tech cave in their house. She began the picture, but aggravated the knee injury from *Moulin Rouge*, and had to back out. Jodie Foster took over, though Nicole remains "there": it is her voice on the phone, the new girlfriend, spoiled, sulky, petulant, when the desperate Foster calls her ex-husband for help. The weird poetry by which films reproduce life is random, absurd, but like a dream no one can stop.

The Others

And so, after about a hundred years of moviemaking, a picture—a big, serious picture—was set on the island of Jersey. But why could it not take more advantage of that rare place? I know there must have been other pictures put there before (François Truffaut's *L'Histoire d'Adèle H.*—*The Story of Adele H.*—is set partly on Guernsey), but I cannot think of one. Why do I complain? What has this got to do with an unusual movie admired by many intelligent people? Just the notion that with a good film every detail should count. So, if you've gone to the trouble to think of Jersey, you might as well have a reason for it, an explanation for choosing this rather out-of-the-way island.

And it's not that Jersey is dull (are islands ever less than interesting and dramatic?), or was so in 1945, the time at which *The Others* is set. Jersey is one of the Channel Islands, a British possession, though it is far closer to France, in particular to the west coast of the Cotentin Peninsula, more or less on a line from Cherbourg to St.-Malo. The place-names on the island are a mixture of French and English, but during the Second World War the island was occupied by Germany. There was even a kind of concentration camp there, as well as degrees of collaboration.

I'm not sure exactly when the Germans were cleared out of Jersey, or what sort of reprisals followed, but by the film's 1945, apparently, the war is over; Jersey is settled and calm again, so that old ghosts have come back. It's just that Grace (Nicole Kidman) is a young mother living in a large lonely house with her two children, waiting and hoping that her husband, Charles (Christopher Eccleston), will return from the war. He does return in due course. Grace goes out in the fog, trying to walk to the nearby village, and she bumps into him—as exhausted and nearly as tattered as Ashley coming back from the Civil War. She takes him into the house. He is more than weary, and he has some unspoken rebuke for Grace. Still, they seem to make a kind of love one night, whereupon he declares that he must go back to the war.

I am not being crass or facetious in my way of describing the "plot" of *The Others*; it is a film in which the dream, or the nightmare, collaborates with the actual. We are meant to feel undertones and subtexts. Just as in all great horror movies, there is the understanding that, if the fear and the suspense are to be justified, if they are to be more than tricks, then the whole thing must lean toward some meaning. I want *The Others* to mean something, and I can think of few recent films so crawling with subtexts.

The film came into being because, somehow or other, Tom Cruise had noticed the 1997 Spanish film *Abre los Ojos* (*Open Your Eyes*), directed by a young Chilean based in Spain, Alejandro Amenabar. In *Abre los Ojos*, a very successful young man gives up one woman for another, and is then terribly disfigured in an accident caused by the jilted woman. In his slow recovery this man discovers that he committed suicide a few years earlier and is now living a "lucid dream." This is very difficult terrain to negotiate, especially outside Spain, but Tom Cruise was fascinated by the film, and he bought the remake rights. In what followed, his remake (written and directed by Cameron Crowe, but produced by Cruise's own company), *Vanilla Sky*, the most searing sequences involve the hero's very mixed feelings over his own damaged face, his former beauty, and the scarred remains. One has to think that that is part of what attracted Tom Cruise, and though *Vanilla Sky* is a very bad film, striving and incoherent, its yearning bespeaks a large anxiety at being good-looking.

It seems that Cruise was so impressed by Amenabar (though he did not retain the Chilean for his remake) that he asked him what else he was making, or hoping to make. Whereupon Amenabar mentioned *The Others*, and it quickly became a production by Tom Cruise and his partner, Paula Wagner, translated into English, in which Nicole was cast as the central woman. Some saw the project as Tom's gift to her; others thought the offering might be more barbed. They also noted that as the Cruise-Kidman marriage came to an end (just after the shooting of *The Others*), so *Vanilla Sky* retained Penélope Cruz from *Abre los Ojos*, and Ms. Cruz in turn became Tom Cruise's lover. As it was, Nicole went to film *The Others* right after the close of *Moulin Rouge*, her knee not fully recovered, her family life coming apart.

"*The Others* was a scary time, too," she says. "I didn't like the way the story and the two children reflected on my own situation. I was in a bad state, and I had to make that psychological journey of a mother who kills her own children. I wanted to drop out, and I tried to get Julianne Moore or Sharon Stone to come on board. I was having nightmares about it. But they said they would sue me. I kept telling them I did not want to do it. I was willful and stubborn, but they said I had no choice."

Produced in partnership by Cruise/Wagner Productions and two Spanish companies, *The Others* was shot in the area of Cantabria, just outside Madrid, but the very significant house where it takes place is isolated and forever garbed in mist. It is a little more decorated and emptier than an English house. Still, the weather and the overall melancholy are northern European. Grace lives in this large, many-roomed place with her two children, a little girl, Anne, and her younger brother, Nicholas. These children are English and their mother, Kidman, has a pretty good English accent, even if it is not firmly rooted in class. Indeed, she sounds like an Australian girl based in Earl's Court who has taken a job as a ladies' companion in South Kensington, and who has worked to develop a voice that will not give her away. But it is a voice not yet at ease, in the special languid, superior manner that sustains the English upper class. Kidman is very striking as Grace, but you feel the effort behind the accent; indeed, it is part of the much larger anxiety that grips her character.

The children are pale. This is understandable, for they live in a house where the bright winter light never hits them directly. They are said (by Grace) to suffer from a rare sensitivity to light. They cannot go out, and must live in rooms where the heavy curtains are kept drawn. From the outset, however, there is an inextinguishable hint that the children's condition may be less a matter of their own health than of their mother's neurotic fixation. She asserts their problem. She guards against it. She will be horrified when the curtains all disappear from the windows. But in a film that is meant to be perceived visually above all, there is a fascinating contrast between Grace's nerve-wracked beauty, shining in the winter light that does not trouble her, and the gaunt, parchment faces of her children. And here it is important to stress that the daughter, Anne, is plainly suspicious of her mother.

The hovering house takes on a distinctly Irish character when three servants arrive. They are very much a team: Mrs. Mills (Fionnula Flanagan), in charge and trusted with the talking; Mr. Tuttle, the gardener (Eric Sykes; he seems to grow dead leaves); and the clenched, fearful, mute Lydia (Elaine Cassidy). Because Mrs. Mills is the mouthpiece for the servants, and because Flanagan is so marvelously expansive, confident, and orotund, she does bring something of the classic Irish ghost story to the picture, by which I mean a fair element of spookiness, to be sure, but well mixed with humor or teasing—the understanding that ghost stories are not entirely serious.

At first, these servants seem obedient enough; they do not dispute the odd arrangements of light and its denial. But Grace is so jittery, so wary, so certain of trouble—I suppose the word is paranoid—that she discovers how her letter to the local newspaper advertising for servants has not even been sent yet. So how did this lugubrious trio happen by? Ah well, says Mrs. Mills, we were just passing; this could be funnier than Amenabar allows, and it is a sadness all through the film that he does not seem aware that Eric Sykes was once a comic genius of the most delicate kind. He could have so many more moments of daft wonder to add to the uncertainty.

But Amenabar is busy making a tasteful, restrained horror film, one in the general area of Val Lewton, the inspired but short-lived RKO producer who made *Cat People* in the forties and several other minor masterpieces of morbid psychology. And so the idea spreads that there are "intruders" in the house, and no one suffers from this agony more than Grace, who is not just the center of the film, but the divining rod bending toward terror or the threat of it. Nicole has a very good forties hairstyle, and she entirely justifies Amenabar's declared confidence that her staring eyes are the best register of alarm or dread. In costumes that are purple, chocolate, or gray, with strong vertical ribbing that stresses her height yet makes her seem bound up, or imprisoned, Nicole gives a brilliant performance of pent-up nervous energy waiting to explode. And it is a mounting pity as the film goes on that it cannot really provide the story or the psychological setting that would justify her hysteria. Moreover, hysteria left unattended can become monotonous and grating. As Hitchcock knew, intense anxiety (think of *Marnie* or even *Rebecca*) has to be sustained eventually by external dangers.

I mention Hitchcock because it's clear that Amenabar intends that scale of reference. But in that case he should have studied Hitchcock more closely. To all intents and purposes, Kidman's Grace (are we meant to remember Grace Kelly?) is close to dementia because of . . . well, there's the point, because of what? A horror film has to be about something. That is why I think of what Jersey could have offered: a furtive wartime love affair between Grace and a German officer (all done while her husband was away); at the close of the war, the German is killed; Grace saw this murder, and it and the cruel reprisals against her "collaboration" send her into shock. So now she cannot let her children see the light—in other words, she cannot face the truth, or them knowing it, and she has a dream that is as much a nightmare that her husband will return, dead but bleeding with accusation against her.

No, none of this is in *The Others* (and I may be accused of remembering Alain Resnais's great film, *Hiroshima Mon Amour*). The film's story goes off in a quite different direction in which the three servants are ghosts who like to come back to the old house where they worked in 1891. And . . . well, I could go on, but in the spirit of Irish ghost stories that often feature a shaggy dog or two, I won't, in part because if you haven't seen *The Others* you have a fair claim on wanting your surprise kept intact, but also because I am bound to admit that that "surprise" is so cockamamie, so tall a story, that I can scarcely remember it. Still, Kidman's own report of her unease over the film's dread is understandable. The harder thing to credit is that she was compelled to make it.

So, really, all I want to say is that *The Others* is one of those failures that you nag away at in your mind just because so many things in it are so splendid and so promising—like the creak in a secret door that starts to open. Fionnula Flanagan and Alakina Mann (who plays Anne) are very good. And Nicole is, for an hour at least, on the verge of a great performance. As I said, her Englishness is not quite right, but her personification of hysteria (it is there in the very first scene) is brilliant and disturbing. Grant that somehow the film had found a way to wear its Jersey, grant that there had been a touch of St. Helier Mon Amour and the shrill, on-edge disturbance of the household could have been made meaningful. In that case, I see no reason why Mrs. Mills—an amiable ghost, such as you can easily meet in Ireland—might not have been the gentle guide who helped the young mother give up her guilt and take down the curtains in the madhouse.

I can think of another film, another madhouse, and I hope this is not going too far. It occurs in the home of an actor and an actress, the place to which at night the married couple return from making films like *The Others* and *Vanilla Sky*, with Amenabar desperately trying to keep the two dreams apart. But, of course at night, in the way of dreams—especially the dreams of two people in one space—there is always the possibility of crossover, embrace, or twisted sheets, and the unexpected discovery of awkward truths. Imagine a Tom and a Nic tossing and turning, driven by the dreams of movie roles that are not quite clear yet. They stagger into wakefulness, in the same blue moonlight, wracked by the same jitters. And a terrible new likeness is born when they look at each other, that of helpless strangers. (A treatment, please, twenty-five pages, by Monday.)

The Hours

I n July 2005, in *Newsweek*, falling in with the public's increasing disil-
lusion with big movies, David Ansen asks, "Is anybody making
movies we'll actually watch in 50 years?" Fifty years must seem a very
long time, and Ansen is not cheerful. Yet he lets his tastes show. As for
Tom Cruise, he reckons eight films will last: *War of the Worlds, Collateral,
Magnolia, Jerry Maguire, Rain Man, The Color of Money, Top Gun,* and
Risky Business. For Julia Roberts, he picks four: *Erin Brockovich, Notting
Hill, My Best Friend's Wedding,* and *Pretty Woman.* Yet in Nicole Kidman,
he sees only one keeper—*Moulin Rouge.* As for *The Hours,* he says, "it
moved me, and putting on Virginia Woolf's schnoz made her the darling of the Academy, but I have a suspicion that it's a movie for the
moment, not for all time."

Of course, not even the immense horizon of fifty years includes "all
time." Yet *The Hours* is plainly the movie and the experience that alters
Nicole Kidman's standing in the world, and the way we may be inclined
to think about her. It was also the best opportunity she had for redis-
covering herself. Whatever people think about *The Hours* as a whole
(and there are mixed opinions), nearly everyone admits to that first hal-
lucinatory uncertainty—is this Nicole Kidman or someone else, an
unknown? And that absence of self also assists the idea that the three
women, without complete meetings, are one. Not that I mean to suggest that Kidman had given up herself to be Virginia Woolf. There are
lots of ways in which her performance merely flirts with Mrs. Woolf—
not that flirting in the movies is out of place. But it is far more to the

point, I think, that the first and abiding impression is that she is no longer Nicole Kidman. Something like self-effacement has occurred, and there are many comments about how much that had to do with a false nose. The nose is clever, professional, and interesting, but it is the eyes that are most arresting. That is where the performance lives, in a gaze that has abandoned every hint of the seductive, the sexy, or the rather amusing delight in being Nicole. Inevitably, perhaps, people remark on this loss of self, or the concomitant onset of anxiety or pain, as something that may refer to the facts of her life—to the divorce from Tom. I think that's foolish.

The best explanation for Nicole's gravity is *The Hours* itself, and a startling imaginative depth that has come from nowhere. (We do not really believe in the trite equation of personal unhappiness and artistic seriousness. If we did, we'd have to wonder how and why the real Virginia Woolf laughed so much.) This is a work of searching gravity and unity, rarely attempted in mainstream cinema. If *Moulin Rouge* is *cirque du cinéma*, then *The Hours* is *cinéma du noir*, and enough to put the clichés of *film noir* to shame.

The Hours is the first time Nicole has played a supporting part. I am not saying that to be wicked—because we know that she's going to win the Oscar for a leading role in *The Hours*—but because by any stretch of the Academy's own definition and in our response to *The Hours*, this is a story in which every character and player is supporting the larger thread of the work. And it is an immense gift to the artistic conscience of actors to let them play small parts sometimes. There is no better education in the nature of drama or art.

For there is a boldness in the assumption of Michael Cunningham's novel that requires the power of movie's editing—and which runs the risk always of artiness and pretension—and which calls into play eventually (after two other scores are abandoned) the roiling, running piano music of Philip Glass, which is like a rippling effect that washes over the three stories seamlessly, and which speaks to continuity and the bonds between strangers as well as the meaning of water. And so *The Hours* proposes to offer us Virginia Woolf as she starts to write *Mrs. Dalloway* (1923–24); Laura Brown in Los Angeles as she narrowly avoids her own suicide; and Clarissa Vaughan in New York in 2002 (Clarissa is Mrs.

The Hours

Dalloway's first name) as she prepares a party to celebrate the poet she has loved, no matter that just before that party, the poet, Richard Brown, will throw himself out of a window. He has AIDS. But his true despair may be inherited, for he is the son of Laura Brown—he is the Richie who seemed to know even as a child what a precarious hold he had on his own mother.

Cunningham's novel (which won the Pulitzer Prize and was a best seller) is very movielike. David Hare, its adapter for the screen, will go through many drafts, maybe as many as thirty, but his work is often local or detailed. The line of a movie is there, naked, in the novel, if there is a modern movie audience prepared to sit still for the great conceit about these strangers being linked as securely as, say, Rick, Laszlo, and Ilse in *Casablanca*. Beyond that, the audience has to accept Virginia Woolf and the elitism of at least a marginal sense of *Mrs. Dalloway*. (This is not to be knocked; it is Nicole's biggest problem, for she has hated the book as a child, though at least she has tried to read it.) And then the audience must stomach a kind of rapture for suicide, without feeling that that fatalism is just a privileged, homosexual tendency, or a defiance of all the ways in the twentieth century in which the gay life has been made difficult.

Still, it is a vital part of Cunningham's approach, and of any attempt to make the movie, that the three women are sisters or interchangeable. At the end of the film, when Julianne Moore's Laura comes to meet Meryl Streep's Clarissa, Laura must be seventy-five. Ms. Moore wears the makeup very well (that is not sarcastic), and she just about gets through in what is a very difficult scene. She is helped enormously in that effort by the astonishing attention paid to her by Meryl Streep, who was fifty-three when the film opened. But that's enough to indicate how easily those two roles could have been swapped: Streep could have been old Mrs. Brown, and Moore (who was forty-two in 2002) could have handled the demands of Clarissa, who is in her early fifties. Correspondingly, Moore could have played Virginia Woolf, and Kidman could have played Laura Brown. And in truth, who can think for one moment that Meryl Streep could not have played Virginia Woolf? After all, at Woolf's death—and a good deal of *The Hours* shows her walking toward the River Ouse in Sussex, putting stones in her pockets and entering the water—she was fifty-nine. As it is, *The Hours* rather slips that point: Kidman's makeup in the film is famous, but walking toward the Ouse she looks no older than the way she does poised to start *Mrs. Dalloway*. But her walk—flat-footed, hunched shoulders—imparts a shape that we have never seen to Kidman's vaulting body.

If, for the sake of argument, David Hare (more naturally a playwright) had thought to reappraise *The Hours* for the theater, then any production of that play might have thought to let the three actresses have their turn at all three parts. The intensity might be excessive, and unduly schematic, but you could make the film in such a way that in one two-hour stretch the three players and the three roles are in a dance. I prefer it not that way, but surely in stage rehearsal it might have been tried—to the benefit of everyone. I stress this not in disapproval, but as a way of spelling out what happened with the film. Still, in a happier world, the Oscar for leading actress in 2002 might have been awarded to the ensemble—to Streep, Moore, and Kidman. That is more understanding of the work involved than singling out one actress. And it is a way of negotiating the plain fact that the three actresses are only playing supporting roles or aspects of one character.

How much better it would be for the health of our cinema if such arguments prevailed for actors and audiences to consider. But it does help one see that *The Hours* is a work that exults in the community of actors, in the very strange life they share and the terrible competition they can hardly escape for a few prized parts. This is also a film in which the three actresses have hardly a romantic, let alone a sexual moment, and in which they and their characters live on the wrong side of forty. I would suggest that just as Marlon Brando in *The Godfather* was not just the literal father of the family, but the model of its way of acting, so *The Hours* is a kind of tribute to the tradition or example set down by Meryl Streep. One way or another, she had pioneered all three roles, not to mention the assumption that such lives could make a compelling film. There is a kindness in the film in that the great English actress Eileen Atkins plays the New York florist to whom this Clarissa goes for her party flowers. In her time, Atkins had played Mrs. Woolf on the stage as well as adapting the script for the 1998 movie of *Mrs. Dalloway*. That kindness might have inspired one more—the thought from Kidman on the eventual Oscars night that this film was a tribute to the example of Streep. Never mind that on Oscar night most actresses are without a script and they are untidy at best, crying their own tears.

The Hours would end up a joint production of Paramount and Miramax, but it was initially the design of producer Scott Rudin, who purchased the rights to Michael Cunningham's novel, enlisted Stephen Daldry as director (after his debut movie, *Billy Elliott*), hired David Hare to do the script, and conceived of Nicole to play Virginia Woolf. Just as one wants to give Rudin great credit for seeing this as a movie, still his commercial instinct began to build it around the starriness of Nicole as Woolf (a piece of casting likely to be regarded as original yet dangerous). Moreover, though the finished film would cost only $25 million (a restrained figure), Kidman seems to have been hired on at $7.5 million. In other words, she was the major budgetary item; she was always the box-office identity for the picture. In short, Streep and Moore cannot have been engaged on anything like the same terms. And Kidman did take persuading. Her youthful experience of the book and Virginia Woolf did not encourage her. It seems to have been David Hare's script that tipped the balance. And it was only then that Streep and Moore were hired.

But the crisis in Kidman's personal life occurred between her signing on and her actual filming. That meant that Streep's story and Moore's were shot first. In turn, that allowed Kidman to come to the project not only when it had begun to take on shape and texture in Stephen Daldry's mind. Nicole did not look at footage of the other two actresses, but time had made it clear that Virginia Woolf was the fount of the story and not just a character. Some may minimize the importance of that, but I think that in many ways Virginia Woolf is the true author of the whole story. It is a book she never writes. Her *Mrs. Dalloway* is Laura's essential reading; and Mrs. Dalloway's name and the nervous excitement of her "party" have been inherited by Clarissa. It's not that Kidman was expected to take on shadings or mannerisms of the other two women (as De Niro certainly did in uncovering the earlier life of Vito Corleone in *The Godfather Part II*). It is not that these characters are related, but it does mean a great deal that Kidman's Woolf knows where the picture is going. As many people attest, it is not that the Virginia

Woolf sequences involve so much crucial action, but they require a degree of knowledge in the character's eyes. In many works of art, the energy of the line may depend on the artist's confidence in where it is going. So I'd say that Kidman's Woolf might not be as bold without the advantage of Stephen Daldry knowing the rest of the story first.

"With Stephen Daldry, I realized that the chemistry on a film is with the director," says Nicole. "It's a platonic love affair. It's not the result—it's the process. I was not in a good place, and I did not really want to make the film. I could not feel myself getting in a place and coming up with a performance. I was in a deep depression. And I found a cottage in the woods, two hours out of London, near the location, next to a golf course, surrounded by trees. I was all alone. I slept there and it made me feel safe. And I could feel myself getting into her flesh. I latched on to her and I fell in love with Virginia. I started smoking like a fiend, roll-your-owns, the way she smoked. It was a strange, strange time, and I wasn't interested in the other characters. But I went with Virginia to a place where life might stop for art, and it's a scary place."

Naturally enough, Kidman researches Virginia Woolf—with a great deal more sympathy than the schoolgirl could ever muster. She schools herself to write with her right hand (as Woolf did) for the scenes where we see her actually penning the opening of *Mrs. Dalloway*. On the other hand, in listening to BBC recordings of Virginia Woolf speaking, she and Daldry and anyone else know immediately that it would be disastrous to mimic that very closed upper-class voice. Its authenticity cannot possibly surpass connotations of snobbery and responses of laughter. Speech, the articulation of words, must have been vital for Virginia Woolf (and she was a lot more chatty than the film suggests), but from the outset Kidman fixes on a new voice: gruff, lower than her own, not Australian, not authentic, but resonant.

In the matter of appearance, the same decisions are taken. Nicole Kidman does not look like Virginia Woolf. Woolf was longer in the jaw, a lot more innocent or haughty in the eyes, far finer in sensibility. But how many know that, or would recognize her? In truth, Kidman's Woolf has moments of looking like Princess Anne or even Lady Diana; she resembles pictures of Charlotte Brontë. She wears a rather dusty-looking auburn wig—her hair has never had less sheen. She wears a false nose—but it is not a Woolfian nose. It is, instead, an alteration that helps us forget Nicole Kidman.

What emerges, under the studious treatment of production designer Maria Djurkovic and costumier Ann Roth, is the Richmond home of Leonard and Virginia Woolf. Virginia regards it as a kind of prison, or exile—so far from London—but on film, in so many lovely shades of blue, brown, and mauve there is always the possibility of these English interiors looking like a treasure house from the *Antiques Roadshow*. Mrs. Woolf speaks of her illness; she can make children laugh at her apparent distraction or absentmindedness; she is close to being intimidated by her own servants. Yet we hardly know what this mental illness is. Rather, it is presented as the opposite of creativity, of work and writing. And Kidman's Woolf is no weakling, no victim of self-pity. Far more, she is a prisoner who has learned to guard her inner life. So the eyes are fierce, angry, bitter over time or calm lost and over the need to keep up a bare domestic front. I don't think this portrait matches too well with what biographical scholarship has made of Virginia Woolf, a woman who was likely set back fatally by sexual interference at the hands of brothers (a thing not mentioned in this film), and who certainly found some rescue in a romantic life with women. Kidman the actress, and the movie, have made the ruthless decision to fix on this unstable woman's commitment to work. That's what makes her not just stronger but more creatively robust or selfish.

What that means, I fear, is that Kidman's Virginia and her killer eyes are hardly candidates for that obedient passage to death that frames the film. Of course, we know that Virginia Woolf killed herself. In fact, the Woolfs had equipped themselves with suicide pills in case the Germans invaded Sussex (and the rest of England) in 1941. Yet this Virginia, I suspect, might have proved a sturdy figure in some resistance movement, tender in sensibility yet prepared to learn how to break a Nazi neck. All I mean to say is that in her inward stronghold Kidman's Woolf is so strong—such a potential opponent—that her suicide seems imposed. Inevitably, it makes a crushing rhyme scheme with that way in which Ed Harris's petulant poet slips out of an open window. And it is in Harris's character, I fear, that *The Hours* is most repellently tidy and foreboding.

In the same way, with the movie's tremendous grip on life itself and its love of incident, I'm not sure that the illness or despair of Laura is adequately explained. There she is in Los Angeles in 1951, the mother of one adoring boy, and pregnant with another child (Julianne Moore was pregnant as the film was made). Her husband (John C. Reilly) is fond yet obtuse. But is that enough? Is it, perhaps, that deep down she needs to be writing her own *Mrs. Dalloway*? Or is such therapy simple-minded? She nearly kills herself, but too irresolute for that (we learn), she will leave husband and son—and in the unduly reductive process of a sparse film, that loss cannot be separated from Richard's bitterness, his self-pity, his suicide, his obscurity as a writer, and perhaps even his gayness. In other words, the deeper one looks into the undergrowth of the film, the shakier its fabric is, and the more composed its death wish can seem.

I speak as someone who loved the film on first viewing and only gradually came to see its false poise, its limits on energy. What that means, I think now, is that I was so moved by the film that my emotional loyalty could withstand every shaft of logic or regret that I let strike its target. I suppose I was ready, primed, for some heady expression of my feelings for Nicole—and maybe life had so organized itself that she was ready, too. But I think I was always watching the film as a story created by Kidman's character and I was exhilarated by what felt like her liberation in 2001. Remember that Kidman filmed her sequences in the summer of 2001, just before the great external assault on our society, the thing that is supposed to have changed everything, but at a moment when she and her friends may have been pleased to think of her stepping forward into a new self.

There is one other thing I have not quite mentioned, and I think it is vital, no matter that she has not always followed through on it. In being Virginia in *The Hours*, in acting out this woman's burning need to be alone in her room, writing, Nicole Kidman for the first time in her work set aside all those pressures in her and in all actresses to be liked. There is hardly anything so damaging to an actor—on stage or screen—as that overpowering urge to secure the affection, the support, the sympathy of strangers. Without necessarily being in a position to spell this out, she had advanced into the imagined territory of the greatest filmmakers. If such people existed any longer.

The Hours opened in the days between Christmas 2002 and New Year's. It was expertly handled by Leslee Dart of the PMK agency and by Miramax, a company that had by then acquired a rare instinct for pursuing Oscars. And from the outset, it was assumed rather than argued out that the film starred Nicole Kidman. The very strong review in the *New York Times*, by Stephen Holden, began:

> In *The Hours* Nicole Kidman tunnels like a ferret into the soul of a woman besieged by excruciating bouts of mental illness. As you watch her wrestle with the demon of depression, it is as if its torment had never been shown on the screen before. Directing her desperate, furious stare into the void, her eyes not really focusing, Ms. Kidman, in a performance of astounding bravery, evokes the savage inner war waged by a brilliant mind against a system of faulty wiring that transmits a searing, crazy static into her brain.

From before the film's opening, it felt likely that Kidman would win her Oscar. *The Hours* was an Academy kind of film: it had literary credentials, a somber tone, and craft laid on with precious attention. It was also a serious, good film. Kidman had been nominated before for the very different *Moulin Rouge*. She had plainly gone a long way to overcome her personal unhappiness. She had emerged as her own person and as someone ready to take bold decisions. She had remade herself as a screen performer, and she had shown an extraordinary attitude as Virginia Woolf. In truth, in terms of drama or narrative, she had not been asked to do much more. Her part could be seen as less testing than those of Julianne Moore or Meryl Streep. But they never felt like candidates for the Oscar. In part, that was because Moore had another film to offer, *Far from Heaven*, in which she was onscreen most of the time. The other eventual nominees for the Oscar were Salma Hayek in *Frida*, Diane Lane in *Unfaithful*, and Renée Zellweger in *Chicago*.

Nicole won everything. First she took the Golden Globe, where the competition did include Meryl Streep in *The Hours*. Then she won the

BAFTA (British Academy of Film and Television Awards) award. Then the Screen Actors Guild prize. By the night of the Oscars, March 23, 2003, there was little doubt about the Oscar. There was far more concern over the U.S./U.K. invasion of Iraq that had begun just a couple of weeks earlier. Or that's what Hollywood pretended. In the event, Kidman seemed surprised by her Oscar, but she was not quite enough of an actress to make the surprise feel natural. On the other hand, her feelings may have been out of control. She had to say something worthwhile, no matter that she was now restored as the giggly Australian girl—so far from the Virginia Woolf in her lair, using a sharp pen to leave her mark:

"Stephen Daldry—you took a huge chance on me, I am so grateful. David Hare, you gave me magnificent words to say. I am just absolutely thrilled to be standing up here tonight. I have to say, though, it was, Why do you come to the Academy Awards when the world is in such turmoil? Because art is important. And because you believe in what you do, you want to honor that. And it is a tradition that needs to be upheld. My whole life I've wanted to make my mother proud, and now I want to make my daughter proud."

So perhaps the Oscar was generous—the Oscars are, just as they are savage and indifferent to their losers. But the victory had another consequence: if Nicole ever strayed too far from the toughness of being Virginia Woolf, that departure would not be forgotten. It's still not clear, as I write, how far she has learned that lesson, but her stage had changed.

She would say that she believed Virginia Woolf had come into her life as help or guidance. She had worked very hard and had clutched at superstition (holding one of Woolf's handkerchiefs in her pocket). She got Hare to add a scene—the one at Richmond railway station—that did not figure in the novel. She is there with her husband (the excellent Stephen Dillane), in a scene Kidman found very hard, according to Hare. But she found her answer (and her help) in making it personal: "The scene at the train station was the reason I wanted to do the film. It's about a woman saying, 'This isn't what I want to be. I have the right to make choices for my life that are going to fulfill me.' I loved Virginia.

I just love when she says, 'I'm living a life I have no wish to live. I'm living in a town that I have no mood to live in.' "

And yet, is David Ansen necessarily wrong? When I look at *The Hours* again, I cannot easily surmount the film's ellipses or problems—the way the Philip Glass score becomes liturgical, and in turn the pious air that is cast upon the series of suicides. I still feel that this Mrs. Woolf is too fierce and strong to go into the river. I still do not understand Laura Brown's tragedy—that is not to say I don't believe it, but I do not understand it. And when I reread what Nicole said about what the role meant to her, I can hear so little of the sisterhood that seems to me aesthetically vital. *The Hours* cost $25 million. In the United States it grossed $41 million, no matter it won several awards, including the Oscar for Best Actress. Outside the States it is said to have grossed $15 million—so about $56 million in all. That makes it a marginal venture as far as profits are concerned. And surely there are many things about the film that might make you think, why ask about profit? It was good that it was done. It was remarkable that it was so well noticed.

And there's truth in all of those claims. Yet I cannot help but look ahead a little, to the mood of *Dogville*. If someone came to me and asked how would you film an adaptation of *The Hours*, I could see two ways: with great actresses, immense craft, tender resources of costume and decor, inspiring music, deep reverence—in a word, the way it was done; or on a bare stage, where the three time periods are marked out like playing areas, with actresses swapping the parts around.

Why do I heed the unknown, the second way? Perhaps I do because it remains unknown—the unseen always draws us on in film study. And the best films—including those as daunting as *The Hours*—leave us wanting to know more, or to live longer in the screen. But also because then the budget might have been $2.5 million, say, and because then a true sisterhood (among the actresses) would have forced a kind of play or merriment to break up the texture of what is a very composed funereal monument.

Dogville

*D*ogville is an extraordinary enterprise, the kind of film people might make when the movies are no longer enough. And that is worth considering in 2003 when the picture opens to rancor and controversy at the Cannes Film Festival. There are those who regard it as an attack upon America itself. And in so many ways that might amuse the writer-director Lars von Trier, for not the least of his insights is that when the small, isolated, impoverished, but self-satisfied town of Dogville, U.S.A., suffers a visitor—the fugitive Grace, arriving in a long black coat with tattered ostrich at the neck and the cuffs—they learn how to take her not quite as a gift so much as an attack, and a reproach.

Nicole Kidman is Grace, and just as it is plain that her adventurous instinct has allowed *Dogville* to be made (and to become an international event), so no one really has made such a decisive gesture since Ingrid Bergman did in 1946 when she gave up a Selznick contract, and such fantasies as *Gaslight, Spellbound,* and *Casablanca,* to go to Italy to make a film with Roberto Rossellini, because she believed in his startling neorealist ways. The picture would be *Stromboli,* and it led to a love affair, adulterous scandal, twins, condemnation, and nearly a decade in which Bergman was like a flag on Rossellini's pole, increasingly torn in the wind, before she came back as an outcast, and as a nervous, coughing fugitive who said she might be Anastasia, the daughter to the Tsar. A second Oscar greeted her contrition.

Nicole's adventure is briefer and more controlled. Far from being

Dogville

romantically involved with the austere but tricky von Trier, she manages to extricate herself from the sequels that are talked about as part of the *Dogville* project. Nicole may be an inquiring mind—and nothing takes away from the cold beauty of the *Dogville* experiment, or her odd saintliness in the film. But she is a cover girl, too, and someone who needs to know that whenever a film earns just $150,000, it better be quick and there had better be a couple of locked-in deals at $10 million or so to oil it.

Ingrid Bergman in the years just after the war was not just a genuine romantic and a scatterbrained political conscience as well as a woman desperate for sex and integrity. She was a wreck, through and through, someone who never possessed Nicole's cool intelligence. I have spoken of this control before, and you may think it is a small matter. Not so; Nicole is clever enough to have organized a terrific career, one that has held now for more than a decade. And it is part of that trick that she seems to have her cake and eat it, too—she does *The Stepford Wives* and *Dogville* without anyone in public asking the obvious question: Is she crazy? And it is not asked because a saving impulsive warmth erases it, the one in which she is simply opportunistic, Virginia Woolf and Little Miss Flirty-Eyes on a magazine cover. Does that mean she's dishonest, manipulative, unstable? Of course not. But her eyes in the magazine pictures ask you that very question. Whereupon you say, of course, you hadn't quite realized how "smart" she is. Very well. But smartness is not intelligence, and many people who believe in giving themselves to a project and a role believe deeply—with every ounce of brainpower they have—in suspending the intelligence that can control and intellectualize everything. Because intelligence muffles instinct and spontaneity; because it shadows true acting. When Ingrid Bergman behaved like an idiot in 1946, that was the final proof of her passion for acting. No one has pinned the idiot on Nicole yet, but *Dogville* flirts with the prospect, and von Trier dreamed of sequels, with Nicole.

Dogville is a small town in the Colorado Rockies, high up at the end of a road. It has a church without a pastor and an abandoned mine, and it has a tiny population that could be a cross section of the nation—one black household, a family with children, a blind man, a souvenir shop, and the Edisons, father and son, Thomas and Tom, where the old man reads *Tom Sawyer* and young Tom aspires to be the fill-in preacher—or the voice of moral rearmament—in the town. It is easier to be that than the writer he also dreams of being. Then one night this Tom hears shots in the valley far away and not long afterward Grace appears, needing a place to hide. He sells her to the town, first on a trial basis, then as a member of the community.

But Dogville is not to be found in Colorado; it is notorious in the career of Lars von Trier that he has never been to the United States. So how do you know the place enough to challenge it? some ask. He replies, Who in America in 1943 knew Morocco well enough to make *Casablanca*? He could add, Which actress has written not one line of Virginia Woolf, yet is able to become her? In other words, Lars von Trier stands up for the imagination.

And so his *Dogville* is made in an old machine hall in Trollhattan in Sweden. The place is thirty by sixty meters, and it has a black-lacquer platform that is the town, and a diagram of it. Our first view, from directly above, is like that of a sketch map or a board game. There are approximate markings of streets and properties. There are a few flats, or doorways, to flesh out the abstraction—enough to look like a child's idea of a ghost town—and there is a cyclorama behind it all, a sky that goes flawless black or snow white to signal night and day. It is a stage set, you might conclude. Well, yes, but something more complete than that, and something that takes on a prisonlike actuality in the three hours of the film. It is also a method that brings a drastic but invigorating economy to the filmmaking, and which requires that any viewer regard the film's story as a lesson or a parable. It is fundamentally un-American not because of the things said against America (by way of Dogville) but because of the savage, satirical denial of lifelike fantasy, and the implicit mockery of a culture that cannot look at a movie unless it has that air of transportation to it, a belief in the illusion so great that you don't have to consider the point.

Von Trier is part of a northern European movement called Dogme that has laid down authoritarian laws about the necessary primitivism of filmmaking—necessary if only to escape the various lies of the illusion just referred to. Dogme is interesting, but it is also for many of its followers a blatant grab at attention and publicity, a way of getting to make films cheaply. So it is interesting to ask ourselves why Nicole Kidman takes *Dogville* on, just at a point where she has secured the kind of salary level never given to actresses before.

So consider what I said at the outset, that *Dogville* is the sort of thing people might do as they see the age of movie coming to an end, not just as an easy entertainment, but as an aspect of the easy or comfortable world. It may be that the old illusion is itself wearing thin—that it has gone stale on its own adherents, so that it depresses them now too often and cannot hide the shams and frauds, and because it is no longer as easy as it was to make the bargain inside one's own head that, yes, the world is very bad, but still I will take a couple of hours of consolation or mercy.

That old faith in moviegoing is slipping away. We feel we have seen every story so often before that now all we can notice are the clichés and the camp play on them. And as the sense of story goes, so we realize that photography—that trembling imprint of life—is itself giving way to electronic and digital reworkings of imagery so that films are no longer like life. Instead they become increasingly deranged with noise, violence, the celebration of cliché, and their own money. Something in us—especially in movie lovers—hates this.

And at the same time we are not sure what we can expect to last. Isn't our America—and it belongs to us all—plunging into an un-American war in which wholesale lying and duplicity are leading weapons, in which wrongful imprisonment and torture are regular instruments? And all this for a culture and a nation that clings to the shattered figure of God as all of its essential, man-made democratic salvations—education, health, language, honesty, memory—fall away into disuse and betrayal.

Is this what Nicole Kidman thinks? She is too canny to say so and not radical enough to go this far. But part of her acuity and her cuteness is hearing what is out there in the air, of knowing enough people who are more than smart. And around this time, an idea clearly comes into Nicole's mind—that maybe all this, this being Nicole Kidman, must end, that the part of it that has always been a trick will fade, that someone else will come up on her just as she overtook people like Meg Ryan, Julia Roberts, and Sharon Stone. After all, she has children and family, and she begins to talk of retirement—idly, experimentally, but with feeling—and of going back to Australia, a place where she is more at ease, or so she likes to think. And, if the very worst does come to the worst, well, Australians have always known that their country was a last natural stronghold, a place so far away it would survive the fallout clouds longer than other countries, a place where convict practicality might survive.

I do not mean to make too much of it, but even as a gesture *Dogville* tells us how au courant Nicole is. A further proof is that she makes the film—holds it up as a central pole sustains a tent, and is its life and feeling—without ever quite laying her hand on von Trier's testament and saying, I believe. In the mid-1940s, Ingrid Bergman is condemned on the floor of the House of Representatives and scolded from so many pulpits. There was a time when, even if she had returned, she could not have been employed. Her sin was not political, but it occurred in the age when to be un-American was enough to ruin careers. It is a very cute arrangement that allows Nicole to make the film without picking up a speck of anti-American dirt.

And everyone attests to her conviction and enthusiasm. It is an intense six-week shoot, with cast and crew housed alike at Ronnum Manor House. Nicole is in one degree not alike: she has an outlying building to herself, secure and secluded, and her old friend Russell Crowe does fly in for one weekend, from Berlin, on a private plane, without the story getting out. But she joins in the making of the film with her usual determination and likability. It is not just that she is the star, but a star likely to help win over the illustrious cast—including Lauren Bacall, Patricia Clarkson, Blair Brown, Ben Gazzara, and Chloë Sevigny—and the children who are part of the cast, too. She never has a moment's doubt about the concept in the shooting and she is as loyal and supportive to von Trier as anyone could be. And it is the most costly film ever made in Scandinavia—whatever the code of Dogme says. Nicole is always ready for the crazy method of shooting, with von Trier himself often operating the camera, darting in and out for little shots that can never be cut smoothly into the flow of the film. Smoothness is not everything.

She gives a fine, watchful performance as this stranger in town who wants to be liked and who takes mounting abuse because of it. She wears shabby, secondhand clothes; her hair is cut roughly to chin length; there is not much makeup, but she looks lovely and it is easy to feel that this loveliness is an inner, spiritual force shining out of her. She is the figure of good in this parable of a selfish, mean-minded world that has lost all idealism. Her bright blondness serves a purpose, the way the light in Colorado can cast a natural halo. And she is a great trouper. When the story calls for it, she puts on the collar of slavery and allows herself to be tethered to a great weight so she can hardly move. That is Grace's affliction or humiliation, but Nicole takes it on without complaint. And she is on camera for nearly all of the film.

Even if you haven't seen it, you can tell how odd a film it is. It is too long, by far—with John Hurt's wintry narration, the fable's simplicity should be enforced, not prolonged. It is very odd to see Lauren Bacall in the posture of someone hoeing at weeds, and startling to see the bleak superciliousness in her face, no easier to hide than the shallow kindness in Nicole's face. There are horrible, giddy camera movements that do nothing but stress amateurism. But there is a serene masterwork hiding in there, a true fable about the terrible reactionary spirit in small-town America. Need we underline the way in which, lately, that spirit has hardly been content to stay home, but has moved to cities of more power and authority?

Dogville should be seen: it has an icy wit and a formal daring that are entrancing. At the very end there are heavy-handed allusions to American poverty that seem clumsy and juvenile. But the film's own narrative ending is remarkable and important. Grace is increasingly exploited and humbled by the town. Not even Tom Jr., who supposedly loves her, will come to her aid (he says he doesn't want to lose his status of being fair). But finally Tom makes a call to the gangsters from whom, apparently, Grace has been running.

Does he do that to save her—for there is a hint that the gangster boss, Mr. Big (James Caan), cares for her—or does Tom intend that they destroy her? The gangsters arrive in their black cars. Caan, it turns out, is her father. He rebukes her for being arrogant (this is not very well handled). But the logical buildup of the film will not be denied: those cars and the guns wait to deliver. Grace consents to the execution of everyone in Dogville and she goes away with the gangsters.

It is clearly possible for us to argue over this ending. It may mean that the force of organized power in America can and will eliminate any opposition—even if it comes from the heartland of its own support. It may mean that the world of Dogville deserves destruction. And it can mean that Nicole—even saintly Nicole—is truly the child of gangsters. In other words, is there a suggestion here that if you live long enough with the system, with the magazines, with Miramax, then you are—even if you try to run away from those things—their helpless possession? *Dogville* is a fascinating work, something we would probably not have had without the restless smarts of Nicole Kidman. At the same time, it is a message to her—and not that comforting.

As the shooting ends, an exhilarated von Trier toasts a sequel—with Nicole. She is carried away; she has felt the fervor. "Yes!" she cries. But in the event it does not happen.*

---

*The sequel, *Manderlay,* appears in 2005. But now Grace is Bryce Dallas Howard—it does far less well than *Dogville.*

Cold Mountain

There is always more luck in these things than the intelligent person would like to know—and that is another way of wondering whether Nicole Kidman wants to seem farseeing or not. Several times a year, in effect, she is asked, Would you like to be her, or her, or even her? Now, for anyone who has ever felt cramped or jaded in their only self, this may seem a heady invitation, especially if the offer reassures you that after 6 p.m. and the last "Cut!" of the day, or on weekends, why, you can go back to being yourself. And perhaps sometimes you can. I spoke to Bruno Ganz recently, the Swiss actor who played Hitler in *Downfall*, and he said what a relief it had been at the end of the day to hang up "Hitler" in the dressing room and go out to dinner as Bruno Ganz. But I looked at his sad, dark eyes, and I wondered, especially as his Hitler began to make him more famous.

It is Nicole's nature to be sturdy, cheerful, robust, a real person, full of common sense. She doesn't let herself be seen pondering or calculating. Because then if you make a mistake, you can begin to look foolish. She aims for something more like the attitude of a golfer on the eleventh green at Augusta facing a very tricky downhill putt of eleven feet, curling to the left. You can read the green as long as you like, or for as long as the rules allow. Wherever the sun stands there will be shadows on the green, or lines of light that may conflict with the undulations in the ground or the nap of the grass. You have to decide what the putt will do and then you have to exercise the finest physical control to deliver the putt your head has chosen.

But your ball lips the hole, gathers pace and runs past it eighteen feet into the collar of less tightly mown grass. You three-putt the hole.

Then you have to walk on to the twelfth not shattered, not hideous, not humiliated, not as angry as Hannibal Lecter, not quite forgetting it all. But calm. Because on the twelfth you may have a very similar putt and you have to come to it with eagerness, not dread.

Of course, we are talking about a golfer who may have so ordered himself that he does not go through life trying to be content, or trying to see that those near him are content, who does not have to worry too much about anything except knocking small balls into holes that are about two and a half times their diameter. And that sort of order can be madness. An actress, a human being (one with two children), can hardly go through life trying to get these other, imaginary people "right" if she is "wrong." This is speaking about the dilemma very loosely. But Nicole works hard to seem balanced, to be aware of and deeply determined by other things—by life, the children, common sense, spontaneity, and being Australian—even if sometimes she might concede she is trying an insane habit: being other people.

But that's no reason not to work very hard at choosing which people to be. She has to read the greens—the scripts and the way the projects are shaping up. There are so many other elements in the choice, so many more than a golfer faces and so many for which she can hardly be held responsible—or not until the picture is being demolished by critics. There is her part—is it right for her? There is the larger story—does she believe in it? There are the questions of the writer, the director, the producers, the company—is she going to be comfortable with these people? Her deal is a part of that, of course, but not the only part: she wants to be respected, she wants to feel she will be listened to, and given time when she needs to stop and think. Who else will be in the film? Whom must she kiss, or make love to? Whom must she talk to for days at a time in a tiny cabin at the top of the mountain—or wherever? Where will the film be shot? Can she have her children there?

Not that anyone at the outset can answer all these questions—and Nicole is likely to be there at the outset, because her saying "Yes, I'll do it" makes it so much easier to get the funds to put the rest of a project together. The earlier she says yes, the more chance she has of influencing the other things. And even if she has no single-minded wish yet to be a producer, far less a director, she knows there are matters best not left to the real producers—not if she wants what she needs.

But even then, if every omen or collateral matter looks promising, she can't tell. She may not know what a director is really like or whether there will be chemistry with the co-star who comes in late to replace the guy she was so happy with. She does not know that the location for the picture may be changed, late in the day, from one continent to another. And because movies do not belong to actors—except in the minds of the people who love them or condemn them—she does not have control over every little thing enough to assure that it will be all right.

Take *Cold Mountain*.

Charles Frazier's novel, his first, is published in 1997 by the Atlantic Monthly Press. In many ways, it is a throwback to a kind of novel not much seen in the last thirty years or so. It is a piece of history, deeply felt and researched by a writer from the mountains of North Carolina. It is a Civil War story, yet it is patterned on the *Odyssey*, and on a lone figure returning from war in hopes of finding the woman he loves. It is an introspective book, plunging into the wells of the solitary characters (Frazier sees people as being alone). It is very well written, in a deliberate, literary way that seeks to evoke the voice of the 1860s, yet it is filled with incident, action, battle and skirmish, and longing. It is a best seller, number one on many lists for many weeks, yet it also wins the National Book Award and is the American Booksellers Association book of the year.

Before those awards, before publication even, Anthony Minghella is spending a few days with Michael Ondaatje in the latter's Canadian cabin. They have become friends during the adaptation of Ondaatje's *The English Patient*, which wins Best Picture in 1996 as well as directing and screenplay adaptation Oscars for Minghella. In the cabin, Minghella notices a proof copy of *Cold Mountain*, which has been sent to Ondaatje so that he might say something supportive to go on the book's jacket. Minghella picks up the novel—having vowed after *The English Patient* not to take on another adaptation—and is "mesmerized." Nicole Kidman, as they say, is sleeping somewhere far away, unaware, oblivious, not yet reading the green, not yet being read by Minghella.

It will be the summer of 2002 when Kidman goes to Romania to be Ada Monroe in the Miramax picture, budgeted at a little over $80 million ($15 million for her), the most costly film Miramax has ever made. Even so, it was to bring the budget down as much as possible that Miramax made the call to shoot in Romania as opposed to North Carolina. In the years of Nicole's sleeping, Minghella has met and talked with Charles Frazier, has tried to absorb the novel, its history and variants as Frazier recalls them, to say nothing of the story of the Civil War in those parts. He has spent time on his own, walking in the Blue Ridge Mountains—he has tried to be the book's hero Inman. No one ever thinks of him for that role, but every director is his own hero and every other part as he writes or explores the terrain. And Minghella is an uncommonly literate and sensitive man. He has also made Patricia Highsmith's *The Talented Mr. Ripley* in the intervening years (one more adaptation), and he is by now very familiar with the odd ordeal of wanting to be faithful to a text while yearning to do something unique.

He is also quite inward enough a man to see that a predicament recurs in his own work. It cannot be just chance, but lovers are cast apart—by separation and/or death. In *Truly, Madly, Deeply*, his debut, one lover comes back to talk to the other after his death. In *The English Patient* two great lovers are separated and then brought back together by death. In *The Talented Mr. Ripley*, or in Minghella's version of it, Tom Ripley and Dickie Greenleaf come close to seeing their own union—it is identity as much as love—then Tom kills Dickie and is haunted forever after. And now in *Cold Mountain*, we will have a film in which Inman and Ada are lovers who scarcely meet.

And in the intervening years, from 1997 to 2002, among many other things, two planes enter the twin towers of the World Trade Center in New York, and in a way that is imperfectly related (Intelligence never gets it straight) a war will be begun in Iraq. For anyone sleeping (like an actress) or slowly determining his plan for a film of *Cold Mountain*, such events may be shocking and cruel, yet they are distractions from a greater, more constant, and more intimate task. In the Hundred Years' War, in the Black Death, in the Dark Ages, stonemasons kept a little light to carve acorns and oak leaves in the stone of cathedrals. Not even an explosion vast enough to take away London is going to stop a Virginia Woolf from putting down that first sentence of *Mrs. Dalloway*—or warn her that the small pleasure of the sentence may not hold back her troubles.

So who is Ada Monroe and how can Nicole Kidman become her? And why do I have an early tremor about putting Nicole in a film with "Cold" in its title? Is it playing on her weakness, the thing some people flinch from?

The novel does not say how old Ada is, but having been raised in Charleston she has come with her widower father to the country of Cold Mountain. It seems an odd and unkind direction for the father to take. For Ada had already "been educated beyond the point considered wise for females." She knows French and Latin and some Greek. She plays the piano and paints in watercolors. She is well read and "filled with opinions." But opinions don't go far on Cold Mountain and it is not a thing Monroe the father seems to consider—but who will Ada meet there?

He is not long in the movie, but Donald Sutherland gives a fine air of the lofty father who does not notice others' points of view. As a farmer on Cold Mountain, he is impractical. He reckons to put cows and sheep together in his fields. Why do that? ask the locals. Do you want wool or meat? Neither, says Monroe, I want atmosphere. Neither Frazier nor Minghella cares to look too closely into a way of life in which Ada may have been mere atmosphere for her father. And that is why her age is important. Kidman is thirty-four, and while she looks glorious or ravishing she does seem thirty-four. Yet a daughter of that age, especially one as versed in the Brontës as Ada is said to be, especially one filled with opinions, is hardly likely to have taken the move from Charleston to the country with such docility. On the other hand, a daughter of twenty-two—and Ada in the book could be that age—might be too immature to protest.

So it is more a problem than a question. An Ada Monroe in her thirties, I think, might easily look at her father's inclination to be a country preacher and farmer and elect to stay in Charleston. Surely Charleston is a place of music, art, society, and opinions? Not to mention a better place for Ada to find a husband—or, if you want to see her as more advanced or independent, a great love affair. As Frazier organizes his book, he hides the problem as much as possible: we only really meet Ada after her father's unexpected death, and without an exact sense of her age. She is alone in the wilderness, and that is easier to take if you don't have to see a thirty-four-year-old with an experienced look and a mind of her own. Even with her father dead, couldn't Ada go back to Charleston? The question is not asked. Frazier is set upon casting his Ada adrift in this strange world—and that is made easier to accept if she is actually very young. Equally, her affection for the Inman who has gone off to war is more the passion of a young, inexperienced person. In other words, despite her academic record, she behaves like a country girl, yet one cut off from country skills or knowledge.

Minghella begins by giving Kidman and Renée Zellweger (his Ruby) a tough physical regimen, or so they all say. Just how many weeks of unrelieved labor expensive movie stars will endure is another matter. Still, the two actresses walk the land, they shift timber, they work with animals, they get a tan, and they start to sweat. Though whereas Zellweger's Ruby is a rich nut-brown hue, very plausibly a country girl, someone who has kicked animals aside, grown hard hands from labor, and ruined her own complexion, Nicole stays Nicole. It is a first warning sign.

Living with the inner Ada, the one left alone by her father's death, Frazier dwells on her silent inadequacy: "she had discovered herself to be frighteningly ill-prepared in the craft of subsistence, living alone on a farm that her father had run rather as an idea than a livelihood." But a mind capable of that shrewd analysis of her father is hardly likely to see no way out of her plight. Left alone, Ada is humiliated in a fight with her own rooster. As she bathes her wounds, we have a vision into the kind of abandon she is going through:

> She ran her fingers through her hair to rake out the boxwood leaves and then just let it fall loose below her shoulders. She had abandoned both of the current hairstyles—either gathered all

around and swept into two big rolls that hung from the sides of a woman's head like the ears of a hound, or pulled tight to the scalp and bunned at the back like a mud-tailed horse. She no longer has need or patience for such updos. She could go about looking like a madwoman in a bookplate and it didn't matter, for she sometimes went up to a week or ten days without seeing another soul.

Doesn't that carry the implication of a person whose own soul pales or shrinks without a community of souls? I think it's rich and fascinating, and very close to the somber, nearly spiritual fatalism of tone in Frazier's book. I stress that, for if you don't feel drawn to the tone of the language then I'm not sure the novel is really worth adapting.

To be precise, it is a phenomenon of the film, *Cold Mountain*, not just that Nicole Kidman's hair stays butter bright, shoulder-length, and lustrous throughout the years of the Civil War, but that she seems to have daily access to shampoo in the inner folds of the southern Blue Ridge Mountains. This is all the odder in that as her friendship—it is a sisterhood, really—develops with Ruby, poor Ruby's hair looks like rags and wire. By the way, it is worth adding that Renée Zellweger is, according to Anthony Minghella, more drawn to this book than any of the other actors. Indeed, Zellweger found the book very early and tried to option it for herself (for Ruby or for Ada?) and found that it was already sold to Minghella. But she has worked on the book, on an accent and on her role, and when the film opens it is more or less the conviction of everyone who sees it that she is "right" as Ruby down to the last detail. She will win the Oscar for Best Supporting Actress. But her approach is so complete that it cannot help but make Ada look more effete or precious.

In the book-length interview, *Minghella on Minghella*, the director talks about quite different preparations made with Nicole Kidman: "I sent Nicole Kidman a poem called 'The Glass Essay' by Anne Carson, which had been as big a compass in writing Ada as anything that I'd read elsewhere. 'The Glass Essay' is both a meditation on the Brontës and the writing of *Wuthering Heights*, but also on the loss of a relationship with, funnily enough, a man called Law. It's also about a relationship with a father who's dying. This convergence of themes in a bleak landscape of snowy Canada seemed to have so many clues, and is also a most beautifully written poem. It seemed to be a real secret text for Nicole, which she immediately understood when I sent it."

Shortly after that, Minghella adds this intriguing extra: "The other model for Ada ... was myself. A certain development of the inner being and a perilous starvation of the outer being, an inability to function in the world and make sense of practical challenges."

I said earlier that in the mountains Minghella would be Inman—his eyes seeing the way ahead at twilight, his legs walking maybe twenty miles a day, his spirit attempting to fathom how Inman feels. This is so natural, so necessary, that it's foolish to suppose a male director doesn't also identify with his heroine and his female characters. It is part of the mystery of filmgoing that we cling to all the people in a story and both the sexes—assuming there are just two. It may be strange to hear Minghella, a very effective film director and producer (as well as chairman of the British Film Institute), laying claim to his failures with "practical challenges." But that doesn't mean he doesn't feel that way about himself, and doesn't mean that he tried to read into Ada's record poetry that he cherished—as if she could be him. This is not far from the common, perhaps even the inevitable, way in which directors fall in love with their actresses. No, this is not a charge laid at Anthony Minghella's door, so much as the wondering how it can be avoided. And how any actress, Nicole or whoever, does not begin to feel herself necessarily in love with the person who is guiding her. Ada is yearning for Inman, but only Minghella can show her the way.

Moreover, "The Glass Essay" is a fine poem—Kidman reads it onstage at a special event for *Cold Mountain,* at Royce Hall on the campus of UCLA, and she reads it well enough but not with what I'd call secret understanding. I'm sure the poem helps her performance—but her hair is devastating to it, and I wonder who wants her to look so nice that her hair seems like something ready for the cover of *Vogue* or *In Style*?

Well, one answer to that is that in the movies you put the light where the money is. Never forget that *Cold Mountain* is the biggest financial risk Miramax has undertaken, or that it is clearly intended for a shot at the Oscars. Don't exclude the knowledge in all parties that probably the two most successful films ever made in America—taking contemporary dollar value—are *The Birth of a Nation* and *Gone With the Wind*, not just Civil War movies, but stories told from the point of view of the South. And they featured great romances, with Scarlett O'Hara one of the most celebrated characters Hollywood ever let loose on the world.

But Scarlett is so full of energy—she was from the moment Margaret Mitchell started writing about her. Famously, audiences love her and loathe her, in that she is as devious as she is candid, as selfish as she is brave, as calculating as she is romantic. Frazier is a better writer than Mitchell, yet Scarlett is a more challenging character than Ada, and she has this great advantage as a movie character: Scarlett does things and says things, whereas Ada lives inwardly. She is placid.

I think you have to say the same in any comparison of Rhett Butler and Inman. Rhett (*he* has a first name) is a lovable rogue who was Gableish long before Clark got the part; you think of Rhett and you see Gable's cocksure grin. You think of Inman and you see Jude Law's concentration, his sinking inward even. Anthony Minghella will note this, as he watches Jude Law looping the dialogue: "In post-production, when we did our first ADR [dialogue looping] session with Jude, he was standing in the booth looking up at his performance on the screen, and I looked at him and it was as if Inman's kid brother had turned up to impersonate him; there was no relationship between the face on the screen and his; there seemed to be fifteen or twenty years' difference in age."

It is a touching moment, because Minghella had been very early in seeing the potential in Jude Law (his Dickie Greenleaf is so riveting a performance that most audiences sigh when Dickie is killed off). And Law is very fine in the movie—no matter that Tom Cruise was Minghella's first thought, or hope. We do feel Law's wounds and the damage done to his handsomeness by time, privation, and the terrible things he has seen. Still, Law has problems: does he not seem just a touch younger than Kidman? And doesn't Inman suffer from the same passivity that affects Ada? Yes, Inman makes his great journey home, but the journey has taken away other energies. For example, he does not take sex when it is offered, and he does not fall in love with the young mother who lives alone. Never forget the old rule that people in movies need to do things.

Is there chemistry between Ada and Inman, or between Kidman and Law? I don't think it's exactly the fault of anyone concerned, but no, not quite—largely because they have so few scenes together, but also because the two characters have been driven so inward that they are rather shocked by the opportunity to be together. There is reunion, and it is well staged, at a distance, with neither person quite recognizing the other. I have to add that Kidman in that scene in a very handsome hat and a long black coat and boots looks alarmingly like what this year's well-dressed woman might wear on a pheasant shoot. The glamour that never leaves her face and her hair carries over into costume—she is a knockout, whereas at the close of this ruinous war she ought to look haunted, shabbier, and simply less radiant.

In the book, Frazier advances very shyly on what one may call a love-making scene. The shyness is in part the result of the numbing left by war and the real strangeness of reunion after absence. But these two people are virgins still, raw and clumsy. This is the novel, with a tender air of sleepwalking and of distance in which time and history have erased the urgency of passion:

> He took his hands from where he held them to warm at the fire and touched his fingertips to his face to see if they were still cold as the nub ends of icicles. He found them unexpectedly warm. They felt not at all like the parts of a weapon. He reached to Ada's dark hair [isn't that more likely?], which lay loose on her back, and he gathered it into a thick bunch in his hand. He lifted it with one hand, and with the fingertips of the other he brushed the hollow of her neck between the cords that ran down into her shoulders, the fine curls of hair. He leaned forward and touched his lips to the hollow of her neck. He let the hair fall back into place and he kissed her on the crown of her head and took in the remembered smell of her hair.

The novel's "sex" is slow, remote, and not arousing. Bodies cannot quite shrug off the nearness of dead bodies after a war. And there is a quiet melancholy in the way time has fallen on them like rain and sun. The description is longer and it is much more about inner feelings of recognition and resolution than what bodies do. It is a beautiful, grave passage and yet it gives a hint of how Ada and Inman are not simply living beings but monuments to survival. And it is not sex yet—they are too numb for that. But the delay is beautiful and delicate.

A few pages later:

> Inman sat up with his blanket around his waist. He had been living like a dead man and this was life before him, an offering within his reach. He leaned forward and pulled the clothes from her hands and drew her to him. He put the flats of his palms on her thigh fronts, and then he moved his hands up her flanks and rested his forearms on her hipbones and touched his fingertips to the swale at the small of her back. He moved his fingers up and touched one by one the knobs of her backbone. He touched the insides of her arms, ran his hands down her sides until they rested on the flare of her hips. He bowed his forehead to the soft of her stomach. Then he kissed her there and she smelled like hickory smoke. He pulled her against him and held her and held her. She put a hand to the back of his neck and pulled him harder, and then she passed her white arms around him as if forever.

The meaning of these passages is in the rhythm and the reticence, in the near ritual of touching and the evocation of peace. We know where the people are going, but without any sense of excitement—not that there is anything amiss with sexual excitement, but Frazier is seeking a subtler mood here. Alas, the lovemaking sequence in the movie is far more movie than 1864, and it knows no way of catching the pacing or the mood of the prose. In fact, Minghella trimmed his own sequence down because he felt how anachronistic it was, how easily it gave a feeling of Inman and Ada as sexual experts, swept away by their passion. That is how movies often work, and it makes a travesty of the careful accumulation of period in so many other ways. In the movie the characters fuck. There's no other way of putting it, as the big movie attempts to deliver star skin.

·　·　·

In many ways, *Cold Mountain* the movie is a testament to fidelity in adaptation, and Minghella's respect for literature leaves him regularly subscribing to that aim. Yet I'm not sure that fidelity is always the best approach, or even the one most loyal to the book. I have tried to demonstrate that the thing most vital to Frazier's book—the structure and measure of the prose—is not to be found in the film. So maybe a greater boldness with plot would have been in order. After all, there is no need to make a film of any book—for the book does exist.

The most stirring and moving passage in the film (for me) is the one where Inman lives with Sara and her child (the woman played by Natalie Portman). Similarly, the most potent threat in the film is the way Teague (Ray Winstone) and his Confederate Guard loom over Ada and the community of Cold Mountain. So consider this narrative adaptation: Inman falls in love with the young mother, but cannot save her from being killed; Ada is raped by Teague and becomes virtually his slave—he takes over the atmospheric place in her life once filled by her father. When Inman comes back, he kills Teague and frees Ada, but their youthful love cannot admit to what has happened or to the penalties paid by war—that he has loved someone else and failed her; that she has been raped and brutalized. So they are reunited briefly, before Inman's death, but they are preserved in romance by that death.

Would that work—or work better? Anyone taking on the project has reason to wonder about other roads worth taking, or considering. In fact, as Minghella works on the adaptation, he does change "Sara's scene." He makes an addition: the death of the baby and the suicide of Sara. This is shot, and it is clearly painful and shocking. In many ways, that is why the collective on the film—Minghella, editor Walter Murch, executive producer Sydney Pollack, and Miramax—take out the death of the baby and the mother.

It is too much to suffer in a film that they mean to close in the future, in a happier time. In the cockpit of postproduction, Murch and Minghella are struggling toward their oak leaf. They feel that Miramax is nearly the enemy. But the word spreads of something Harvey Weinstein's brother, Bob, has said on seeing the work-in-progress: "I like it, Anthony, and it's really good and everything, but just what is it about? I enjoy it, but in the end, what is it about? It's not a war film; it's not a love story."

In the ordeal of finishing—working on the acorns and the cathedral—that may sound like a harsh producer. But it is a wise insight into the film, and the fear that it is wandering, and that proper, appalling tragedy has been resisted—in just the way Nicole stays too pretty. It has to be said that *Cold Mountain* does not work when it opens. It is a big picture, still, and Miramax gives it its best push. But critics and audiences alike come away with feelings of disappointment and Miramax begins to restructure its business. The film has great things, but not coherent greatness. There are obvious failings—like the excessive prettiness allowed to Ada—and maybe everything else wrong flows from that. But perhaps this very successful novel is closed against a movie adaptation.

Here is the point: in writing his novel, Charles Frazier might write the whole thing two, three, or more times, and burn every "bad" draft because his own remorseless editing eye knew it was wrong. A film is never like that. A film can be wrong before the first day of shooting, with mistakes in the conception, the script, or the casting, yet beyond repair because all of those things are locked in by contract and inviolable agreement.

To go back to my first analogy, the golfer on the eleventh green at Augusta may pause over his putt with the piercing realization that he is actually a baseball player.

Cold Mountain opens in December 2003. Its final budget is $83 million, with half as much again to be spent on promotion. It opens like a big picture, but the reviews are off at the very start. It will gross $95 million in the United States and $173 million worldwide—but it probably needs to bring in over $215 million to be in profit. There will be video and DVD down the road, but *Cold Mountain* is not a smash hit. Jude Law is nominated, and Renée Zellweger gets her Oscar. But the picture receives not even a nomination for Best Picture, Best Director, or Best Actress.

The Human Stain

S ometimes the vagaries of motion picture release make it seem that someone is "everywhere"—and that's fine, so long as the work passes inspection. But it happens that Nicole opens in *The Human Stain* just six weeks before *Cold Mountain* premieres. Six weeks is long enough for the film to vanish. *The Human Stain* grosses just over $5 million in the United States. It never reaches more than four hundred screens. Despite the lineup of Philip Roth, Robert Benton, Nicole, and Anthony Hopkins, it is regarded in advance as a disaster. There are no awards for the film. But it is only timing that makes the disappointment of *Cold Mountain* seem like an echo of recent calamity.

I taught at a college once in New England. It was not "Athena College," the place Coleman Silk has to quit in Philip Roth's novel, *The Human Stain,* but the same daft whims of political correctness that oust him applied at my college, too, and there were country roads nearby with lakes or ponds only a few feet away where a car might slide off into the water and through the thin edge ice. So I think I know what I'm talking about when I say that if Nicole Kidman had been working as a cleaning woman at a local post office, milking cows on a farm, and doing mop-and-pail duty in some college buildings, well, it wouldn't have been long before she was "rescued" and brought back into the fold of romance. There's not a lot else to do in those college towns except drink, listen to Red Sox games, and speak to the young about the mysteries of existence. For Philip Roth, Faunia was a wild woman of the woods; but in the movie she's someone bursting to be on the cover of *Interview* magazine.

In the novel, Coleman Silk, dean of faculty and a classics professor at Athena, is teaching a class. In the fifth week, he notes that two students out of fourteen are never present, so he asks the twelve, "Does anyone know these people? Do they exist or are they spooks?"

It turns out that the absent pair are black, and their single piece of indirect class participation is to hear that this word "spooks" has been tossed in their direction. Whereupon they bring charges of racism against Coleman Silk, and when he mocks the charges, his robust common sense is not quite shared in the community or on the investigating committee. He has ruffled feathers in the past. He is not supported. So he is out of Athena. And that shock kills his wife. I'm not sure that we need to believe all of this—it is rather more that Philip Roth is making a point about our foolish and dishonest habits—but it is still easier to believe than that Nicole Kidman, looking about as dowdy as a sunset over the mountains, would be anonymous or undiscovered as a cleaning woman for more than half a day.

Talking about our bad habits and our foolishness, *The Human Stain*, the film, is a deserving case. But it is one that brings testing questions to an actress who certainly helps the marginal project get made—and who comes in for some blame when it proves a disaster. Though when I say "disaster" I am speaking from the same dictionary as the one in which "spooks" is automatically racially hostile. *The Human Stain* the movie has errors or holes as large as those in *The Portrait of a Lady*. But it is decent, distinguished, and moving in ways not considered by others Kidman makes. As Stanley Kauffmann notes in the *New Republic*, the fault may lie with the novel itself: "it seems built from a blueprint to which both action and character must conform."

So Coleman Silk is seventy-one, alone and bitter, but deeply humane, when he sees Faunia Farley at her janitorial work. The wondrous name is Roth's invention, but so is this: "Whatever miseries she endured she kept concealed behind one of those inexpressive bone faces that hide nothing and bespeak an immense loneliness."

I am not going to kid you by arguing that that describes Nicole Kidman's everyday look in 2003, or even the slightly faded appearance she found for Robert Benton's *The Human Stain*. Oddly, however, it is not a bad description of Kidman as she is in *The Hours*, where "bone" could come to mind along with the failure of reserve or lack of expression to mask loneliness. Kidman's own face—I am wary of using that concept, because I hope I have shown already how far her face is in the service of imaginary beings—the one that magazine readers can recognize, is not etched in loneliness. It is a face accustomed to being looked at—by herself, maybe as much as by others. It is a pampered, cherished face, and one that can respond with coyness, flirtation, and ordinary seductive designs in the air between you and her. This does not mean that she is unacquainted with loneliness, or not sometimes distressed by her own slightly bereft status as someone who is excellent impersonating others, but that loneliness still needs to be worked out as a construct or a design for a story.

Faunia Farley is not a common person or an obvious role. Raised in a big house south of Boston—in a family that might have created her name at Scrabble and her history in a soap opera—she suffered her parents' divorce when she was five, and then she was molested by her stepfather and not believed by the mother. She told a psychiatrist, but he believed the mother, too. So she ran away at fourteen. That was the last of her schooling, and she ended up married to a rotten farmer, a Vietnam veteran, Lester, who beat her. They had two children who died in a fire. She keeps their ashes in a can under her bed—that and an old Chevy are her only possessions. She can't read—or won't. She must have learned, but when her life turned against her she gave it up, the way she gave up Lester, when he beat her so regularly.

The director Robert Benton willingly takes the blame for Nicole's "look" as Faunia: "I had seen a cut of *The Hours*, and I loved it, but I was just wary about showing her plainer again. So I let her be more herself. She'd have done it. Oh, sure. There's no vanity. She'll do whatever you want, very quick, without a question. And I've never seen anyone who complains less." Of course, there's also the chance that Benton—a generous, kindly man, and very fond of Nicole—simply wanted to make her look good. If Nicole needs to make a platonic bond with her directors, don't think they are immune. Introducing *Cold Mountain* in Sydney at its premiere, Nicole called Anthony Minghella "the most wonderful man in the world," and he dubbed her "the most beautiful woman." To make a movie, to give your life and years to it, often requires such faith.

The Human Stain is a remarkable novel, for the unrestrained affair between Coleman and Faunia comes at the end of a life in which Coleman has done terrible things, to himself and others. As a young man, fearing rejection, he has turned his back on being black—and, somehow, he passed in white society. Faunia is the first person to whom he confides that dire history, and she accepts it. (Alas, there is an unintended subtext: well, we're both actors, aren't we—we play implausible people.) They are content, it seems, driving along the snowy road at dusk, with Lester waiting to edge them off the road and into the lake. The film begins with Coleman's face as he is driving, with Faunia asleep, leaning into him. And the novel is told by Nathan Zuckerman, a neighbor and a friend to Coleman, who in turn learns of the truth and decides to write a book about it, the book we are reading.

The film made by Benton and scripted by Nicholas Meyer is easier to enjoy if you have not read Roth's book. Benton now admits that there's a gap between Roth's sharp voice and his own greater tendency to kindness. It's not just because Nicole is not Faunia, or even because Hopkins raises doubts about whether Coleman Silk could pass as white that need not be so palpable or troubling in the book, but because Roth brings a depth of intelligence to the story, and a willingness not to cast or enforce judgment, that is not really current in any American movie, where automatic judgments rule. So, in a way, it was folly to make the film, and many reviewers stressed that point, which meant that they missed the great humanity that is there, above all in the decision Silk has made for himself. And in that sense the best performance in the film is Wentworth Miller as the young Silk, the man who makes the decision, and who is a more intriguing example of hidden black being than Hopkins can manage. But the older Silk has been "lost" nearly fifty years, and he has claimed that he is Jewish—enough of a part to play.

Nicole has brown hair for the film, shoulder length, which is some kind of a concession, I suppose. The *New York Times* remarked on her "struggling to stifle her natural radiance." But in Roth the character's hair is gray and straight; even at thirty-four, Faunia has had too many winters and too little light, too much loneliness of the inward kind, growing slowly outward. She wears bad clothes—not even J.C. Penney's but from thrift sales. She has not much makeup on, and yet there is a moment the film cannot resist when Coleman Silk comes home and Faunia is stretched out quite naked, amber, curved, ripe and Giorgione-esque. Moreover she lies on her side, one great hip an arc in space, her pubic hair somehow covered, in a way that hints at a lot of nude posing. Kidman's look and her unequivocal sexual readiness bring the Mediterranean and summer days into the harsh winter of New England, but they substitute pinup availability for Faunia's raw soul.

If I ask myself who could have played that part, I come to an actress easily put in Kidman's class (and one Nicole admires)—Cate Blanchett, Australian, but harder, tougher, a great deal less used to admiration or posing. Am I saying that Blanchett is the better actress? Not necessarily, but she is surely better casting as Faunia—someone who could easily show us the awkwardness, the unpenetrated plainness that Coleman sees through. Not that Blanchett has really done this on film before— has she not been asked?—but she might bring a rougher, more ordinary texture to the sexual scenes, if the director wanted that. In the book, Coleman tells Zuckerman that his pleasure, and Faunia's (more to the point), owes something to Viagra. The movie does not go in for that product placement and it portrays movie love as if everyone involved was the apple of their own eye. And so, alas, awkwardness, failure, inadvertent comedy, and profound misunderstanding in sex go unnoticed in our films, which only makes it harder for people in life to think they are living.

But here's the point, there are people in life, cleaning out post offices or university buildings, unknown or unnoticed by the people who use those buildings, people who might have love lives, sexual careers, and be figures in great stories. But in the movies time and again they come down to actresses like Nicole Kidman—whereupon everyone sighs and feels the innate gulf between movies and ourselves.

As *The Human Stain* is about to open, *Interview* magazine wants to put Nicole on its cover (and we are not going to be churlish about this;

she sells magazines; and she does the sitting with enthusiasm). For those of you who know *Interview,* you will not need to be told that it is a magazine for those who are young and those who think young. In other words, to put Kidman on the cover with Anthony Hopkins, no matter that he is a great actor and very famous, would not be "possible." It would have a connotation of sex between the old and the young that many of the young could find distasteful.

So they put Nicole on the cover with Ed Harris, over fifty, balding, and in the film the actor who plays a monster. Still, there they are on the cover of *Interview,* in rich color, photographed by Bruce Weber, with her as blond as corn and him with his hand in the act of caressing her face. Modestly, the cover calls the thirty-two-page portfolio inside "Sensational!"

The portfolio offers short interviews with Harris and Kidman and many pictures in which they are a bizarre fall-foliage loving couple. I know that Nicole has a grand time doing these things, but still there is something close to hilarity in a full-page color photo of Nicole sitting cross-legged on a plain country bed, her black bra showing beneath a stone-colored, thickly knitted sweater (sweater by Versus, bikini by Ralph Lauren). And her face gazing soulfully toward a fond light arranged by Weber. Turn over the page and there she is on a full two-page spread, stretched out, her blaze of blond curls mixing with the burnt grass of September, her plaid shirt boldly open to show us a lilac-colored bra (shirt by H & M; bra by Victoria's Secret).

These pages allow for a little light text, in which, at random, I find these sayings from Nicole: "These different people that I play become the loves of my life"; "Even as a child I always felt very protective towards the people that I love"; "We can exist with a little more compassion and understanding and forgiveness of others' flaws, which is what I try to teach my kids."

Now, it is possible that Kidman thinks up these bromides, that she ponders over them, and came slowly to their full articulation. Yet does *Interview* not see the fatuousness of this thirty-two-page portfolio, or realize how any reader going through may begin to look for the source or the designer of the quotes, which are really as pretty and specious as the bras Nicole wears? And when does an actress not see that if she is going to attempt to be Faunia Farley in *The Human Stain*—instead of saying, No, it's not me, it's wrong for me—she has to go away and submit herself to the kind of gradual effacement that led to Kidman's Virginia Woolf, until indeed her sheer unrecognizability makes us begin to wonder what life is like for Faunia? As opposed to having to witness the daydream of an actress helplessly lending herself to the follies of movie promotion.

Birth

The point about being the best-known movie actress in the world, about commanding $15 million a throw (without much further argument—and it is the argument that saps the soul), and about having "clout," in short the point about being Nicole Kidman or even a "Nicole Kidman" type, is not just letting the opening of *Birth* (2004) coincide with a splashy campaign for Chanel No. 5, it's having the iron in your soul to know that *Birth* deserved even fonder attention.

After all, Robin Wright Penn was the director's first thought—a fine actress, and so much more economical. Then Kidman, through her resources, heard about the script and called the director, Jonathan Glazer. They met in Los Angeles. "Before I got there," he would say, "I knew I'd recognize if she was right pretty quickly. There was also the concern about the exposure her celebrity would bring and whether I was happy with that. But she got the script almost entirely and she had a very peculiar response to it: she talked about it as if she'd written it herself."

I push Glazer about that, and he says, "Nicole understood the part at a low frequency. At base level. So all the changes I made, all the stuff I threw at her at a moment's notice, she absorbed. She inhabited the idea to the point that she could tell the story with her face. She understood that tacitly. How to get the inside on the outside." That kind of instinctive rapport is fascinating, but still it comes as a surprise when Glazer says he didn't talk about birth or mourning with Nicole because "I didn't want to subject her to too much analysis."

Birth

Nicole recalls it this way: "I had an understanding of the grief and way Anna's understanding of her life is altered. Why is it called *Birth*? Grief is a new birth, I suppose, in which Anna sees her loneliness and we recognize the things that make us. I see it as a story arc. She thinks she's better, but then she realizes that the struggle is still there. But she'll get through it, I think. Still, it's horrifying. Because Anna breaks down. Jonathan created these moments, but it's not a linear film. It tries to get at a different, buried part of our consciousness. Some directors do that, but they tend to be European."

Of course, that zeal and inward sharing charm a director and reassure him. But it may only signal a higher challenge to an actress: that if the director would rather not talk about the innermost things then perhaps she needs to do the film herself, all of it.

But *Birth* turns out to be a commercial disaster, almost ignored in the season of awards and prizes. So something extra is needed: the capacity to trust your own film while carrying on. What happens with *Birth* is a failure of fair play, the neglect of something deserving—and Nicole has an old-fashioned face and a middle-class nature, one that can be undermined or hurt by the lack of fairness. *Birth* is one of those failures where you have to determine whether it is you or the world that is wrong. And that ages you more than any cosmetic treatment or any amount of Chanel No. 5 can withstand.

Birth, as they say, is a turning point.

Of course, there are always explanations for how and why movies turn out "wrong," or uncertain, and it is not that the explainers are lying or making things up. The world of moviemaking is so constructed that anything and everything can go astray. And sometimes the fatal misstep comes so early that every further action taken on the film leads it farther away from a proper journey. It is a rare hell to be making that disastrous journey, and to know minutes or hours after the misstep that it was wrongly taken and that now immense energies will be required simply to finish the ungainly project. But afterward, when this mishap has occurred, no one cares. Do not expect sympathy. The audience has done its bit; they have sat in front of the bare screen and tried to believe in what passed there. They have felt betrayed. As Glazer puts it later, "I think it touched some people who wanted to be touched. I think it was a failure for some people. So what. The effort was worth it. Worth everything I got and everything I didn't get. Sometimes a heart can be felt even at a distance."

Birth onscreen begins in the half-light of winter's dawn, in Central Park in New York City. The camera is tracking a jogger, a man, whose face is obscured. He runs on, enters a tunnel, and collapses. These beautiful tracking shots (done on Steadicam by Garret Brown himself, the inventor of that method) are not without moment or momentum. The half-light aches with compassion. The dogged attention has us waiting for importance. The music (by Alexandre Desplat) is far away, but foreboding—and this is the first Kidman film, I think, with a great score. The park at that time of day is spectral and uneasy. The tunnel where the collapse occurs is like a mouth or a womb—I don't think that association would be farfetched even without the title *Birth*. At the very least, the death we witness is like a threshold. And the sound of the runner's steps and breathing are the intimacy that make us attentive.

If only we knew this man, or cared for him.

A "mistake" has been made in that the man who has dropped dead as he runs has no place or face, no life or voice, in the story we will be told. Imagine, instead, that against the soundtrack of the running steps and the breathing, we had seen the head and then the face of a woman waking up, alone in a double bed. Imagine her long hair spread out over her pillow, and the pillow beside her, the place where her companion, her husband's head, rested, before he went out to run. We see her face listening to the sounds of his run. There is no need for any specific, indicated expression to fill her face. Let it be that she is simply imagining something, anything. But then the sounds of running stop. The camera sinks in upon the face a little closer. A hint of anxiety appears in that face, like the face of an actress who has not been told what to do but who realizes that she is still being filmed, and who is trained to stay "on," or in the story, so long as the camera is silently turning over.

A phone rings. The woman reaches out and picks it up. The camera moves away from her to the bedroom window through which we can see the stippling of the park in the pale light. So her face is gone when we hear the unforgettable and terrible scream that is her response to whatever has been said on the phone.

I'm just making pictures, of course—you can dispute or debate my choice. But with this opening at least we know who this film is about, and we have a chance of caring.

In *Birth*, ten years pass from the morning when the runner drops dead. A young woman, Anna—thirty-five, say—lives in Manhattan on the Upper East Side. She is Nicole, with burnt-brown hair cut very close; it is not cropped, not quite Jean Seberg in *Bonjour Tristesse*, and hers is an expensive haircut, but it is a cut and a style we have not seen before on Nicole Kidman—it suggests either an emotional freeze or a life on hold. She is well dressed, in expensive, designer clothes that are also simple to the point of severe, while emphasizing her slender, boyish figure. I said she seemed thirty-five, but she might be a little younger. And she lives in Manhattan in a very good apartment, surrounded by her family.

It is the night of her engagement party. Her husband, Sean, died ten years ago, while jogging in the park. But now she is about to be married again—to Joseph (Danny Huston), who is pleasant, attentive, sensitive, and even anxious for her. But is he right for her? (It is a very subtle movie chemistry, to show a couple together, yet not matching.) There is a hint in his protective attitude that she is or has been an invalid, and this helps explain why her extended family is so close and so alert on her behalf. There is a mother, a brother, a sister-in-law, and an aunt, as well as an old family servant. They watch her as if expecting madness, or magic.

Not that Anna seems ill or insecure. We don't know what she has been doing for ten years; we can believe that she has done nothing, for she seems to exist at that level of Upper East Side comfort where there is no need to be doing anything. It should be stressed that we have no sense of the quality of Anna's marriage to Sean—they had no children, but we have no way of judging whether or not they were happy. Still, we see her and Joseph visiting Sean's grave—the scene is full of distant reverence—and it seems to serve as her recognition that the past is over, that she is not just free but ready to marry again. In theory, she loves Joseph—there is a ceilinglike view of them, naked, making love. Yet that does nothing to alleviate the feeling that he is one of her attendants. Anna is like one of those slightly unstable heiresses in a nineteenth-century novel—there is an uncanny feeling of Henry James on the edge of the supernatural. Joseph is like a lawyer who has grown fond of his ward. The relatives (and they are all like a fence or a barrier) seem to be waiting for some sign of distress, something that would justify their veiled apprehension.

But it is not clear that Anna loves or desires Joseph. Their lovemaking scene is tender and arousing; but still it has some sense of the man applying a last healing treatment to the woman. And it is a sign that the facts of many scenes in *Birth* are not as profound as the emotional atmosphere. Instead, she seems a little numb or frozen. The close-cut hair is part of that, but so is Nicole's air of a repressed girlish flirtation, an energy that she seems afraid of releasing.

It is a measure of the movie's stealthy air that no one can be quite certain at first whether this apartment and the family belong to Anna or to Joseph. The family is Anna's, but her condition may leave Joseph the more natural or satisfactory member of the group.

It is at the engagement party that a little boy will appear, the ten-year-old Sean (Cameron Bright). He has never met Anna, but he says that he is her "Sean."

Sean does not belong in the apartment building; he is not of the class that lives there. He is not a refined little boy; he is not learned, precocious, or clearly marked by spiritual gravity. He is a solid, blunt kid, with a crewcut closer than Anna wears her hair, a wide, fleshy face, slightly aggressive eyes. He wears a windbreaker and a sweater. There is no magic about him—by which I mean to say that we have met more arresting children, in film and life. Haley Joel Osment was such a child in *The Sixth Sense*, so that his visions were never really surprising. Cameron Bright's Sean, by contrast, is not alluring or seductive. But he has force, in just the way any street kid in a smart apartment has force if he stays unashamed of his poverty. The Upper East Siders cannot answer or deflect his directness. And, as it happens, he gets in the building only because he knows the doorman.

The narrative of *Birth* is so constructed that we do not quickly understand what this Sean is doing. We see him observing the gathering that is Anna and Joseph's party. We see him watch and follow a woman guest (Anne Heche) who turns away at the last moment, buries her intended gift in the park, and buys a replacement. This is more than a little mysterious, because of a harrowing gravity in Ms. Heche—early in the film she seems to be in possession of secret knowledge and her face seems carved out of damaged soul.

So Sean presents himself to Anna—and says he is Sean, her Sean, and that she should not marry Joseph. At which point—even on the brink of becoming Joseph's, or letting him have her—Anna is tempted.

This is not the easiest thing for an audience, no matter that *Birth* is being put together with great craft and a kind of buried purpose that is intriguing. Nothing suggests a slice of life, or everyday New York realism. The lighting is very controlled; it is white and it tends to fall from above, a little like the snow in the air in the park when the jogger dies. This brings a religious or spiritual sense of occasion, something that is borne out in the somber, stately music, the smart but color-restricted decor, and the way in which the film moves forward with large omissions of regular information—like what Anna has felt for ten years, and what these family members do other than watch and wait for Anna.

What also works against the temptation has to do with Nicole Kidman. It is a part of her nature and her being—her look, if you will—that she is rational, sturdy, filled with common sense, good cheer, and confidence. Let me make a comparison here with Julia Roberts. Roberts is four months younger than Kidman, and yet in a film that opened in very much the same season—*Closer*—Roberts managed to look a good deal older than Kidman.

What do I mean by that? Well, at the most obvious level it is a way of observing that in *Birth*, Nicole is "properly" made up to be pretty, youthful, and appealing, whereas the photographer Roberts plays in *Closer* makes far less use of makeup, as if to say she no longer believes in it (she does try to capture exposed faces in her work), and because there are matters of age, loss, and pain in getting close to forty that she is no longer prepared to conceal.

From her first real impact—in *Pretty Woman* in 1990—Julia Roberts was ravishing. For this observer, she always had a more natural grasp of "beauty" than Nicole Kidman had. And this was accentuated by her overwhelming smile, to which in her early years she gave vent with nervous regularity. She was teased about it, and I daresay at times she lost her confidence. And at those times and in certain films that catered to it, it was easy to see a stricken creature, afraid or hurt, a victim—something far from the young whore who had become a lady (or at least a doll) in *Pretty Woman*. But in time, Julia Roberts the screen performer learned to trust her eyes more than her mouth. And by the time of *Closer* (a film where she relied less on makeup and pretty clothes than ever before), there was a naked emotional vulnerability.

I am putting it this way for a couple of reasons: to refer to the vague but unavoidable competition that goes on among actresses, and to indicate how remarkably untroubled Kidman's Anna seems in *Birth*. Actors and actresses make a common assumption in their approach to work, and it is one that we, along with Rembrandt, take for granted: that in time, with loss or experience, the face grows toward its own deepest character, and becomes less pretty but more interesting.

I'm not sure this is always so in life. There are so many disguises available these days, and so many of us have imitated the subterfuges of acting. So the principle may not be universal. Still, that has not stopped us from believing in it, and that is more important for my argument than the facts of life. We believe that that change occurs, that it is inevitable and tragic but a condition of mortality. And so in any art that enlists the human face, we look for experience.

And, of course, Nicole Kidman has already demonstrated the kind of facial transformation that is not just arresting, but exhilarating. That is what she did for *The Hours*, where her eyes seemed to belong to someone we had never met—and that is why it was possible to think they were Virginia Woolf's eyes. You can say that those eyes were troubled by headaches or something far worse—the obsession that was bordering on mania. You could say they were English eyes (as opposed to Australian eyes), eyes so often disappointed by rain, overcast weather, the chill and the damp inside even expensive houses, and the obstinate remnants of the class system forever betraying any hope of liberty. I don't think I'm going too far to say that the eyes in *The Hours* knew that experience just as they were credibly the eyes that had despaired over some sentences in *Mrs. Dalloway*. They were migraine eyes, the smothered eyes of a tortured and forlorn moralist.

And once an actress has done that much with her eyes, how is she ever going to be just cute and seductive again?

But the face in *Birth* is one that has not grown in the ten years of mourning. The close haircut is less harsh or severe than undeveloped, boyish, or adolescent. Are these decisions? Do we have the right to read them as information? How else are we meant to engage with movies except by looking at faces and trying to imagine their life? And if the face of Anna in *Birth* were not Kidman's but that of Julia Roberts in *Closer*, so much would be apparent. The mourning has never lifted for Roberts's Anna. The grief remains. The woman sleeps badly. She has not found anything real or useful to do. She is drifting, wandering, sleepwalking, and if she ever pauses to look in a mirror she must see that her youth and her hope have gone. She is one of the walking wounded. You might even go so far as to wonder whether she had been left a little unbalanced.

But Kidman's Anna is childlike, arrested, waiting; she could be a sleeping princess—and that does lead one to anticipate the possibility that she is waiting for a child or for another case of arrested development. I do not mean this as a weakness. It signals a readiness, just like the impassivity in Deneuve or Garbo or Louise Brooks.

Of course, there's another challenge in the prospect of what may follow when the little boy says he's Sean—it is that any of us are going to be expected to entertain this cuckoo.

And here we come to a remarkable and distressing paradox in the American or the mainstream movie: that while the medium is founded on fantasy involvement, still so much of its material is held up to short-sighted and depleting schemes of what is plausible. The audience, the customers, have always gone to see movies to make an imaginative journey—that of rising from their seats in the dark and going up to exist on the bright screen, in the sublimity of heightened behavior. But as if we're ashamed of yielding so much to the fanciful in America, we then go to great neurotic lengths to persuade ourselves that the action of movies is "plausible." And so the medium is innately dreamlike, while the content is ostensibly photographic and lifelike. Thus, we hope, we keep faith with our existence as a hardworking, rational, scientifically minded, capitalist culture—as opposed to people living in a dream.

The history of *Birth* is, allegedly, that one day, while working on another project altogether, the young British director Jonathan Glazer (*Sexy Beast* was his only previous feature film) had the idea for a movie:

"There's this little kid and he tells a woman he's her dead husband—and he's ten years old."

How could that "situation" be explored? The little boy could have a diabolical plot in mind, an intrigue meant to extort money (or love) from the widow. That begins to presuppose a second possibility: that the widow is destabilized from her loss, uncommonly vulnerable and open to the suggestion. A third way to go is to accept that this is a story about reincarnation. Or to put it another way, about a woman and a little boy, both of them sane, who believe in reincarnation, and even take it for granted.

Someone apparently suggested to Jonathan Glazer that this was an idea that might repay some consultation with Jean-Claude Carrière, in Paris. Born in 1931, Carrière is a most accomplished screenwriter, who has worked with a great diversity of directors. For example, he wrote the script of *The Tin Drum* for Volker Schlondorff, of *Danton* for Andrzej Wajda, of *The Unbearable Lightness of Being* for Philip Kaufman, and of *Valmont* for Milos Forman. That is enough to confirm Carrière as versatile, sophisticated, and literary, as well as a master of adaptation. But there has been another side to Carrière—his prolonged association with Luis Buñuel. Indeed, Carrière wrote these films by Buñuel: *The Diary of a Chambermaid, Belle de Jour, The Milky Way, The Discreet Charm of the Bourgeoisie*, and *That Obscure Object of Desire*. Three of those deserve a place in the roll of the greatest films ever made, and they belong to a tradition that has never had much place in America—that of surrealism, and the calm acceptance of how far life is a dream. In addition, in their deep friendship, Carrière helped Buñuel with his autobiography, *My Last Sigh*. Come to that, Carrière also wrote a little-known film, for the Japanese director Nagisa Oshima, in which a woman (played by Charlotte Rampling) falls in love with a gorilla. And it's reciprocal.

The mechanism so precious in the Carrière-Buñuel collaborations is the way magic, or desire's breath, has eased its way into the forefront of existence, so that it is the companion to apparent realism, without ever being remarked on for its absurdity. In *The Discreet Charm of the Bourgeoisie*, a group of socialites are unable to enjoy the pleasant dinner their hearts are set on. The obstacles are mysterious, absurd, but persis-

tent and obsessive, and in time the thwarted meal becomes a mon-
strous object of desire, excluding all else in life, but without ever disturbing the calm tenor of the matter-of-fact. In *That Obscure Object of
Desire*, a respectable middle-aged man is obsessed with a young
woman and cannot see that she is "played" by two actresses, one a
teasing prude, the other a cruel wanton. And in *Belle de Jour*, Catherine
Deneuve (perhaps the cinema's most exquisite child bride, or case of
arrested development) takes on the afternoon occupation of whore in a
Paris brothel that caters to eccentric tastes. (What other tastes are
there? We are talking about desire, beyond shame or guilt, beyond oddity, starkly self-sufficient.)

This is a mood or a light—I mean, surrealism—in which if a boy says
he is Sean, your beloved, you can only comply, and recognize that
annunciation as a gift sent to uncover your buried desire. As I start to
describe the story of *Birth* in this way, I see its potential: Anna responds
to Sean's suggestion exactly as Joseph and the adults in the apartment
find it preposterous. For Sean's suggestion unlocks the prison they have
made for her.

This is jumping ahead, but isn't there an extraordinary promise or
energy disclosed in the leap forward? Suppose that Anna's curiously
childlike or suspended emotional condition has to do with the kind of
imprisonment in which she finds herself? As soon as one uses that
word, then the rather stealthy treatment of the attendant family
becomes clearer. As degrees of imprisonment or incarceration (of withheld liberty), the bleak, laconic solicitude of Lauren Bacall clicks into
place as cleanly as a well-oiled lock turning. The presence of as considerable an actor as Arliss Howard as a minor relative is made more persuasive, and the fact that Anna's sister-in-law is pregnant emerges as a
comment on her childlessness, her childlike state, and her terrible vulnerability to a child (Jonathan Glazer had a child two days before
shooting began).

I realize that most contemporary, everyday residents of the Upper
East Side may be the first and loudest in any effort to discern magic or
fairy tale in their upholstered lifestyle, the one with twelve-foot ceil-
ings, twenty-four-hour doormen, and price tags on everything. But
suppose that this lush yet hushed apartment is also a kind of castle

where the princess is held captive by those caring for her. That idea immediately helps one understand the tone of the apartment, the enwrapped, dull tastefulness of its decor, and the rather mournful, sentinel-like movements and gestures of the other members of the family; the way their own life has atrophied guarding against life or risk in their princess. There is a stricken calm in the place, a deathly clasp, that is striving not to alarm this strange wild child. It is so complete that you could easily not grasp what constitutes her wildness. But I will call it "desire," by which I do not mean a merely erotic longing, or some kid's longing for love. I mean desire in the more primitive sense: the great urge to throw off order, the need to take decisions for oneself even if they are disastrous. It is the idea of sight as it might weigh upon a blind woman; or it is the prospect of madness in this enclosing apartment—the urge to rip down walls and deface the cool, nurturing colors with the stain of blood and shit and every other bodily fluid. *Birth* might have started with a scene where Anna menstruates—images of bright, lusty blood in a tasteful bathroom—and then shown her strenuous care in tidying it all away so that no one in the place might know. Of course, the American movie audience is not expected to accommodate menstruation as a part of life in films—but that is as good a measure of our society's suppression of desire, and life, as you are likely to discover.

Grant that "shocking" scene, and grant that it occurs within a private bathroom within the tomblike apartment (so that we see one cell opening up to reveal a larger one), and the whole jogging-in-the-park opening has to be abandoned. The first Sean (there is still no need to see his face) should be a happy youth driving headlong to his wedding. He goes faster and faster because he is late. And he is killed within sight of the church. The fresh spill of his blood on a broken windshield gives way to Anna—in her wedding dress—with very long hair, the hair of a needy virgin, screaming and tearing at herself. Then cut forward ten years to the cropped-hair prisoner (don't prisoners traditionally suffer abuse in their haircut?) noticing her menstrual blood, as if it were something new, dramatic but guilt-making.

One point of this revision (call it a viewer's cut—why should we not have our versions?) is to expose how far the coming marriage to Joseph is less a liberation than an affirmation of imprisonment. It will be the last unbreachable door in the secure confinement of the princess—and there are things in Anna that seem to want that fate. She is not quite a modern woman, more a victim of melancholy or warping passion such as we associate with the Victorian age. Put that way, and the rather clammy, oppressive air of Danny Huston as her suitor becomes a touch of inspiration. (I see now that Huston could have been Nicole's Gilbert Osmond.) Indeed, the marriage to Joseph is like those gloomy prospective marriages in *His Girl Friday* and *The Philadelphia Story*, the union that the film's ardor must prevent, for it stands for habit, sobriety, and form (suitability even), the gravest enemies to marriage as the ritual of expressed and shame-free desire. And so it follows that whereas in *Birth* (the movie made by Mr. Glazer), the new Sean comes forward with a mysterious claim of rescue or absurd alternative, in my version it might be nearly as much a case of Anna recognizing the better way and claiming it for herself. Blind to life in so many ways, the princess cannot be denied her one chance of insight in the surrealist code. And it is most appropriate that that desire be visited upon a figure as "impossible" or "outrageous" as we can think of—a child, someone with her own short hair and gamine look, but without her social grace.

In this interpretation, Kidman delivers some extraordinary, haunted looks of childishness, waves of feeling that wash over the uncertain constructs of Mr. Glazer's plot. There are shots and scenes in which Nicole Kidman is not just amazing, but in which she brings *Birth* within sight of a great film. Of course, it is a matter of dispute or opinion whether those moments are a source of tragedy or hope: Do we conclude, alas, that this sort of film never could be? Or is it a way to wonder what might yet be? Perhaps it is just the resigned admission that Nicole was thirty years too late to take her deserved place at the center of a Buñuel film. One great merit of that dream association might have been the elderly Spaniard's assurance to her—his weary insistence, even—that she had no need to flirt. Looking as she does, she had only to let the camera be like air on her face. Let the eyes go calm. Forget that old seductive clench, for clenching is always the first sign of closure, or of the difficulty of entrance. The greatness of Buñuel lies in his awareness that Catherine Deneuve trusted herself enough to let her face be passive, still (never coy), so that the face could be quietly, serenely fucked.

This is vital in our screen goddesses. By no means must they ever give away any hint of our strenuous doings at their doorway. At her age now, Nicole Kidman needs every encouragement to give up on girlishness.

There are ravishing moments in *Birth*. I am thinking of the long passage in the concert hall where she is simply listening to Wagner. This is one of the great shots in surrealist cinema, and so potent that one wonders why more of the film was not given over to Kidman listening to music. (It is Wagner's second prelude to *The Ring*—though it was shot with the actress listening to the first prelude.) There is no kind of commentary possible to that scene; one cannot and should not pace out the way from these frames to those that her mind changes. Rather, we are watching a kind of absorption, a chemical process, or one in which a whole life (or the prospect of it) comes into her eyes in the way menstrual blood needs to escape the body. May I say that in a film called *Birth* it should be the ideal to have as many moments as possible rendered as organic process. Thus at the very close of the film, it is suddenly and beautifully right that Anna—in her wedding dress—flees from the final marriage to Joseph, takes to the ocean (at Fire Island), and begins to be soaked by the salt water. There should be much more of it, of course—nothing should be modest or controlled. She should become a sea creature, and we should feel that at last her desire (and the anguish with which it was denied for so long) has found life and visibility.

Whereas, feeling squeamish about actually taking on reincarnation, the film has felt compelled to find a mystery answer to the whole intrigue. And so we are led to suppose that Sean has come upon secret letters (the love letters between the first Sean and Anne Heche, the guest at the engagement party) so that he knows how to proceed in inserting himself in Anna's life. In turn, this calls for a subplot in which that first Sean and Ms. Heche had an affair. Despite the quite brilliant playing of Heche, this is not just a sidetrack but a disastrous evasion of what the film should be about—Anna—for it leaves us without an answer to the question, Did Anna know about the first Sean's affair? We do not want that answer, or the question, for they both detract from the frozen emotional life of Anna. A film has to know what it is about, otherwise it cannot begin to get into the essential mystery of the elements—like what happens to Nicole's face as she hears the Wagner, what happens to a great face. And make no mistake about it, granted the regular perils of that flirty cocked eye and the knowing seductress grin, in *Birth* Nicole Kidman offers up to the air and the light a quite majestic face, the imprint of what might have been a great movie.

I have not done *Birth* justice. Indeed, I find that on every successive viewing—and it is the film I return to over and over again in doing this book—I like it more. Or I am more moved. For just as one learns how to watch the dream—be open, be calm, suspend judgment—so more and more scenes become infinite and mysterious. Perhaps it is greater than I thought at first. In which case, its failure is not just to be pinned on itself, in error, but on the medium. For as films grow steadily worse, maybe we are less able to discern the good ones. But I think it is the best thing Kidman has ever done, and the work that meant the most to her. If that is true, she should work far more in dream and far less in such "sensible" projects as *Bewitched*.

B*irth* fails. Though it opens in the fall of 2004 after a controversial debut at the Venice Film Festival, it collapses from its own inertia. The audience may not know how a great film works, but they can feel the afflatus of collapse, or the pathos of mere silliness. They can feel that *Birth* has no backbone, no consistent intent or purpose, of the kind that they cannot escape. The film does very little business and it only plays at a few theaters. By November in America, it cannot be found, except at one or two New York theaters, as if those real Upper East Siders could not quite escape some echo of their own cell life. The Golden Globes nominates Nicole for Best Actress in a drama, but no one supposes that she has a chance of winning, and in all the year-end talk about the Oscars no one thinks of her as a possible nominee. Indeed, that Christmas season of 2004, there she is onscreen in the coming attractions for *Bewitched*, doing that famous nose twitch and giving the audience a very knowing eye. It is a moment at which this writer begins to realize that such cute self-awareness could yet endanger Nicole, as well as his affection for her.

Jonathan Glazer believes that Anna never knows that the Anne

Heche character had an affair with her husband. Nicole's view differs, but it is no discredit to the film that there can be such a disparity: "Anna doesn't know, but she finds out. I think the startling thing is that the boy loves her—like she's never been loved before. And that's what's so sad. You can't always be with the people you want. You have to move on and that's part of the sadness. The film is strongest in the way it ends. I love that last image of Anna soaked in the sea in a wedding dress. My mother loves the film, too—and she likes very little."

Being Interviewed

Nicole appears on *The Ellen DeGeneres Show* in 2004. She is the guest, of course, but Ellen does a tease opening where she is minus a star, a big star. Then Nicole—rather nicely untidy—knocks at Ellen's dressing-room door. You see, Nicole's car broke down and she wonders if she could "hang out" while she's waiting for the repair job. Sure, sure, says a distracted Ellen—and then there's the double take, Oh my God! It's Nicole! *She* can be my guest. "Corey Feldman couldn't make it!" passes as a joke. "You could borrow some of my clothes," says Ellen, the famously plain dresser. Nicole sighs and says uh-huh—she happens to be wearing a tight-waisted maroon corduroy jacket and jeans with a glimmer of some café-au-lait vest, low-cut, beneath the jacket.

And then Ellen says, "It doesn't matter what you look like." It's a weird insight—is it an ad-lib?—in all the staged setup. And Nicole simpers, because she hardly knows how to stand up under its undeniable truth, not with her hair down and "untidy"—untidy by so-and-so—and with her towering six inches over DeGeneres.

It's a talk show, I suppose—though Nicole is promoting *Birth,* and Ellen tells her the film is brilliant in a way that suggests she was honestly moved or shaken by it. And you do not know how planned this talk is. It's not scripted, but maybe Nicole's people and Ellen's have met in advance to go over the topics. Ellen is looser than many talk show hosts, and one of the things Nicole talks about is her taste for danger. She talks about having been three and a half months at sea to do *Dead Calm* (which Ellen has also seen).

"Did you get seasick?" Ellen asks.

"No," says Nicole—she sounds proud of this—"I never get motion sickness." She throws in that she's "been up in that g force thing." No one explains but it leaves the impression that Nicole has the right stuff, no matter that she is slender and fragile.

But then she's off, and she does seem excited. "I like doing dangerous things," she says. "I love to do skydiving. I love to dive with sharks. I want to do it in the cage with the Great Whites." She admits that on a picture she has to restrict these habits, because of the insurance. And you may ask, Well, isn't she always on a picture? But there are stories of her and Russell Crowe hiring out a helicopter and being flown low over Manhattan at night. And I ask myself, In skydiving, does she do it with a helmet or with that blond hair streaming out? I mean, why wear a helmet when you're skydiving? And then, funnily enough, a wave of her hair hits her lapel microphone, and there's a bumping noise like a small collision. It startles everybody, and Ellen says—this must be an ad-lib—"The average person's hair is not that heavy."

And so suddenly, out of the danger of vacuity the talk has slipped into something Nicole does seem afraid of. Ellen has asked about her children. "Do they know their parents are huge?" The thing about Ellen is that she can say things that pass as celebrity junk stuff, but which have an odd poetic resonance. (Are Tom and Nicole huge because they have heavy hair?)

"They are embarrassed," admits Nicole and she curls up to act out the awkwardness. "They constantly deny us." She is talking as if the kids' parents were still married. "Which is OK. If they've got a soccer game they say, 'Don't come.' And if I go, it's 'Don't touch me.' "

She begins to say, and I think she is beginning to realize, that she is already in trouble if these kids watch *The Ellen DeGeneres Show*, or if other kids tell them about it. Of her daughter, Bella, Nicole says, "Don't call her up." Ellen has her hand on the phone—"If you do, I'm dead."

I'm sure it's all so, and one might wonder how Nicole reconciles a taste for "doing dangerous things" with motherhood, or the pains she takes to shield her children from photography with her own position as possibly the most avidly photographed woman in the world? But Ellen has another good question. She wonders what the kids feel if Nicole does a movie with kids in it, with child actors, like *The Others* or *Birth*, where she does take a bath with a ten-year-old boy and entertain the notion that he is the spirit of her husband back from the dead.

"They don't like it," says Nicole.

And Ellen doesn't ask the question—face it, she wouldn't have a show if she did—What would you do if your kids asked you to stop acting? Which doesn't mean that we and Nicole don't sometimes wonder.

At the end of the interview Nicole says in the third week of January she will be going to Indonesia for UNICEF. Why is she going? To be there, to show concern, and to show that stars feel for the world, I suppose. To show that she and we know about the tsunami. To be famous today drifts very close to politics. Even if the star has no known political allegiances, their bearing witness can be significant. Did Nicole ever see how close she was to Princess Diana?

"100 Donne Più Belle"

It is the cover feature of the December 2004 issue of the Italian *GQ* (2.90 euros, but fetching eleven dollars in the United States): Who are the hundred most beautiful women in the world? But long before the reader (whatever his language) has worked out this quest, the emphatic answer is there on the magazine cover—a full portrait of Nicole Kidman, her head of curly brown hair separating the *G* and the *Q*. She is shown seated, her left thigh drawn up at a right angle, and bare. She is wearing a skimpy dress in wide-mesh black crochet—there are many glimpses of the flesh within. And she is looking out at the camera and at us, her lips half an inch apart, her long left arm stretched down to clasp her ankle or her black shoe. She is not quite smiling; rather, her face has that old seductive nostalgia, as if daring anyone to doubt that she was (that December) the best-looking woman the magazine could get.

I put it that way because the Italian *GQ* has not organized a poll of Italians, or even citizens of the European Union. Nor has it actually gone to the lengths of researching the range of contenders for the title, not just in small Umbrian towns, in the Hebridean isles, in Phuket, Sydney, Anchorage, or in the farmlands of Nebraska. In fact, of the hundred women chosen by the magazine, there is not one who is not a "name" by the standards of this sort of magazine, not one who is not famous (somewhere) in show business, its adjunct, modeling, or the broader fields of simple celebrity. There is not one woman, apparently, utterly unfamiliar with the process of being photographed by Italian

GQ (or similar magazines), and not one who might not have been on the cover, in terms of her being willing to expose a good deal of famous flesh. One measure of this shared attitude is the look in Nicole's patient gaze that is still able to ask of us, So, you dare to photograph me, do you? You have the brazen lust to look at me?

Just to establish the context of Nicole's victory, I should tell you that the final list also includes the Venezuelan model, Aida Yespica, at no. 2, her fulsome breasts quite bare, and at no. 3 Gisela Bündchen, who has just made her first film, and found a way of keeping a strange crocodile-skin bathing suit attached to her glossy body. Others included are Scarlett Johansson (4), Liz Hurley (5), Angelina Jolie (6), Cameron Diaz (9), Sharon Stone (16, and at age forty-six one of the more arrestingly attractive of the ladies), Paz Vega (26), and Julia Roberts (38). There are some I had not heard of, ladies who owe their place to modeling or to a few European films or scandals. In the top ten, only Liz Hurley admits to being older than Nicole. Six of the others are still in their twenties.

Of course, Nicole's victory is an editorial decision, and I don't think it's being unduly cynical to suppose that victory was contingent on her willingness to present herself for an exclusive photo shoot. As well as the cover, Nicole gets eight full-color pages inside the magazine, with four other portraits from the cover shoot by James White. One of those pictures is just the cover flipped, with the information that the crochet dress is by Gianfranco Ferre, the earrings by Neil Lane, and the hair-styling by Jimmy Choo. In the other three pictures she wears what is called a tuxedo kimono (it is only a jacket) by Ferre again. She sits on a plain wooden chair, her bare legs gathered at the knees, the lower legs splayed outward. The kimono is not sufficient to hide the inner curves of her breasts, and again her look—one of tempting disapproval—is meant to balance the insolence or outrage of the shot with her secret desire for it. The look is more sultry still in a closer shot where her left hand is drawing the lapels of the jacket together to hide any nudity. And finally there is a head shot, with a whisper of smile, the chin dipped into her shoulder.

In the nature of such things, we must suppose that the pictures (their look, or their atmosphere) would be dictated by the photographer and by the editors of the magazine. And, presumably, the flirty, sex-kitten kind of attitude they embody satisfied those various notions of what "beauty" might be, if "beauty" was going to sell the December issue. At the same time, Nicole Kidman is clearly the most famous, or powerful, of the one hundred women selected. Her only rivals in that respect would be Madonna, Julia Roberts, and perhaps Angelina Jolie. But Madonna is not the white-hot outrage she once wanted to be, and Roberts and Jolie do not command the same level of salary for a picture. They are not in demand as Nicole Kidman is—they did not win the editors' accolade, though they might have if Nicole had declined the arrangement.

Not to miss the obvious, she did not have to accept her victory or the required shoot, just as she is surely powerful enough to decline some of the clothes, some of the poses, and some of the looks suggested by others. It follows from that that she knows enough about the process of posing for a magazine to be able to guess what the clothes, the "direction," and her own look would mean. She is also, surely, enough of an actress to offer or suggest a quite different look.

Actors and actresses, famously, do as they are told—isn't that how movies and magazines are made? Well, yes and no. Anyone who has actually observed a glamour shoot knows that the woman in the light can exercise a great deal of control if she is so inclined, or she can relax in the ideology (it's more than an idea) that she is a paid performer, an actress, someone willing to conspire in someone else's look. This modest defiance of the scheme of obedience applies to movies too, of course, where a highly paid actress can resist a director's plan and a cameraman's light, and insist on her own image.

So at the very least, you have to recognize that the woman who played Virginia Woolf in *The Hours* and who gave the impression of being capable of writing *Mrs. Dalloway*, is, a few years later, ready to pout and let her breasts show and sit still for nothing less than cheesecake. It is hard to believe that she was compelled into this, or driven there by poverty. So it is easier to conclude that she wanted to do it, to have these pictures (and the cover title) in her résumé.

Then also bear in mind that two of the eight pages inside consist of a collection of shots from Nicole's nude scenes in movies. Some of these may come from official stills, but most of them are of images snapped from the screen, of moments so intimate or revealing they were not put out in stills. Thus, one of those shots, showing her gingery pubic hair in *Billy Bathgate,* has the air of an illicit paparazzi shot. And these images—including the sex scene from *Malice;* the black-and-white erotic dream from *Eyes Wide Shut,* as well as the brief dressing scene; and lovemaking from *Cold Mountain, Birthday Girl,* and *The Human Stain*—are a peep show of nakedness, every shot a postage stamp, but clear and arousing, and ample evidence of her very lovely, supple body.

Did she give her consent to this spread? Was she asked? Should she have known and guessed that the Italian *GQ* might do that? Or did she turn a blind eye? Does she threaten to sue? Does she return her "title" as somewhat sullied? Or does she guess the dirty trick and take it into account? Does she give herself to the photo shoot—it must have been a full day's work—or does she ask for a fee? I do not know the answers, but to be Nicole Kidman all of these questions have to cross your mind in negotiating the tricky ground of publicity without lending coyness or a brutal edge to your pout.

Scent of a Woman?

When a woman's schedule is said to be desperate or ridiculous, as she hurtles from one picture project to another, and when she conscientiously considers the needs of promoting a film as indistinguishable from making it, and when she is also the mother of two children resolved to give them as much of herself as they require, to say nothing of the creative artist needing to replenish herself—simply to rest—and to read, to listen to music, to travel, to dream, to reflect upon the teachings of Scientology, perhaps to have boyfriends and give them the time of the day and night that fondness deserves, it says something that she could find a day, or two, to pose for the pictures in the Italian *GQ*, to summon that sultriness and give it to the camera, when that venture had no other discernible benefit for her than to prolong her celebrity and compromise her soul.

But there is more. There is Chanel No. 5.

In the fall of 2004, Nicole Kidman appears "everywhere" in print, and sometimes in a filmette, directed by her friend Baz Luhrmann, intended to advertise the most famous perfume in the world, Chanel No. 5.

This book has made no arrangement with Chanel, though I have occasionally purchased No. 5 for my wife. It has a pleasant smell—but so does gin. Still, in the cosmetics sections of large stores, and in need of a gift, I have sometimes thought of perfume, and found that Chanel No. 5 was the one that most readily came to mind. That is how a century of advertising works. When I tested the smell of that particular perfume (the number seems to help avoid confusion or error), I found it pleasant, piquant . . . there are so many other words one might use. I thought it might be seductive, I suppose; I deemed that it was a romantic exchange, or would be considered as such by my wife; and I reckoned that the price was in itself a kind of testament to magic.

Of course, I take it for granted that many women prefer Chanel No. 5 to other perfumes. And I don't think many men are ready to spend the hours it would entail at a cosmetics counter smelling every available perfume. Most men, I daresay, select a perfume they've heard of, one that may impress their lady as much as it does them. They buy the label, and, apparently, they enter into the rather strange conspiracy that believes the scent of their beloved needs to be improved, sweetened, or masked. For couldn't any woman given Chanel No. 5, even Nicole, look the giver in the eye, and ask, Don't you like the way I smell?

As a matter of fact, that saucy caption would work very well with the attitude, or with that provocative, half-robed pout, in the pictures of Nicole in the Italian *GQ*.

Do not forget that in the arts of photography and movie, we cannot smell our lovelies. Yes, there was a brief gesture toward that breakthrough in the fifties—Smellovision, it was called—but it was chaotic and entirely disruptive of the atmosphere of film performance. The extreme emphasis on visibility, and the concomitant availability, has always been cut off from the pungent variety of odors, or scents, that the natural human being gives off. More than that, once upon a time at the movies a kind of perfume was sprayed in the air (to help kill germs, or to mask the agents serving that sanitary purpose), just as in many modern magazines—*Vanity Fair, Vogue, GQ*—the glossy paper is sometimes impregnated with a perfume being advertised in that issue.

And so it is that movie denies us so many of the smells that are a part of human existence and experience. Flesh smells. It is a mass of organic material; it is living, and all living things generate an energy that the nose can detect. Hair smells. Breath smells. In popular adulterous movie melodramas, a faithless spouse is eager to take a shower before being with the wife or husband. Blood smells. Saliva smells. Sweat smells. Cum smells. Every human being has odors in the erogenous zones that are not exactly sweet, and which may deter the inexperienced lover until he or she acquires a nose and a taste.

When we have children or when we attend to our elderly relatives, we may have to clean away their shit and pee. The new parent doubts that he or she can manage that task. But then the odor, the texture, the waste in the shit—the very toxic things—all become covered with the love that develops in a parent for the infant. Lovers will experience the same odd passion, even if polite society does not choose to talk about it too much. It is possible that parents and lovers alike—for their roles are alike—will become fascinated or enchanted by the "unwholesome" smell and linger over it. This is natural. And when a baby is born, coated perhaps in the scum of the placenta, no one in the delivery room thinks to add a few drops of Chanel No. 5 or any other perfume to the fresh body. Lovers may put on perfume and cologne after they have made love and when they want to be seen out in the world together. They may even adopt the same sweet scents to show their union. But sooner or later they will gorge again on the darker or more natural flavors of their own bodies, the ones that give a hint of decay or death. Is that how brave love wants to be?

The Chanel commercial is a movielette, if you like, a flurry of romantic clichés in which Nicole and her lover—or the flags waving to signal rapture in the heady air of the advertisement—are together, separated, and then melting together once more in No. 5. The shorter our movies become—and commercials are our ideal short form—the less possible it is to avoid the conclusion that there are only a very few stories, and they have become like atmospheres. Weather systems, like hurricanes, are often given romantic, female names. We may live to see a "tsunami Nicole," as much a marriage of nature and metaphor as *Il fait beau*.

The word goes around, like an ad for the ad, that it cost $15 million and that Nicole—for her part in the campaign (the press ads, the ubiquitous image), including the little movie—has been paid $2 million. Which raises the question, Does she actually need $2 million, or "$2 million more"? Does she need it in a season awash with *The Human Stain, Cold Mountain, The Stepford Wives, Birth,* and *The Interpreter*? And there will soon be *Bewitched*. In other words, she has six pictures likely to open in the space of two years—with *Dogville* somewhere there in the crowd. It is very rare for a major star these days to open in three pictures in one year. It suggests a desperation to keep working—as opposed to not working, to taking the time to reflect upon larger things. It suggests a decision to strike as often as possible before the actress cannot escape the condition of being forty. And the same merely professional imperative might urge Nicole Kidman—no more certain of the world's future than any of us—to put aside as much money as she can while the glow of youthful desire (or of being desirable to the young) is still unmistakably upon her. In other words, at thirty-seven or so she is already making the calculated attempt to be appealing to people younger than her age.

And in that wave of income, does she truly need another $2 million? Or is she unable to resist the fame, the fuel to her own desire, of being an international symbol of sophisticated sex appeal? The queen of seduction? Someone, just like a queen or a goddess, who is there all the time? For true celebrities cannot afford to have quiet times or off-seasons. (At Christmas 2005, when there were no Nicole films to talk about, there she was still in magazines—without the need to be named.) They have to be spoken about all the time. So monetary greed (something not to be discounted just because we may like Nicole, or be like her) may be less compelling than the need to place her existence in the public realm, the need of being in pictures, depicted, in magazines. One begins to wonder in this Kidmania whether she could muster the resolve to turn down any such offer. The storm of her own echo is upon her, and she must be smart enough—intelligent, even—to know that once that sound, that reiteration, begins to subside, it is dying. She is like a ball thrown in the air, enjoying the stillness and the view at her own apogee. Only the drop awaits her. Unless somehow she is going to defy gravity.

And over the century or so of movies, the temptation or the possibility has appeared to some stars that at that apogee their ball might discover some new, sublime thrust, so that instead of dropping, they escape earthly atmosphere and common gravity and ascend farther at an insanely mounting pace. It is a moment at which the making of movies can fall aside, like the first stages of a moon rocket, and utter fame takes over. This is Marilyn Monroe or James Dean dying—a really lasting role and the insolent refutation of aging. Or it can be something like politics or religion. We think of Ronald Reagan, of Eva Perón.

Put yourself in the position of the marketing director for Chanel No. 5, with Nicole as your demanding figurehead always asking, What else? What else can I do? At the end of the year 2004, there comes the other tsunami, the real one, the undersea earthquake off Sumatra and the havoc inflicted on the surrounding shores, near and far. But on those jungle shores, already beset with poverty and all its impediments, there is very soon the slush of death and human ruin, not just the recovered dead, the bodies known or those that can only be photographed in the hope that survivors might one day identify them, but the literal swill of death, of body parts, of corpses putrefying in the equatorial heat; the kind of death that sooner or later bulldozers must squeeze into the waiting earth. The death with a terrible smell.

Baz Luhrmann reports that he made the Chanel commercial exactly the way he wanted. He had "artistic" freedom. Except that he was making an advertisement for a prettification.

You cannot quite sprinkle Chanel No. 5 on those slippery piles. But just as political leaders will go to the devastated area, to dramatize awareness and sympathy, to offer some kind of calming presence, is there ever the idea—if only in her own very eager mind—that Nicole, an island girl, should go, and be seen there, tall, willowy, un-made up, her hair wild, weeping, touching the living children? Would the world laugh at her for her vanity if she went there? Perhaps, but why is it then that some similar creatures take names like "Madonna" if there is not the impulse, at least the temptation, to transcend oneself, and to be identified with the great moments of the world?

You may be saying that such melodrama would be grotesque, that only a living fascist theater could support it. Perhaps. But what are actresses for if not to help us find the gripping ritual in which that rare thing, "Terror," distracts us from the steady disadvantage of poverty and being deprived, of being plain and dull? Every actor or actress has a dream—usually too lavish or shameful to admit—of a role in a film that coincides with the tragedy or the rapture of the world, that literally everyone will see him or her and take that image as a sign of God or all the gods marching on earth. Ronald Reagan—so much less of an actor than Nicole—carried that hope into real life. And reality collapsed. In hindsight, we may think of the Civil War as something Scarlett O'Hara survived. Yet she never existed—except as a heroine of our fantasies. More and more, our politicians pick up the aura of actors, so why should real actors not seek to rival them? To be the Chanel woman is to be a woman in the air, a figment, but a fixture. And if perfume alone cannot mend the world, then will an actress decide on action? The decision turns on the affection of strangers: *Do they like me? Do they respect me?*

As it is, in January 2006 Nicole is appointed Goodwill Ambassador of the United Nations Development Fund for Women. It's far more a calling than a job. But in June, she selects the *Ladies' Home Journal* for a cover story that declares her commitment. There are pictures (by James White), more romantic, withdrawn, and masked, and this wish—"I'd love to be able to move into something that's more far-reaching." She says she means to educate herself about UNIFEM's work, with Noeleen Heyzer, the executive director. "I think India is the first place we're going to go and we're also looking at the Republic of the Congo and Cambodia."

In the modern portrait of a lady, there needs to be something of sainthood and the political spokesperson. You can hardly be famous without taking on a little light meaning.

Clothes and Costume

The news breaks, and perhaps some have been waiting for it. On January 12, 2005, the papers carry the forty-fifth annual listing of the ten worst- and best-dressed people as determined by "Mr. Blackwell." The news coincides with the reporting of the award nominations of the Screen Actors Guild. Nicole Kidman and *Birth* do not figure in this list; neither does Anne Heche. The nominees for Best Female Actor (that term is preferred to "actress") in a leading movie role are Annette Bening in *Being Julia*, Catalina Sandino Moreno for *Maria Full of Grace*, Imelda Staunton for *Vera Drake*, Hilary Swank for *Million Dollar Baby*, and Kate Winslet for *Eternal Sunshine of the Spotless Mind*.

On the other hand, Mr. Blackwell's ten best-dressed women are Nicole Kidman, Natalie Portman, Barbara Walters, Kate Winslet, Annette Bening, Oprah Winfrey, Scarlett Johansson, Gwen Stefani, Teri Hatcher, and Jennifer Garner. Many on that list are actresses, or screen performers, yet the assumption surely is not that they are being nominated for their onscreen costume, but for the clothes they elect to wear in what might be called "ordinary" or "normal" life, a category of existence that could include awards events or big openings where they are often wearing clothes offered and loaned by leading design houses, as well as those personal public appearances—like being seen and photographed at a restaurant or a party—where it is more likely that their clothes are their own, and do indeed reflect their own taste, their fashion sense, or some notion of what suits them.

But if only because so many very well-dressed women—those

lunching at the Ivy, for instance, or those seen at Manhattan social events—are not included by Mr. Blackwell, whose sense of fashion is restricted to the famous, it becomes clearer that, for actresses, any kind of exposure to the air, of being "out" where lenses may see, is a kind of professional appearance. And so Nicole's being on Mr. Blackwell's list is another sign of her professionalism, even if she might say in response, Good heavens, I just wear what I like, what I feel comfortable in.

But that nonchalant liberty is all too likely to receive the back of Mr. Blackwell's hand, and the mannered reproach of his prose. Meryl Streep makes his worst-dressed list (nor does she get a Screen Actors Guild nod for her ferocious mother in *The Manchurian Candidate*), along with this rebuke: "In dowdy glasses and lumpy tents, Meryl is A Series of Unfortunate Events" (an arch reference to her appearance in *Lemony Snicket*). Similarly, Britney Spears is dismissed as "A clothes encounter of the catastrophic kind."

And how are human beings, who may also be female actors, to deal with this tripe (the papers are also wondering about the Brad-Jennifer split, and whether they had a prenuptial), when in Indonesia, say, garments are being tested for the smeared DNA of people who were wearing them when they drowned?

In its February issue, *In Style* magazine has Nicole on the cover with the come-on, "Nicole: Her Real Life." This lettering is just offshore of her bosom in the cover picture, a bosom held in by an elaborate 1920s beaded dress with jeweled shoulder straps. Her hair is shoulder-length and she is giving her closed-mouth, generous but seductive look at the camera. And with the long fingers of her right hand posed on her hip it is a very striking photograph—a natural cover, as they say—and apparent evidence that a great actress can be a pinup at the same time.

Inside the magazine, on pages 332–33, the story, "Nicole: From Head to Toe," starts with a double-page spread in which she is stretched out on a pink sofa against a slightly paler pink background. Her head is up on the endrest of the sofa, her blond hair piled up but off the face, and she is giving the camera a very nice open-mouthed smile. Nearly all of page 332 is her feet (Dolce & Gabbana pumps, the legend says) and her apparently unstockinged legs. But then she is wearing Ralph Lauren Blue Label shorts and a Gap sweater. The big hooped earrings are by

Fred Leighton, the clunky coiled bracelet is from Kenneth Jay Lane. It is a perfectly decent arrangement for the picture, but the small, sans serif info on the clothes does stress the selling angle and that she was willing (again) to go along with it. Still, the promo for the interview that follows is a little ambivalent. Let it speak for itself: "Don't be fooled by the reclining position. Despite her playful poses and cushy niche atop the Hollywood heap, NICOLE KIDMAN is a stand-up woman: philosophical, focused, loyal. She's also the unfussy Aussie she always was—cooking, conspiring with her kids—and at last ready to entertain romance. Ask her a question or two (and we did, everything from dating to her iconic status) and she looks you straight in the eye."

I'd think it a waste of time to quote this flimsy fluff if the flimsy and the fluff didn't make up so much of our culture now. You see, things like Mr. Blackwell's list and even the Screen Actors Guild awards for the best acting of the year are part of the same stream of nonsense that fills newspapers and magazines and so many television shows geared to "entertainment" and celebrity, and which gently assists in the systemic avoidance of more serious material in our news. You may say, That's unfair—after all, the tsunami got terrific coverage. Every television network sent cameras there. The organization of the charitable appeal has been immense and far-reaching. The few bits of amateur film of the tidal wave coming in like a monster were shown over and over again. Why, you hear people saying, We know all about the tsunami. And it is true that we have heard geologists, meteorologists, and many other authorities discuss such things. Yet on April 6, 2005, there is a color picture—a bleak reminder—on the front page of the *New York Times* that shows a place in Indonesia still as devastated and as unaided as it was an hour after the tsunami struck. Except that now, survivors, kids, and dogs have learned to pick among the dried wreckage for seeds of a new life.

I do not blame Nicole Kidman for this, but I cannot absolve her of some responsibility, either. Just as we play a part in this process as readers and consumers, so does she. She has the great weight on her slender shoulders of being attended to, of being liked and admired. She deserves her reputation for unlikely or difficult roles (from *The Hours* to *Dogville*), and she deserves the respect we give her for her insight into the troubled, creative ferment of Virginia Woolf or the ordeal of a young woman in the mountains waiting patiently for war to end and her lover to return. Those things are attached to her now just as much as the unstoppable urge of the dying Satine in *Moulin Rouge* to sing, to dance, to stay in love, to be an entertainer; just as much as Nicole Kidman's decision to stretch herself out on a pink sofa against a slightly paler pink wall, and to give the camera an Ann-Margret look. Ann-Margret is now sixty-four and though very handsome, she has lived enough to be past giving her own brief look to too many cameras. That is a lesson Nicole Kidman is good enough to learn.

The matter of clothing, where we started, with Mr. Blackwell, is a useful way of penetrating this subject of responsibility. So it's very telling, and casually degrading, that Nicole Kidman arrives for an *In Style* shoot with "costume" to wear, no matter that she takes a pose that is classically like that of pinups, in which nakedness is the implicit suggestion. And if you'll wear any designer's clothes for the sans serif advertising, that is not so far from the question, Will you go naked? "Nakedness" in acting is very often a high term of praise—to be nakedly revealing of a character's soul, mind, or inner being is something greatly to be desired. But the movies, as an art, have been so steadily corrupted by commercialism and sensationalism that actresses—female actors—have often had to go naked. In other words, choice is purchased. This is the kind of thing that was contracted for, and took six days, with just a model, Nicole, and Kubrick on camera in *Eyes Wide Shut*. But it is something she had dealt in in several other films—in *Billy Bathgate*, in *Malice*, in *Birthday Girl*, in *Cold Mountain*. In other words, Nicole Kidman does do nude sequences and she does do sans serif advertising for clothes.

In passing, I do wonder what a strange film *The Hours* could have been if, for a moment at least, that grave face of Virginia Woolf had been revealed to have Nicole Kidman's very cute, knockout, body attached. Or did Virginia Woolf never take off her clothes?

The recurring question asked of female movie stars—Will you do a nude scene?—is not so far removed from asking, Will you wear designer clothes for these magazine shots? It's quite possible that a Kidman, or whoever, takes her choice of the designer clothes and never wears anything she might not have bought for herself. But the magazine's need to have the sans serif legends is a measure of her compliance. Because if putting Nicole Kidman on your cover implies that the audience is truly interested in her, then would it not be more revealing to ask her to wear her own clothes, to come looking as good or as comfortable as she thinks she can? Better that than the implicit horror of *In Style*—that Nicole Kidman is really content to wear yellow shorts and a brown sweater on a pink sofa, with a faintly paler pink wall behind her. Yes, you can argue that it's a deliberately garish 1940s Technicolor look (isn't that more or less Ann-Margret, who was born in 1941?). By the way, that's the year Virginia Woolf died, and it gives me the odd urge for the surrealism of Mrs. Woolf on that pink sofa—she doesn't need to stretch out, to do a look, let alone smile. It would be enough to see her tired eagle's face there, in dust-colored clothes with just a touch of Liberty prints no matter how imprisoned she felt by fate.

In other words, in *The Hours*, as Mrs. Woolf, Nicole Kidman doesn't wear yellow and brown or pink. Conjure up the image—aren't her clothes drab, self-effacing, "intellectual" if you like? Don't they leave the impression that Virginia Woolf was so busy thinking of a first sentence for *Mrs. Dalloway* that she hardly registered the clothes she wore or picked out of the wardrobe? She didn't dress for a look—she didn't dress or shop to "suit" herself. I'm not sure how true that is of the real Virginia Woolf. She lived in London, she had money, and she lived with painters and with people who enjoyed design. (The books of the Hogarth Press, the Woolfs' publishing imprint, are very good-looking.)

Still, it is the mindset conveyed in *The Hours*—which is far from a stupid work—that Virginia Woolf was so single-minded an artist and a writer that she dressed without vanity, or even choice. She was absent-minded, let us say. That is oddly like the vast majority of the earth's population, people who, whatever their "aesthetic," exist in an economy that eliminates choice. Some people wear clothes because they are the only clothes they possess. They need to wait naked while their clothes are being washed—if they do wash their clothes. Many more have such scant choice that it amounts to none—in other words, if they have two suits they are two versions of the same suit, and it "suits" them because of the anonymity, the facelessness, the universality of their lives. Have you noticed that poor people dress very badly? Can you live with that strange sentence, or does it arouse feelings of unnatural social dis-gust—one way or the other—that you feel bound to resolve?

Still, brown and yellow on pink and rose begs us not to be fooled—this is still an upright, unfussy Australian (clearly reckoned to be more down-to-earth or less devious than Americans by *In Style*) with a readi-ness to look you straight in the eye, even if she doesn't know you're there, and doesn't know who you are.

Now, Nicole Kidman has arrived at the Oscars in her time as the hysterical personification of appearance—and that is not meant to be critical. But I have seen her (on television) appear in a gown, by Lager-feld (and someone was there to supply that information), where the off-white of the dress, the bone-white dazzle of her shoulders, and the blondness of her hair were so integrated as to be nearly spiritual. Again, I'm not mocking. For surely there is a kind of code, or an innate register, by which we measure soul and appearance. It's vital to the movies, even if we know it's an act. That's why the pained look Nicole had as Virginia Woolf was like genius, and it's what won her the Oscar, above and beyond anything the character did or said. It was the look. For it startled us and made us feel the journey the actress had undertaken. In answer-ing why, we began to learn about Virginia Woolf. Which is why that journey cannot simply be disowned or hung up in the studio wardrobe closet with the costume.

And at the Oscars, Kidman has looked like the best-dressed and most beautiful person there. That is what the fatuous Mr. Blackwell is noting. And it takes courage as well as imagination, for she could turn up at the Oscars looking like—well, looking as she did on *The Ellen DeGeneres Show*, which was perfectly decent, absolutely street accept-able, quite nice. But it would have devastated the crowd at the Oscars—the real one beside the red carpet and us at home on television—and it would have led to talk that Nicole was snubbing the Oscars. Is it snub-bing Ellen DeGeneres then to look like that? If Nicole has a lunch date with you and she comes looking like that, are you dismayed?

The Oscars are different, and Nicole was merely accepting the possi-bility and the real challenge—Maybe I am the best, the biggest, and the brightest. Maybe, even, I am the spirit of this ridiculously contrived occasion. And if I am going to win for being Mrs. Woolf then I need to turn up looking like someone Mrs. Dalloway wouldn't have allowed in the house—not because she was shaken by the sudden shift in time, nor because of social offense, but because this vision was so patently a fraud.

What I am trying to get at is the difficulty an actress has in dress-ing—an illness, if you like, or a malaise, hideously underlined when Mr. Blackwell says she is among the best dressed. For an actress—even a female actor—has given up selfhood. She can wear anything so long as it suits her imagined character—she can look like a Bloomsbury blue-stocking; she can look like a Russian con artist; she can look like Ada Monroe in the Carolinas; and on *The Ellen DeGeneres Show* she can look like "Nicole Kidman" (or her kid sister). She can pull that one off, but perhaps she feels the terrible problem—it is intellectual or spiritual as much as a matter of style or economics—of looking like herself.

The Interpreter

*T*he *Interpreter* proves just the kind of addled nonsense that "film stars" still make—which is to say that it is nothing that Nicole Kidman should be involved with in 2005. To be blunt, you shouldn't do *Dogville* and *The Interpreter* in the same lifetime; it's like supposing you can marry the ideals of Frank Sinatra and Arthur Miller in one lifespan. Of course, a single actress came very close to that. But she died—in part because her profuse, untidy "everything" was hopelessly contradictory; because the muddle was organic and disruptive.

You can tell yourself that, once upon a time, the story of *The Interpreter* may have been presented to her as something much more interesting: She is a young girl raised in Africa, a farmer's daughter, confident with the heat and the animals and admiring the black rebels in her country, a land where once the small white ruling community exerted its control over the large, underprivileged black population. Then a change comes—the famous wind of change—and blacks get the vote, the leadership of their country, and the very responsibility that some whites alleged they never could handle. And so, in the space of a few years, this woman goes from being a gun-carrying supporter of black rebels to a potential enemy of the new black leadership that is proving itself harsh, tyrannical, and as antidemocratic as the whites were once.

Such things have happened. For nearly a hundred years there was a country named Rhodesia, after Cecil Rhodes, that special mixture of businessman, imperialist, and spin doctor. That territory was headed toward independence and a democratically elected government when Ian Smith became prime minister, broke away from the British Empire and London's directions, and established a republic (with enforced segregation on something like the model of apartheid). There were U.N. sanctions against Rhodesia more or less adhered to by the free world, and eventually in 1980 Smith stepped down, the new nation of Zimbabwe was formed, and Robert Mugabe took control. Elections have continued, rigged, as Mugabe has made himself more completely a dictator than Smith ever managed.

That is potted history, admittedly, but it is history that the movies have done little to trace. Yet in Rhodesia and South Africa alike, there were many liberal-minded whites who protested their countries' apartheid, and who became exiles or rebel activists. There are some of them, in Zimbabwe, born and raised in that country, as much in love with the land and the place as any other inhabitant, who feel betrayed by the rogue actions of Mugabe (who remains the leader of his country).

There are the outlines of a film that might be set in Africa, an uncomfortably candid look at a country that is hardly working yet and where some ordinary atrocities are hardly noticed. But out of that potential comes this story: Silvia Broome is a native of the nation of Matobo; born and raised there on a farm, she lost her parents in a landmine explosion, the mine being set by the forces of President Zuwanie. But Silvia—so flaxen-haired, so luminously pale, that it is hard to believe she ever knew a day's sunshine on the open veldt—is an interpreter at the United Nations in New York. Through a modest contrivance, she hears or claims to have heard the outlines of a plot to assassinate Zuwanie when he comes to address the U.N. general assembly. That speech is part of his effort to avoid a war crimes trial at The Hague.

A fatal confusion sets in whereby this innately African story has imposed on it the outline of a Hitchcockian thriller. I say Hitchcockian because the United Nations building in New York has a lucky but damning history in film. You may remember that it was employed once, diagrammatically, as a setting in Hitchcock's *North by Northwest* (1959, made before the world even knew the name of Ian Smith). In fact, Hitchcock did not shoot inside the U.N. building, but his combination of sets, exteriors, and the vertiginous view of Cary Grant fleeing the building after a man had dropped dead in his arms, was more compelling than any reality. And a warning to others that this was a location (like Mount Rushmore from the same movie) so familiar and yet so empty of real character that it was just an opportunity for making pictures. But *North by Northwest,* while a great film, is a fragile adventure in which comedy, absurdity, romance, and sexuality play the four hands. It has not the least interest in international politics. But forty years later, the state of moviemaking was too earnest to let itself be seen working with the same blithe irresponsibility. So the director and executive producer of *The Interpreter,* Sydney Pollack, will promote the film with inane solemnities on how the U.N. building is a third character in the movie. Of course, that assumes too easily that the two humans have been established as characters first.

Pollack is seventy-one in 2005, and he has done good work in his time. In 1969 he directed *They Shoot Horses, Don't They?,* which now looks like an incomprehensibly bleak picture set at a 1930s marathon dance contest, full of desperate energy and the unrelenting pessimism of Jane Fonda. He made a tense CIA-type thriller, *Three Days of the Condor,* in 1975, a picture that is often invoked in reviewing *The Interpreter*—but only by people who have forgotten the tension and authentic paranoia of the earlier picture. And Pollack had years of making prestigious hits like *The Way We Were, Tootsie,* and *Out of Africa.*

He has become respectable, nowhere less so than in his own mind. He has taken to being a producer and an actor. He insists that he acts only because no one else could be found to do this or that part, but he acts more and more and he has a mature presence and steady delivery that are past their best date for eating. He has lately directed a string of very bad or artificial films—*Havana, The Firm, Sabrina, Random Hearts,* and now *The Interpreter.* Of those, only *The Firm* (with Tom Cruise) did any business.

But Pollack is much liked and he has formed a production company, Mirage, with Anthony Minghella; *Cold Mountain* was their picture, and it was one more project that, somehow, failed to deliver all its own firepower. But *The Interpreter* will be Pollack's film, no matter that it grows out of a collection of forces. When it opens, it will come from Universal,

allied with several other entities—the German company Motion Picture JOTA, Working Title, and Mirage. It will have three producers,
three executive producers, and two co-producers. Such numbers are
not a guarantee of confusion, but there is a modest law in filmmaking
that too many producers can get you in trouble.

Furthermore, on the finished film the script will have three names—
Charles Randolph, Scott Frank, and Steven Zaillian—as well as two
other names on "story" and "with the help of *The Interpreter* by
Suzanne Glass." Talking about the picture, Pollack will say urbanely
that one writer was dropped and another brought on as one writer
grew tired. That is code for the sense that the script is not working in its
entirety, or that the concept is so fundamentally flawed that it may
never function. Some reviewers will note later that even after so many
hands *The Interpreter* is one of those films that tries to explain the holes
in its own plot (a fatal sign of weakness). Thus, the fact that a former
rebel fighter—a killer, we will learn—is now employed at the U.N. with
access to the building is excused because the checking procedures are
not that stringent. Well, maybe, but it's actually far easier to believe in
the incompetence of the CIA and the FBI in real life now than it is in
works of fiction. That is the curse of novels, stories, and films: they
depend on common sense and ordinary diligence, things not yet available in the land of the free.

The Pollackian version of film history can argue otherwise. It can say:
Look, Universal opened the picture. It was the most successful film of
its opening weekend ($22.8 million in ticket sales). Larry King said it
was "Spellbinding!"; *Rolling Stone* said that it "bristles with the smart,
steadily engrossing tension that marked such 1970s goodies as *All the
President's Men, The Parallax View* and *Three Days of the Condor*"; Ebert
and Roeper gave it "two thumbs up"; and Richard Roeper said, "Sydney Pollack is a master." It earned $54 million in its first three weeks.
Still, the public knew that it stank, that it was so automatic an offering,
so stale and farfetched, as to add its little bit to the mounting awareness
and resentment that too many movies treat us like idiots.

And there is always the possibility that a movie star can pause at
some point in such a picture, turn to the audience, open her eyes wide,
and say, Well, don't blame me, I'm just the actor, even if I did get $5 mil-

lion or $7 million or $10 million for this picture. Actors often polish their own obedience, and Nicole Kidman in *The Interpreter* has a sheen of glow about her, which with her very blond hair is enough to suggest she might be Swedish rather than African. There is a basic Swedishness always lurking at the U.N., isn't there?

I am mocking *The Interpreter* because no other tone is appropriate. If only at some point in the shuffle of producers and writers someone had said: Look, this picture is going to be rather silly, whatever we do with it. Suppose we mine that folly deliberately and remember the absurdist abandon of *North by Northwest*. Of course, there are obstacles. One is the FBI man who comes in to investigate Silvia's report of a plot. His name is Tobin Keller, a nice whiff of the nineteenth century, and his backstory is that his beloved wife was killed in a car crash with her lover just as Tobin was about to be discarded. This is easier to accept in that Tobin is played by Sean Penn. On the other hand, if you can guess that Tobin and Silvia (a better title than *The Interpreter*?—well, warmer) are going to become fond of each other, then you don't need me to tell you that Mr. Penn is problematic. Sean Penn does not exactly have what it takes to make one fall in love with him. Or is it that he has himself monopolized that territory?

There are people who reckon that Mr. Penn is a great and serious actor, and Nicole Kidman may have signed on in that idealism. Acting with him is not as easy, however. Pollack will talk in his interviews about the several lengthy conversations that these two allegedly smart characters have. But those scenes don't come off that way. Instead, they seem like acting exercises in which sooner or later the actors realize the script is junk.

Enough. *The Interpreter* is product. Nicole Kidman looks very pretty, and she is competent in all the basic moves of suspense and fear. She does not look as if she had lived a day in Africa, and she does not seem persuasive as a former freedom fighter who handled an AK-47. She and the film lack the political toughness of being ready to say that Matobo is Zimbabwe. Indeed, it even went to the length of hiring linguistic experts to create the framework of a fictional language in which Kidman could be expert. She learned these strange sounds and says them very nicely. But she sounds like a zombie, and as any actor knows her voice is her beginning, the place where she lays claim to point of view. As a final touch, the Matobo leader, Zuwanie, is played not by a real African but by Earl Cameron, a veteran of British cinema, and a man actually born in Jamaica.

In the busy run of Nicole Kidman's films, *The Interpreter* comes after *Birth* and *The Stepford Wives*—that's three duds in a row, the kind of string that big stars are supposed to avoid.

Gypsy

When David O. Selznick, the producer of *Gone With the Wind*, had his breakdown (it came right after the huge success to which he had pledged his life), he underwent a season of psychoanalysis. Well, it was never as disciplined as that sounds. He saw an analyst, if she would wait long enough; he was always childishly late for his appointments. But once he had started, his initial resistance to the practice fell away. "You seem happier, Mr. Selznick," noted his analyst, whose name was May Romm. And the movie man admitted that, yes, he was. He had worried that the process would be intimidating, difficult, and too penetrating for his taste. But, he said, I like it because it's just like a story conference. We're discussing a character and what he might do. I've always enjoyed that. And the character is me!

Something of the same pleasure, or sportiveness, may fall on an actress in interviews. Of course, it is always claimed that interviews are chores. But just as Nicole seems to revel in the photo shoots that usually accompany them more than many performers, so she has an eagerness in interview—it's as if she's curious to see what she will say, or what will come out. It's as if she has found a way of making them acting exercises or short stories. Who am I this time? Now, I realize that that interpretation could sound hostile; it seems to say she is inventing, or dreaming, rather than "being sincere." That is not what I mean. We all experiment with different versions of ourselves. We are close to acting. And what harsh idiocy is it that could disapprove of that open-mindedness in an actress, or in a person for whom pretending, and becoming someone else, is a daily routine?

So, consider this, from *In Style* magazine, in answer to the Kantian question, "Do you prefer a slightly manic pace or long-range planning and order?"

She says, "I like unpredictability. I still don't really have a place to live. I tend to give most things away; I try not to have too much stuff. A friend of mine just said, 'Oh, I love that bag,' and I'm like, 'It's yours.' I like the idea of shedding things, not being too attached. I also think it's part of getting older. I don't really keep photos: I tend not to keep a lot of things for posterity."

It's interesting, that remark (early in 2005) about not "really" having a place to live. In fact, she has a condominium in New York, a rented house in Los Angeles, and the family home—or several—in Australia where she is always welcome. It's even possible that she has the key to one or two other places—places she prefers to keep secret, and which I have no wish to divulge. There might be a place in London and, well, where else would you like a small secret place if you could afford it? And, of course, if she wanted to, if she wanted to have a place big and stable and predictable enough to keep all her books and all her children's toys, she could afford it. In the divorce settlement with Tom, she got their Pacific Palisades home, valued at $4.3 million, which she later sold for $12 million. She could get a real place to live. And in February 2006, she tells me that she thinks the "gypsy" period of her life—more or less the years since the end of the marriage—is coming to an end. She envisages a home, a stronghold, where growing older may begin. She must be thinking of a second marriage.

And she has several other places to be, to rest, to live. She could move into any hotel in the world and enjoy its best accommodations. So all I want you to consider is how far the not having a "real" place to live—being "a gypsy"—is choice, or character. And it's very important.

Most "homeless people" feel lost, vulnerable, and hopeless—ask them, look at them, or try sleeping in the park tonight. Affluent people who imagine themselves as outcasts without a real home are playing a game, or experimenting with their imagination. They are not quite rebels or insurrectionaries, but they are adventurous people, artists often, or criminals with what may be disturbed minds. For they are try-ing to deny one of the essential conditions of socialization.

To be in a position to live in several places (and have your children with you) amounts to this. You need staff of some sort in every place, staff you trust to know you, and they wait there, preparing for you, ready to come to life as you come in—like extras or small-part players in your scenes. They keep the garden the way you like it; they make sure the pool is ready and at the temperature you desire; they can be relied on to keep the refrigerator supplied with your delicacies and the ice cream flavors the kids take for granted.

The beds in all the places have the sheets you like. The bathrooms have your shampoo. The bookshelves—or even the libraries these places may claim—have your books. And an actress may need books, any actress, not just one like Nicole Kidman, who talks sometimes of wanting to be a novelist one day. An actress may need Charles Frazier's *Cold Mountain*, histories of the American Civil War, the DVD of the Ken Burns *Civil War*. She wants *Mrs. Dalloway* and biographies of Virginia Woolf. She wants the latest on whether and how Virginia was abused as a child. Now, she can order these things up through research or the production office of a particular film, but sooner or later she needs *Mrs. Dalloway* in all her places so that, late at night, perhaps, she can get a slice of that chocolate cake (just a few days a week she allows herself cake) and settle down with the prose of Virginia Woolf. Liz Smith has observed that the happy-go-lucky Nicole can and will eat desserts without a worry about weight—and she gobbles up books, too.

Most of us, where we live, we have our libraries, our children, our clothes, our dog, our legal papers—our resources, our collections. But when an actress doesn't really have a place to live—when she has not committed to any one place, or agreed to abide by the rules of "home" (which may mean a lot to children)—then she expects to have all those things in all her places. Open a drawer in Manhattan or Maui and there is the same fresh laundered underwear. She has turned her life into one that requires decor, costume, and props. Possessions mean less than her "things." She is floating—this is a word Nicole Kidman frequently uses to try to describe her state of being.

And the engine that determines which property she lives in is the rise and fall of work—or the provision of new people for her to be with for maybe six months at a time. But as I've said already, Nicole Kidman is not simply the parts she plays; she is also, to a lesser degree, the roles she has considered and declined or which pass out of her orbit. How? She may be too expensive for a picture. The timing—the coming together of large talents—may mean a project lapses. The money may go dry. More or less all the time, she—or her people—are receiving offers. They come as finished scripts, or just someone like Stanley Kubrick calling to say he'd love to have you in his new project. And in her time and at her age, it is now almost certain that Nicole Kidman is offered more projects than anyone else. Julia Roberts was a rival once, but Julia with twins now seems less driven to work though she made a stage debut, in New York, in April 2006. Nicole—with two children— has not let her own hectic pace slacken. And it's clear to the picture business that just as her saying yes can make all the difference to projects like *Birthday Girl* and *Dogville,* so it can ease into being those lackluster duplications of past movies, like *The Stepford Wives* and *Bewitched*. It will not always be so, but Nicole Kidman can get a movie made—just as sometimes she has to do as she is told.

"When we rehearsed *The Blue Room,*" she says, "I loved it, maybe the best time of my life in that awful room in Brixton. I loved coming in. When there's a lot of money on a project, I get nervous. When there's not much money—I love the purity. Yet as a woman on her own sometimes I have to do it for the money. I begged them, Don't make me do *The Stepford Wives.* We don't have a script! No, they said, it doesn't matter. You need the script. Making a film is so difficult. And how many are good? One or two a year?"

So she reads scripts and wonders. And it is no wonder if, for a weekend or a good deal longer, she begins to fall in love with a notion. It's very clear that she thought deeply about doing *In the Cut*; I'm sure she was entranced for a moment by *Stage Beauty*; and so she says, in advance of anything concrete, that she'd like to work with Wong Karwai. Christopher Hampton tells me that they have had a chat about *Hedda Gabler*. There was an announcement that she would do Hedda on stage. But it fades away and then Cate Blanchett does the play in Brooklyn in 2006, with spectacular notices.

Years go by, years in which no decision need be taken about where she "really" wants to live because she is in this storm of work, of parts she will do and parts she might do. Work is her real home, and sooner or later her children are going to realize that and draw some conclusions. But something else sets in—a preferred instability, a taste for unpredictability, or of not knowing where you'll be three months from now. It is a state of mind where habit may seem deadening, where change is the breath of life. And it can become compulsive or addictive: you have to be someone else, you slightly dread the emptiness of those times of "rest" when you can get away to be yourself, because that self has never convinced you. You are so much more excited by the promiscuity of being someone else.

I discover, along the way, that there is a script David Hare wrote for Nicole. She was interested in the strange life of Lee Miller, American, the partner of Man Ray in the early 1930s, the muse for other artists, a great photographer herself during the war, not far behind the front lines, who saw liberated concentration camps and Hitler's bathroom, and then finally became a sadder woman who gave up her life and work to be a mother and a wife, and a cook.

"I collect black-and-white photographs, and Man Ray is in my collection," says Nicole. "I became fascinated by Lee Miller and I wanted to tell her story. I was working with David and he loves complex, intelligent women and he seemed like the person to tell her story. Sydney Pollack was grappling with it. And there was a lot of trouble with the estate. But it was something my husband owned. . . ."

The script was paid for by Cruise/Wagner Productions, and it is a casualty of the divorce. It is there on Cruise's shelf, probably not much to his taste, but perhaps a major opportunity. There is something else about the life of Lee Miller. As a child, she was raped . . . by a stranger? But then she was photographed endlessly, naked, by her own father. That was years before Man Ray did the astonishing, luminous portraits—the rayographs—of Lee like a new moon in the world.

Maybe Nicole Kidman is already a little too old to be that beauty. But suppose a film could recapture the look of the Man Ray era . . .

Alas, Hare regards the script as lost. "It's something only Nicole could ask to have back. And she won't do it."

The things not done never go away, whereas films made, if they are as bad as *The Stepford Wives* or *The Interpreter*, are more easily forgotten. But mysteries never lose their power: a few years later Nicole is drawn to another photographer, Diane Arbus.

My Belle de Jour

There came a time in the writing of this book when my dreams became crystalline on the bright thread of our heroine. I began to see stories or projects that might suit Nicole. You might assume that those dreams had me, regularly, on the brink of erotic collision with Ms. Kidman. But dreams are seldom so vulgar. Connoisseurs will know that real dreams hover between the ridiculous and the childlike and partake in a very matter-of-fact way in the boring. Indeed, if ever your "dreams" seem melodramatic or movielike, count on it that you are waking up. It is the listless plod of inane events that signals immersion.

I don't know about you, but whenever I find myself dreaming a good deal in my normal sleep I am inclined to be a little drowsy after lunch. I used to think it was just the burden of having something to digest, but my wife put it another way that seemed plausible. More or less, she fancied that dreaming was my exercise. "So you need to catch up on your rest," she said.

She was doing something else, something absorbing as we talked, so her voice had that absentminded remove into which a good many intonations might be read if you were suspicious.

"Are you dreaming about her yet?" she asked.

"Her?" I said.

"What's-her-name."

"Oh, her. Sometimes, I think. Yes. Do I seem agitated at night?"

She looked up, as if to consider. Then, "No, I don't think so. Your snore is as steady as the west wind."

So I found myself in the afternoons—it was typically warm with us that September and October—taking a nap. At first, these passages were serenely unconscious, but I guessed enough not to hurt my own inner workings. And then one afternoon, there I was, an elderly gentleman, it seemed, on a smart Parisian side street, just walking. I had a black cane with a silver knob on the top and its tapping on the pavement made me realize I was walking. That was all at first, though I wondered why I was so much older—I could easily have been in my sixties.

The vagaries of the dream! I took the glimpse into my future as random; I did not bother to regard it as an omen that I might think of retiring to Paris. How am I going to be able to retire anyway? Then a day or so later there I was again, and my old gentleman did seem to me a touch more frail or less sturdy. Was it my imagination, or was he leaning on his cane a little more? I awoke as he was about to cross the street—he was nearly knocked aside by a wavering cyclist (it was a priest in billowy robes)—but I did discern what seemed to be his destination: a discreet, cream-colored doorway in an insignificant building across the street. Somehow, I felt a burning need to know more about that place—though as I woke up, the burning was just a desire to urinate.

The weather improved; in the evenings you could feel a warmth reluctant to go indoors, but ready to sleep out in the open.

Somehow, I took it for granted that I would get inside those nondescript premises—and I had no intention of being disappointed.

Dreamers assume they are going to eat the pie.

The door to the street opened at a firm touch—there are doors like that in Paris, have you noticed? But I was a little daunted by the long, straight staircase, not just narrow, but with each step about a foot deep, it seemed. So I took a deep breath, wished for a kindly cut, and there I was sauntering around the corner of a small, prettily decorated lobby, with several easy chairs and a few magazines. It appeared to be a kind of waiting room. Without the waiting.

"Monsieur." A rather scathingly well-groomed woman, of early middle age, with close-cut hair and excellent costume, stood up to greet me. She was attractive, but so businesslike that I was not attracted. Her image was quite complete, or perfect, yet she had no shoes on.

"My shoes are being repaired," she said, casually. "These things happen. And what is your pleasure, Monsieur?"

I said nothing. I often find in dreams that the engine of the enterprise knows my wishes, so there is no need to spell anything out.

"I have a genuine Zulu. Seven feet tall. Quite abandoned, with a natural disposition to violence."

"Really," I said.

"Or a Japanese girl. As wicked as any I have ever seen. A truly filthy mind is a rare surprise these days."

"Of course," I said.

"And there is Rose, of course, an English girl, suffused in shame. Her blush is a marvel. I have had customers come from America to witness it. The merest thing unsettles her. Did I mention Alice?" she asked as an afterthought.

"I don't believe so."

"It is an illusion, of course, but gentlemen swear that the very size of her parts alters."

"Fascinating."

"Monsieur?"

"Well . . ."

"*Vous êtes cinéaste?*" she inquired. "You like to watch?"

"For someone of my electric affinities," I said, "it is often enough." I do not know why I said this, or even how. It was like a line I had learned for the occasion, and it had to be said.

The woman gazed at me. There was something gangsterish about her now. "Cute," she sighed. "Of course, I have Belle de Jour."

"Aha," I said.

"She has her following."

"I daresay."

I had only to follow the woman. She did look a little askance at my cane, but I held on to it firmly and she made a face as if to say that some men were always babies. I followed her down carpeted corridors where nothing could be heard except the muffled sound of female laughter from the closed rooms. Then she opened a door. And I saw Belle de Jour. It was her. Who else?

"Do I enter the room?" I whispered to the woman.

"But of course."

"I might prefer to watch from another place."

"Alas, I do not have those facilities," she said. "Really, it is the same, and more convenient. She does not notice."

And she did not. I was able to enter the room and stroll about and, magically, I did not get in the way of the Gestapo officer and the elderly Chinaman who were having their way with Nicole. She wore a very revealing white brassiere, a size or two too small, I calculated—how else was her bosom such a promontory? And her matching white panties were meshed with a garter belt that held up her long black stockings. She gasped and sighed at every intrusion and indecency from her odd Abbott and Costello. You know the sort of thing.

When they were done, they left her with me. She was a trembling heap, on the bed, and I was all alone with her. But really, I wasn't there, not in a way she noticed. It was like being in a room with an intricate screen.

"I cannot see the join," I whispered to Madame.

"The technology is flawless," she agreed. "But she is a marvel—don't you think?"

"Ravishing," I said.

I did examine her then with more of the critic's eye. It was Nicole, of course, but she had that wondrous, depraved impassivity of Deneuve, as if to say there really wasn't the least point in complaining about this treatment. It was in order; it was what she deserved. *N'est-ce pas?* I could even see how Kidman had learned from the great Catherine. She had put her ego aside. The self-congratulatory grin was wiped away by the plain slap of fate. Not for the first time, I thought that perhaps all movie acting aspired to the stricken, unnoticed imprisonment of people in Bresson films.

"Splendid," I whispered to Madame as we handled business.

"You are always welcome," she said. And then, *"Mon dieu!"* Her hands had gone up to the lobes of her fine ears. "My earrings," she said. "They are gone." I couldn't be sure, but I thought I remembered a pair of simple pearl clip-ons.

"They'll come back," I promised.

"Men!" she said with a small, proud smile. "You'll say anything."

I don't know what else may have happened, but I woke up in San Francisco. The weather was still delightful without the heat being oppressive. I made myself a cup of tea and thought over how restorative an afternoon snooze can be.

Then my wife came in. We greeted each other quite fondly. She wondered what I might like for dinner. I gave the matter every thought and I was about to answer. Then she yawned and said how tiring her afternoons were these days. Perhaps she'd let herself have a nap before dinner, if I didn't mind waiting. She took off her earrings and was asleep before I could reply.

That Icy Look?

A man approaches me at a reading for my book, *The Whole Equation*. He refers, with sympathy, to my chapter on Nicole Kidman—he could be a fellow sufferer. But then he blurts out his feeling of betrayal—he's heard about Nicole Kidman and her "frozen brow." I push him, and it turns out that he has no sort of evidence to offer—it is just the talk out there—but he believes she may have had "botox" treatment, in her forehead, enough to still life or mobility from that part of her (along with signs of aging).

I find myself responding like a busy husband—fond enough, but having so much to do to support the family—who also realizes that perhaps he has given up noticing his own wife. Why would she do such a thing? Why take such a risk? Or is there really a kind of cosmetic resource that is safe enough and does leave the legitimate vulnerability of her face (the appearance of thought and feeling) free from any risk of seizing up, of stricture, of becoming like a sheet of ice?

Now, I do not immediately credit the stranger's suggestion, though he seemed a decent, amiable man, rather hurt by Nicole's alleged concession to cosmetic support systems. On the other hand, any author has learned that among those who come to his readings there are those who nurse demons and mania beneath the affable manner. They are like some people who call in to talk shows on the radio—they have a terrible loneliness. I told myself that there could be no reconciliation between the sacrificial urge to be in *Dogville* and *Birth* and the decision to resort to botox (or any other cosmetic intrusion).

At the same time, I was ignorant then of what botox involved, and I could easily see that shining, bright, flawless brow in the central image used to advertise *The Stepford Wives*—a terrible film, the kind of project that was hardly explicable except in the most crass, monetary terms, or out of the nagging demand never to stop working. There was the book—the novel by Ira Levin—the paperback movie tie-in, lying on the floor of my office, with the staring blue eyes and the forehead as clear and inviting as a fresh ski slope. I mean, there is that Nicole, the person who somehow did as dumb a film as *The Stepford Wives* for a few more million. This is how "out there" rumors arise, and it's why after *The Hours* and *Dogville*, say, it's hard to be carefree or casual again.

A Stepford wife, I reasoned—meaning that genre of desperate housewife, clinging to her appeal—might easily employ botox and much more. The man at the reading had said "frozen." Did he mean that metaphorically, or was he trying to speak accurately? Was something like a novocaine for appearance stealthily pumped beneath the skin so that its smoothness could be eternal, or longer-lasting? The more I thought about it, the less likely it seemed for someone as set on being photographed as Nicole. Suppose her brow grew lines one day— would she worry? Would an Australian be shaken by weathering? What else explained her hurry now and her great zest for work better than the urge to get her paydays and her projects tucked away before the natural marks of age or autumn set in? Why work so furiously if you had a secret protection? Why resort to such uncertain rescue when you seemed happily caught up in a race with time?

All that was the fruit of logic. But we cannot quite say that the lady in question is above illogic or acting in a drastically contradictory way— going from eye candy to Virginia Woolf.

You see how thoroughly I could defend Nicole and her honor? Yet as soon as I had worked out this airtight defense for her (a devoted husband is quite ready to be the lady's lawyer—an appealing role, especially with client confidentiality), as soon as I had her in the clear, so to speak, I knew (it was instinct, I didn't have to figure it out) that impulsiveness would explain it. Instinct is how people go off in different directions at the same time. And when I looked at the shine of Nicole in so many different pictures, I could not testify in all honesty that there wasn't at least the possibility of derangement in that oh so bright, white, staring gaze. I mean the look that abandons all the flirt and pout, and looks at you as unblinking as a camera and says, Well, what do you think I would do? Or stop short of?

I did try to indicate that the breakthrough on *To Die For* was some kind of realization that the woman herself—Nicole-whoever—might be ready to die for glory, for being the center of attention. If only for a moment. Wouldn't you? I think that's what Nicole's look is saying so much of the time. It will be a great pity, an abuse of her creative nature and potential, if she never quite gets to play a lovely murderess, a woman who urges some weak man all that way, not simply to gain a fortune, or sexual rapture, or even freedom—whatever those things are. But just to see—Wouldn't you do it?—just the once, just for the sake of it. Like skydiving or swimming with sharks.

And I know I would.

That's why I'm writing this book, I think, to honor desire.

And when you write about an actor or an actress, it is very important to find a way, or a mood, that fits the subjunctive—the might have been. As audiences, we think of actors' careers as the sum of those parts they choose to play. But that is just the simple, tidy way of doing it. In truth, their life is nearly as fully crowded with the parts they only consider, some of which may come very close to being done—think of Fran, the woman in *In the Cut*. There are roles on which the actress may have thought and worked harder than on those she actually plays—parts that fall through at the last moment, or parts that were just the fever of a heady weekend. The director Richard Eyre has told me of such a moment with Nicole. He had offered her the female lead in what became *Stage Beauty*. It was clear that her saying yes would have made an uncertain production a definite thing. And she was hugely intrigued by the role—effectively the first actress, the first woman, to appear on the English stage, and who proves superior to her boyfriend, the actor who has hitherto played female roles.

Nicole wanted to hear what Eyre thought and felt. "She touched me a lot," he says, as he recalls their talks. It wasn't that she was being seductive; it wasn't that anything happened—though some, observers as well as participants, might have thought it had or could or would. And actresses count on being watched.

I ask Eyre, if Nicole had said yes, would that have changed the film?

I suppose it would, he says. Yes, it would. And he was prepared for that. But he says now that he thought she would never say yes. She was trying it on, as it were. She was pretending. She was trying to fall in love with the part perhaps. She was being an artist. And when she said, Sorry, but no, she sent Richard Eyre a very good bottle of wine.

Recast any film and it shifts. Story is set on a different course by mere presence. And surely there is a delicious anticipation—for her as much as us—in wondering what Nicole would be like in a remake of *Rebecca*, *Belle de Jour*, or *Mississippi Mermaid*. For instance, I cannot resist telling you how sublime Nicole is in *Mississippi Mermaid* in the mounting repetition of moments in which she tells the increasingly ruined Russell Crowe, "But, of course, I love you." It is true—I have this firsthand—that the director had a hard time at first coaxing the flirt out of her eyes at these moments. She wanted to be the coy seductress; she wanted to be the femme fatale; she wanted to be a naughtier Suzanne from *To Die For*. But our director persevered. He told her to let her eyes go blank. He urged her to say the line as if she was reciting it—as opposed to thinking of it—because it was a line in history and legend waiting to be said. Nicole asked what her motivation was. And the director said to repeat history. And at last she got it, and those who were there—at the location in eastern Oregon (we are going to the edges)—still speak with awe of the way a kind of wisdom settled in her at that moment that has never yet left her. It lets me recall that scene from *Birth* where Anna is in her bath and "Sean" simply decides to join her there. The director, Jonathan Glazer, said, "I remember talking through that scene with Nicole. I said, 'I'll cut to you when he's taking off his clothes.' And she said, 'What am I doing?' "

I wonder if Nicole doesn't go to see *In the Cut*, "her" film, the one Meg Ryan ended up doing—the nearly complete failure—and watching the crushed beauty of Ryan's naked performance in a mixture of horror and envy: I could have done that!

·   ·   ·

The stranger at the bookstore appears in late 2004 with his distressing question. I overcome my doubts and hesitations—I am studying *Birth* at this time, sinking into it, developing ideas about it that are fetuslike, if you will, and in *Birth*, under its quiet white light, I can see no hint of cosmetic rescue.

But then, there is another magazine cover, which appears at just the moment of *Bewitched*—it is the August 2005 *Glamour*—and there are two pictures of Nicole staring into the camera, seeming nearly to count the split second of the exposure, and I feel (far more than see) the deep-down threat of ice in place, holding beauty together. You understand, I am still nowhere near equipped to recognize these things with authority. My suspicions are worth nothing. Yet I have the hardest time throwing them off. And in *Bewitched*, the lady is shot in a bland, soft focus . . . You could say it is a version of the era when *Bewitched* was a TV hit. You could tell yourself not to notice.

And then the day comes in a supermarket—I can remember the slippage of horror in the bright light and the Mantovani music—when I see the cover of *Red* (September 2005). There she is, our lady, on the cover, three-quarter profile, the chin dipped, the eyes saucy, and the brow . . . It seems polished, lined (in the way a coat may be lined), and just a little too close to those chosen and presented supermarket fruits that are always more battered and used when you get them home.

I feel confused, yet I feel a loss, too. It is not my business? No, I think it is, for I am one of those people who go to see Nicole Kidman. And this book may have a modest influence with others. There are women in the same business—Meryl Streep, for instance, Diane Keaton, Sigourney Weaver—about whom I do not entertain the same suspicions, but can we be sure? I have no right to disapprove of the trade-off that gets a few more lush paydays in return for looking preserved. Though if I notice it, and worry, then hordes may be aware of the change. And yes I do recognize that aging has always employed makeup and distortions of appearance to be creative. And so it should. But I don't know if I can tolerate the urge to stay cute or pretty or young for even one extra season in someone I want to love. Not if I must grow older.

Put it this way: the wondrous retention of youth that she manages in

Birth seems an effort of will, imagination, and intelligence. The cover of *Red* is something else, and I like it less than the unmistakable signs of growing older, or dying even.

And in September, when the TV Emmys are broadcast, Alessandra Stanley writes in the *New York Times*, "Almost all the women, from the cast of *Desperate Housewives* to Mariska Hargitay of *Law & Order: SVU*, wore tight, shiny dresses and tight, shiny foreheads—they looked less like actresses than members of a new, genetically altered cult: Nicole Kidmanites."

Go back to *In the Cut*. The writer Susanna Moore and director Jane Campion felt dismay as, gradually, they lost Nicole's interest, or her concentration. It took years, but the project endured, with Meg Ryan as Fran. By then it was a $12 million budget, which suggests that Ryan received no more than $2 million. Its domestic gross was only $4.7 million.

Bluntly, those who advised Nicole against doing the film were proved correct. But the numbers are never enough in film history. *In the Cut* was startling—it was a novel thing to see a star actress so casually naked, so ordinary or shabby, so devoid of glamour. Kidman's very beautiful body has sometimes shone like a lighthouse in sex scenes. Her own pleasure in herself glows.

When she bought the rights to *In the Cut*, she says she did not tell Tom about it. Talking to *Movieline*, she seemed to know the choice reflected on her in inescapable ways:

"The way she [Susanna Moore] writes is very graphic, but yeah, it's an interesting point that she's making [about female masturbation]. . . . It's sort of true actually. Simple as that. Why did I want to do the book? Because it's a book about loneliness. It speaks to a generation of women in their 30s now who are lonely. I'm now 30, and I've got a lot of friends between 30 and 35. It's a book about searching. That's what appealed to me. On top of that, it's a very erotic book. In the hands of Jane Campion . . . that becomes interesting, because I've never known Jane to be ugly in the way she depicts sex. I bought the novel for Jane. I asked her to produce it with me. As we worked on it we fell in love with it. We're now very passionate about it. It will be a controversial movie, but it will have a lot of depth and insight into women. It's a shocking novel, but the film will not be made to shock. A lot of people have told me not to make this movie, but that spurs me on."

Nicole did not care or see far enough ahead to grasp the risk of making herself dowdy, feral, not shining. I wonder how far she found that difficult in her own thinking—to reveal so much without feeling good about herself. An actress can attempt to determine her career in terms of how popular she is, and how positive she feels about herself. But neither of those approaches actually rivals the quality of her choices. And the nature of choice in the picture business is that it requires you to bet your future and bet your bank. You have to believe in the integrity of caring. Otherwise, movies like *Bewitched* will flutter over your glowing head like butterflies on a warm day.

Bewitched

Being bewitched is not the same as being stupid. But making *Bewitched* in 2005 may stand for the worn-out certainties of a movie business that notices its summer audience has declined in a year by about 7 percent. And *Bewitched* is a warning to anyone who might think of relying on the stardom of just being or remaining Nicole Kidman.

Bewitched ran from 1964 to 1972 on ABC television, with Elizabeth Montgomery playing Samantha Stephens, the pretty, middle-class wife to Darrin Stephens. She was actually a little bit of a witch, though she was trying to give up that dark art to please her hubby. It was the most popular show ABC had ever had until that time. As a child, Nicole adored it. It won Emmys, although it was never seen as being as good as *Get Smart, The Mary Tyler Moore Show*, and *All in the Family*, which were its rivals. Even in its heyday, *Bewitched* was recognized as a derivation, borrowed in large part from a hit play and movie of the 1950s, *Bell, Book and Candle*.

In truth, *Bewitched* was a family sitcom show, a portrait of the vagaries of marriage, in which a little voluntary or involuntary magic served the same kind of role as Lucy's klutziness in *I Love Lucy*. At a stretch, it was possible for feminists to claim that Samantha was "empowered," and thus an example of the kind of woman Betty Friedan was writing about—strong, smart, with many urges to be other than pretty, obedient, and placid. So she was naughty—and she was the engine of the series. She played tricks on her plaintive husband, and the series even dropped one actor, Dick York, for another, Dick Sargent, as Darrin without the public complaining, or even noticing.

Bewitched was a top-eleven show for four seasons, and Montgomery (the daughter of actor Robert Montgomery) found a large popularity, even though she never won the Emmy herself and never translated her television fame into a movie career. But her husband, William Asher, was a producer on *Bewitched*, and sometimes a director, so they did OK.

It is not uncommon today to find movie studios led and controlled by men and women whose formative experiences with the screen were with television when they were kids. This covers a large period: *Bewitched* had its eight years as a prime-time show, and then many more years in reruns and syndication. And so it was that nostalgic people in their forties thought of doing *Bewitched* as a movie as long ago as 1991. It was then that Penny Marshall (an actress made on the small screen, in *Laverne and Shirley*) hired actor Ted Bessell to join her small production company, Parkway. One of Bessell's pet schemes was a movie of *Bewitched*—as Penny Marshall put it, Bessell "just loved the idea of giving up immortality for love." No, that was not exactly feminist, or even naughty, but there had always been a theme in the TV show that Samantha was being nagged by Darrin to stop being bewitching—because it was alien to their Connecticut world, to shopping, and to American middle-class order.

Marshall introduced Bessell to a screenwriter, Monica Johnson, who had done episodes of *Laverne and Shirley*. There were at least three drafts, but Bessell was not satisfied; he enlisted Richard Curtis, the Englishman (*Four Weddings and a Funeral*), to do another version. Several other writers would be hired during the 1990s, including the playwright Douglas Carter Beane. By 1996, there was a reading of his script in New York (with Cynthia Nixon as Samantha) that went very well. A movie seemed on the point of blooming, and Gwyneth Paltrow was in line for the lead part. Then Ted Bessell died.

So Penny Marshall now wanted to make the film "for Ted," who had cherished it. Other producers came along—Douglas Wick and his wife Lucy Fisher. There were several more writers. Soon there were well over a dozen scripts or drafts (and all had to be paid for). There had been over ten years' work and thought and love devoted to *Bewitched*. There are those in Hollywood who have been raised to see ten years on a bit of froth as a disaster preparing to descend. But Amy Pascal at Columbia wanted to make the picture. And in 2003, she reckoned she could get Nicole Kidman as Samantha—for what turned out to be $17.5 million.

An executive could do the spin: a hit show, beloved by Americans; the comedy of marriage, with the sauce of witchery; a decade during which good writers had been building the concept. Still, Pascal realized that all that building didn't quite make a story line to put before Nicole. So she called the writer-director Nora Ephron and asked her for a take on it that might hook the actress. Overnight, Ephron had the notion of a pompous male movie star, on the ropes careerwise, who thinks of doing *Bewitched* to save himself and stumbles upon an unknown co-star who proves to be a little bit of a witch.

Yes, a decade can turn into an overnight scramble, and a property that had always been driven by the wicked nose and sharp wit of its Samantha could turn, potentially, into Darrin's show. Nora Ephron and her sister Delia were hired to write it. Nora would also direct. And Will Ferrell would play Darrin. Almost certainly, Nicole would have been consulted on her co-star, and she may have sensed a problem. Ferrell can be funny, but does he want to be an actor? He is what today passes for a "big star": made on television, chiefly in skits and impersonations and double takes to the camera, but apparently secured on the big screen only with *Elf* (2003). Whatever else, Nicole, plainly, was being asked to be "the girl."

Over the years, *Bewitched* gathered not just four producers and three executive producers, but a budget of at least $85 million. Thus it was set in a mathematical logic that would require revenues (from all sources) of something like $250 million for it to break into the magic of profit. Almost certainly, Ferrell would be paid what Nicole was getting; it would be unmanly for him to be expected to take less. And so there is $35 million to start with, before one has paid the Ephrons, the nine screenwriters, and the overhead of the years. To say nothing of twelve weeks' work in Los Angeles, with Michael Caine and Shirley MacLaine as two of Samantha's witchy relatives. Except that she is no longer Samantha; her name has been changed to Isabel. This is the originality for which some writers get rewarded.

The film that emerges is nowhere near the worst of its year. The Ephrons, plainly, are smart, caustic dames, and there is plenty of humor in the dialogue. Nor is the "new concept" a ruin, in itself. The show-within-a-show fabric seems promising, and the setup allows Isabel to be a sharp pin ready to burst the silly bubble of Jack Wyatt (Darrin's new name). But just because they are unattached to begin with, the movie bumps against the unlikelihood of their falling in love. The TV series began with the marriage and it never allowed the slightest hint that Samantha was anything but crazy about Darrin. Why she might be was never asked—and that may be a big reason for not redoing *Bewitched*. But the marriage (as marriages always do) permitted the comic discord of heartfelt lovers. Whereas one has only to look at two shots of Kidman and Ferrell to feel the heavy, smothering hand of politeness that bonds (and traps) two aliens getting $17.5 million for this foolishness.

There are moments when Nicole tries a nice little Marilyn Monroe act—more than enough to wish that she could have played that role somehow, somewhere (though she is already older than Marilyn ever managed, and so much more secure). The new *Bewitched* gets by—just—but it never acquires a life, a marriage, chemistry between its two stars, or the sheer naughtiness that made Elizabeth Montgomery a delight in the 1960s (an age when women were finding so many fresh territories that Samantha's naughtiness seemed cozy).

There's more to complain about. Nora Ephron, I'm sure, is up-to-date, rational, practical, filled with common sense. She will say, jokily, as the film opens, that reporters needn't bother to ask her whether she believes in witchcraft! How silly! Well, maybe. I'm reminded of Steven Spielberg when *Close Encounters of the Third Kind* opened. That film had a reliable UFO expert as its adviser. And some asked Spielberg if he believed in unidentified flying objects. No, he replied, but I believe in people who believe in them.

There's wisdom there to wipe away the knowing grin on Ephron's face. Elizabeth Montgomery (who seemed earnest, businesslike, liberal, et cetera) left no doubt about believing in Samantha and her luck, and she let us see from time to time that it was both a cute trick and a curse. If you recall *Bell, Book and Candle*, it involves a witch who has to forsake her powers to be in love, and in the movie, Kim Novak brought moments of real pathos to that situation, no matter that the film was a wild and eccentric comedy (it also includes Jack Lemmon, Elsa Lanchester, Hermione Gingold, and Ernie Kovacs in its cast—oh, for the sedate fifties). There is a great prospect in the idea of a woman who wants love but who hardly knows how to set aside her magic so that she can deserve it.

And magic, of course, could be a metaphor for acting.

Bewitched opens in the United States on June 26, 2005, on 3,174 screens. The response is modest. David Ansen of *Newsweek* has the lead quote in the first ads: "Kidman and Ferrell are a kick to watch," he says. Elsewhere he admits, "By the tepid ending, the movie appears to have been sedated."

Still, at the end of June, it seems to be a "hit," or the most successful film of its opening weekend. It grosses just over $20 million (about one thousand viewers per screen). In its second week, as it faces the challenge of Tom Cruise in *The War of the Worlds*, it falls away by nearly 50 percent. In the next two weeks, there is the same drop. In its fifth week, it grosses less than $500,000. Its total domestic gross is under $60 million, and it has been cut down to 405 screens.

And so success comes and goes in the wretched summer of 2005. The young audience—which is more or less the only active audience in such a season—shows no nostalgia for *Bewitched*, and very little recognition of what it is. The world is still conducting itself as if to say that Nicole Kidman is a very big star, but in truth she has had four films in a row—*The Stepford Wives, Birth, The Interpreter*, and now *Bewitched*—that amount to a campaign of disaster (especially when you recall that they were preceded by *The Human Stain* and *Cold Mountain*).

People ask me anew why I am doing a book about Nicole Kidman. I tell them there are great things to come, and I hope that I am right.

Dangerous Age

As I finish this book, I contemplate its being published in the fall of 2006. At that time, Nicole Mary Kidman will be about six months short of her fortieth birthday. Her daughter, Isabella, will be coming up on fourteen. Her son, Connor, will soon be twelve.

She may still be a single mother. That package of life circumstances is demanding enough, you might say, even without the extras that the mother is a great and driven actress, and the two separated parents are among the most famous people alive. This is not a book about Isabella and Connor. But having no wish at all to intrude on their lives does not stop one wondering about their point of view. They are going to have stories to tell, energies to act out. And teenagers are one of those life forces with the power to age all of us.

Tom Cruise had a turbulent 2005. The ordinary follower of his career may recall his startling performance on a few television shows and at some live events as he announced his love for Katie Holmes, an actress, aged twenty-seven. I recall Robert Benton's words, that it is hard for mortals to comprehend the pressure in being Tom Cruise. For a while he dropped his public relations firm, PMK, and gave that job to his sister. His exultation, for Oprah, shattered the set norms of that type of show, just as he plainly rattled the host Matt Lauer on the *Today* show when he launched into a painfully serious attack on psychiatry and drugs. There were those who asked whether Tom was cracking up—or emerging from his armored shell. Yes, he seemed very happy, and yes, he seemed uncommonly agitated by things in this modern world that offend him. At the same time, in *War of the Worlds*—a film that looks better on repeated viewings—Cruise gave a very interesting performance as a deadbeat dad, and he made that disaster movie a steadfast boost for parenthood. His father redeems himself by saving the children. And at the very end, he just waves to his ex-wife, in salute, or identification. You may say that *War of the Worlds* was a story bound to end that way, as well as a film in Steven Spielberg's control. So be it, but you underestimate Tom Cruise's power in the business if you think he cannot lean upon story with his own needs.

Other things were set to happen before this book could be published: Katie Holmes had a child, a daughter, a step-sibling to Isabella and Connor; and *Mission: Impossible III* (is it really only the third?) opened and did notably less well than its predecessors.

The future facing Nicole Kidman is not quite as clear. The year 2005 was not her best. *Movieline* magazine declared that the two worst bits of casting chemistry of that year were Nicole and Sean Penn in *The Interpreter* and Nicole and Will Ferrell in *Bewitched*. I have pointed out already the line of films that have been "disappointing" in some way or other. I don't mean to put all those films in the same basket. But the pattern is there—and Nicole Kidman knows it. Nor is she too proud to admit that some things were done for the money, with fingers crossed. But the woman I spoke to was in no doubt about having learned (again) the need to trust herself, to rely on her natural ability as a character actress, to follow her head and her heart, to trust directors she likes. And to be smart—and lucky. Moreover, she has every right to say (if she wants to) that a Tom Cruise can age a good deal (it may happen one day) and still look rugged, heroic, manly, and a favorite. Whereas if a gorgeous thirty-five-year-old begins to raise thoughts of forty in the public mind she may be dropped in the time it takes the business to discover a new knockout kid. (The other day at a party, a man in venture finance told me that he loves everything Scarlett Johansson does.)

In all likelihood, as this book is published, Nicole will open in a project called *The Visiting*. This is a big suspense film, based on the classic *Invasion of the Body Snatchers* (filmed three times already under that title). She plays a psychiatrist, with a son, who lives in Washington, D.C., and takes a leading part in the struggle against alien invasion (note, in all the earlier versions of the story, the aliens or the pod people win). The male leads are Daniel Craig and Jeremy Northam, and the director is Oliver Hirschbiegel, whose last film was *Downfall*, the atmospheric re-creation of the final days of Hitler, with Bruno Ganz as the dictator in the bunker. I'm not sure how proven a director Hirschbiegel is, but I suspect he was a large attraction in this project for Nicole. (If you were doing that story, would you have Nicole as the valiant heroine or the ultimate alien, with her staring blue eyes and her luminous pale skin?)

She has finished another film, a far more uncertain project. For the moment, at least, it is called *Fur*, and it is based on the life of the photographer Diane Arbus. "But it's only a period of time in Diane's life," says Kidman, "when she chose to leave her marriage. It's a strange fairy tale about a woman who doesn't know yet whether she can be fulfilled." It is directed by Steve Shainberg, and it also stars Robert Downey Jr. It sounds like a dangerous, experimental film—in other words, it sounds far more like *Birth* than *Bewitched*. Not that Nicole could easily resemble the real Diane Arbus. Samantha Morton (the original casting) looks more like the photographer. That film is being edited as I write (February 2006), and that process seems to have taken a while already. There were also rumors out of that set that Nicole was unusually anxious over her appearance.

It's hard to be sure how these films will turn out. But then there seems to be a run of projects of the kind that remind one of the era of *The Hours*. Long before this book is published, she will have shot a picture for Noah Baumbach (who made *The Squid and the Whale*), about sisters in upstate New York. She is to play in it with Jennifer Jason Leigh, who has a very good record as a sisterlike character (*Georgia, Single White Female, In the Cut*). For anyone who admired *The Squid and the Whale* as much as I did, this is exactly the kind of low-budget picture, high on material and character, that one would like to see Nicole doing.

Then, in the summer of 2006 she was set for the new Baz Luhrmann project, untitled as yet, about events in Australian history, where she will be cast opposite Russell Crowe. (This compensates for the breakdown a couple of years earlier of *Eucalyptus*, a film that Crowe backed out of when he found the material lacking interest.) The period for

Luhrmann's story is the 1930s. Nicole will be an Englishwoman seeking to sell a house in Australia. Crowe is the drover who helps her. It is a love story in which landscape expresses romance. Meanwhile, war is looming. With a chuckle, Baz Luhrmann speaks of *Gone With the Wind*. It is worth noting that Nicole has committed to that project without seeing the script. In fact, in April 2006, it had to be admitted that their Australian epic would be delayed—and then Crowe was out, again, and Hugh Jackman was the drover. Much the same can be said of *The Lady from Shanghai*, a Wong Kar-wai picture, on which again there is no screenplay so far. As well as that, she has pledged to do a new picture with Jez Butterworth, the director of *Birthday Girl*.

Of course, that policy of going with proven directors or auteurs is one that a film critic or historian is bound to recommend. But the real historian knows that no schedule is guaranteed, and it is especially hard these days for an actor or actress to determine that all their pictures are brave, fresh, and good. Still, I think Nicole has lined up a team of projects sufficient to carry her past a threshold that has long alarmed her—that of being forty. In which case, it may be encouraging to offer a short list of pretty good pictures and performances where an actress was over forty, or playing it: Bette Davis in *All About Eve* (done at forty-two); Joan Crawford in *Daisy Kenyon* (done at forty-three); Katharine Hepburn in *The African Queen* (done at forty-four); Meryl Streep in *One True Thing* (done at forty-seven); Jessica Tandy in *The Birds* (done at fifty-four); Gloria Swanson in *Sunset Boulevard* (aged fifty-three); and . . . Nicole Kidman in *The Hours* (done at thirty-four, but playing Virginia Woolf at fifty-nine).

Yes, you're right, those parts stand out for rarity as much as interest, and in turn that supports the terrible dread that actresses feel over forty—that maybe they are about to be denied work just as they become more interesting as people. But of course men continue to find very young women very interesting—which can simply mean that men prefer females not too well trained at answering back, arguing, and using their brains.

There are other lists: of screen goddesses who never saw forty—Jean Harlow, Carole Lombard, Marilyn Monroe, Mabel Normand; of those who died in their forties—Margaret Sullavan, Judy Holliday, Linda Darnell, Judy Garland, Natalie Wood; and of those who did little serious work once they were past forty. That is a very long list, and it starts with Garbo, who retired at thirty-six and never quite came back.

What did Garbo do then, for nearly fifty years, except dodge still photographers while clinging to her own legends? She "knew" people, they say; she traveled, or she didn't; and she was close with her family. I can hear the same things being said of Nicole Kidman, but I wonder if this absolutely concentrated person wouldn't go crazy without work. I don't mean work simply as a means of income, or something to keep an active mind engaged; I mean work in terms of the total and uncomplaining addiction to being someone else—as if that terrible pursuit was really her only chance (as slim as herself) of finding redemption or peace.

In the time I have been studying Nicole Kidman, she has had romantic involvements with a few men—Lenny Kravitz, Stephen Bing, Keith Urban. Perhaps there were others. I hope so, because this trio does not seem especially substantial or rewarding. They seem like bold-type names to keep her in the celebrity columns. No, I don't mean that cynically, but it is so much easier in her half-strangulated existence, forever attended by security people and entourage, that she meets only famous or half-famous people. It is so much harder for her to meet real people. Forgive a nostalgic touch, a revelation of sentimentality, but I mean the kind of people who might love her and talk to her for years, as opposed to objects of flirt and brief, passing sexual contact, enough to fuel the beast, enough to encourage the notion that she understands men.

But in May 2006, the announcement comes that she and Keith Urban are engaged. He is Australian, a country singer, a star with his own career, and his base in Nashville. A summer wedding is talked about, but they show every sign of wishing to keep things secret. I hope I am mistaken about Keith Urban, but he would seem to be more a step toward happiness than a career strategy, and I am not sure that Nicole hears the first as clearly as the second. Perhaps she will have children—that prospect alluded to in so many strange ways in her films. I hope she will be happy. Yet in truth I am the kind of caring stranger who would prefer two more great films. Or one? We gamble.

What else can there be? Her life is laid out in professional demands: prepare for a picture; shoot the picture; do publicity; do photo shoots; attend awards events; do TV interviews; see the children; be with the family; exercise every day for several hours, run, run, run—where do you think such slenderness comes from? I do not mean to put those demands in any order of duty or preference, but I think her schedule is crammed and overflowing. I am not sure she has time to be in love or married. Do you remember how long those things take—even if you have servants? And can you imagine how difficult those things can be with your house staff watching, waiting for your call? You say, well, that's all very well, but you wouldn't mind a few weeks of the strain. Don't be so sure. The strain is terrible, not least because in the end it reifies or mocks the closest ties in life, the things you ought to care the most about if you are really a great, sensitive, kind artist.

And Nicole Kidman is—that's why I'm writing about her. I don't say she's the greatest actress ever, or even the best of her time. Though I think she is the bravest, the most adventurous, and the most varied of her time. Just remember these films: *Moulin Rouge, Birthday Girl, The Others, The Hours, Dogville*—that great run. And *Birth*. I know many of you in reading this book have said, *Birth*? What was that? I never saw it, I had better seek it out. Yes, you should, because it is her best and she knows it went unseen, and forgotten. And she knows how far she relies on stupid luck. But it is frightening to know it. In *Birth*, and in a few other movies, she finds a shining, profound intimacy, the thing that may be such a mockery in real life, and it is in the nature of what actors do that the people who see it and are most moved—who, as it were, fall in love with her because of it—must always remain strangers.

Actors make love to people they will never meet. It is their passion. And so the real people in their lives often feel neglected or lost. That is their puzzle.

Postscript

On Monday, June 26, 2006, the papers in Los Angeles report from Australia that Nicole and Keith Urban were married the day before, overlooking the water of Sydney Harbour. She wore a white Balenciaga gown and carried white roses. There are magazines on the stands in L.A. that wonder if the bride was pregnant, too—a little loop of speculation surrounds the pout of her tummy in a photograph. And that day in Los Angeles, the distributor Picturehouse shows me *Fur*, an astounding new film, a film for Nicole's fans, about a young woman who needs to end her first marriage if she is to find her freaky talent as a photographer.

Fur is a story of Diane Arbus, the real American photographer. The film, by Steven Shainberg, is also called a tribute to her and "an imaginary portrait." With reason: the movie contains no pictures by Diane Arbus, a sign that the Arbus Estate has not given its approval to the project. For what emerges is a story of how Diane's marriage to Allan Arbus ended in 1958 after seventeen years. He had been the photographer. She was the daughter of a Manhattan furrier, and she helped arrange the fashion shows that her husband photographed. We see such a show and we see that Diane is a nervous wreck, trying to get the show right, but not doing her own work. "I take light readings, and I iron clothes," she says.

So she is, on the one hand, the frustrated woman, the repressed artist, and the ego wrapped up in the family furs. But then she begins to realize that someone new has moved in upstairs in their Manhattan building, a mysterious masked man who watches her. To the best of my knowledge, and from reading Patricia Bosworth's biography (and Ms. Bosworth is a producer on the film) there is no hint that this upstairs neighbor ever existed. He is the neighbor in a story, he is a man so covered with hair (not quite fur, the hair of illness, but the growth of artistic vision) that he is an invalid. He looks like a lion, or Beauty's Beast. He is named Lionel.

We are in the region here of fairy story, of *Birth*, of the films for her I invented. And *Fur* is so invented it may well be attacked—or laughed at by some. Yet Robert Downey Jr. plays Lionel with exactly the right mix of charm, magic, and insouciance. He is a master sent to bring her out. And so, bit by bit, Diane slips away from her set domestic life downstairs where she wears dresses her mother has bought for her. She discovers the dark world Lionel knows—it is the world of dwarves, Siamese twins, transsexuals, addicts, pimps, whores, and freaks that

Diane Arbus would photograph. Lionel seduces her in so many ways that the marriage with Allan has to end. She is free to begin her work.

I hope you can see that this is a film of great daring. It also has many scenes of beauty and it makes Nicole a woman who is childlike again, going back to origins to understand her life and her purpose. As in *Birth,* near the end there is a great scene on a seashore. It is not a perfect film. On one viewing, it seems to me a little overextended, and I think that Lionel's upstairs world should be nastier, more feral, more that of a beast. I do not think the film will do great business, but that does not matter. It is a film filled with the prospect of beauty, art, identity, and change. There will be people who see it over and over again.

Nicole may be a little too pretty in *Fur*—Diane Arbus was seldom exactly pretty or conventionally glamorous. There was a fierceness in her, prepared to go too far, and this is a film that believes in going too far. The gathering of freaks in Lionel's apartment may be a touch too genteel, too like a social club for outsiders. Whereas outsiders are raw, awkward, and not clubbable. But the decision to take a known figure and to create a dream world for her shames the drab conditions under which most of our films are made. It is the venture of a great, dark, headstrong actress who has no expectation and not too much need for everything to turn out tidily or happily. This is from her black book, the one with demons on the cover to keep innocent readers away. This comes from a woman who lives with lions and wolves.

SOURCES

Angeli, Michael. "Screaming Mimi!" *Playboy*, March 1993.

Bjorkman, Stig. "Thieves Like Us." *Sight and Sound*, July 2003.

Bosworth, Patricia. *Diane Arbus*. New York: Knopf, 1984.

Brantley, Ben. "Fool's Gold in the Kingdom of Desire." *New York Times*, December 14, 1998.

Bresson, Robert. *Notes on Cinematography*. Translated by Jonathan Griffin. New York: Urizen, 1977.

Burke, Carolyn. *Lee Miller: A Life*. New York: Knopf, 2005.

Butler, Robert. "The Kidman and the Hare." *Independent on Sunday*, September 27, 1998.

Calhoun, Dave. "A Difficult Birth." *Time Out London*, October 27, 2004.

Carrillo, Jenny Cooney. "The Eyes Have It." *Time Out*, July 28, 1999.

Chion, Michel. *Eyes Wide Shut*. London: BFI, 2002.

Clarke, Roger. "Grief Encounter." *Sight and Sound*, November 2004.

Corliss, Richard. "An Actress to Die For." *Time*, October 9, 1995.

Cruise, Tom. Interview by Jesse Kornbluth. *Vanity Fair*, January 1989.

———. Interview by Lucy Kaylin. *GQ*, May 2006.

Cunningham, Michael. *The Hours*. New York: Farrar, Straus and Giroux, 1998.

Denby, David. "The Quick and the Dead." Review of *Dogville*. *New Yorker*, March 29, 2004.

Dickerson, James L. *Nicole Kidman*. New York: Citadel, 2003.

Doctorow, E. L. *Billy Bathgate*. New York: Random House, 1989.

Ellis, Lucy, and Bryony Sutherland. *Nicole Kidman: The Biography*. London: Aurum Press, 2002.

Ewbank, Tim, and Stafford Hildred. *Nicole Kidman: The Biography*. London: Headline, 2002.

Frazier, Charles. *Cold Mountain*. New York: Atlantic Monthly Press, 1997.

Griffin, Nancy. "Can This Film Be Fixed?" Review of *The Stepford Wives*. *New York Times*, June 6, 2004.

Hare, David. *Acting Up: A Diary*. London: Faber and Faber, 1999.

Holden, Stephen. "Who's Afraid Like Virginia Woolf?" Review of *The Hours*. *New York Times*, December 27, 2002.

Jones, Laura. *The Portrait of a Lady*. Screenplay. New York: Penguin, 1996.

Junod, Tom. "A Bridge, a Bed, a Bar, and One Real Ozzie Gull." *Esquire*, August 1999.

Kakutani, Michiko. "A Connoisseur of Cool Tries to Raise the Temperature." *New York Times*, July 18, 1999.

Kauffmann, Stanley. Review of *The Human Stain*. *New Republic*, November 24, 2003.

Kidman, Nicole. Interview by Stephen Rebello. *Movieline*, March 1994.

———. Interview by Lawrence Grobel. *Movieline*, October 1998.

———. Interview by Baz Luhrmann. *Interview*, May 2001.

————. Interview by Rick Lyman (on Stanley Kubrick and *The Shining*). In *Watching Movies*. New York: Times Books, 2002.

————. Interview by Ingrid Sischy. *Vanity Fair*, December 2002.

————. Interview by David Gritten. *Daily Telegraph*, October 2, 2004.

————. Interview by Christopher Goodwin. *Sunday Times* (London), April 10, 2005.

————, Interview by Jeanne Marie Laskas. *Ladies' Home Journal*, June 2006.

Koppelman, Charles. *Behind the Seen: How Walter Murch Edited Cold Mountain*. Berkeley, Calif.: New Riders, 2005.

Lane, Anthony. "In Translation." Review of *The Interpreter*. *New Yorker*, April 25, 2005.

Levin, Ira. *The Stepford Wives*. New York: Random House, 1972.

Maslin, Janet. "Bedroom Odyssey." *New York Times*, July 16, 1999.

Maynard, Joyce. *To Die For*. New York: Dutton, 1992.

Menand, Louis. "Kubrick's Strange Love." *New York Review of Books*, August 12, 1999.

Minghella, Anthony. "The House Is Dark and the Children Are Afraid." *New York Times*, August 12, 2001.

————. *Minghella on Minghella*. Edited by Timothy Bricknell. London: Faber and Faber, 2005.

Mitchell, Elvis. "An Eyeful, An Earful, Anachronism: Lautrec Meets Lady Marmalade." Review of *Moulin Rouge*. *New York Times*, May 18, 2001.

Moore, Susanna. *In the Cut*. New York: Knopf, 1995.

Obst, Lynda. *Hello, He Lied*. Boston: Little, Brown, 1996.

Plunkett, Danny. "Through a Glass Darkly." Interview with Jonathan Glazer. *Sunday Times* (London), October 31, 2004.

Raphael, Frederic. *Eyes Wide Open: A Memoir of Stanley Kubrick*. New York: Ballantine, 1999.

Schnitzler, Arthur. *Dream Story*. London: Penguin, 1999.

Scott, A. O. "A Unified Theory of Nicole Kidman." *New York Times*, November 2, 2003.

Stayton, Richard. "Mountain Man (Anthony Minghella)." *Written By*, February–March 2004.

Wood, Michael. "Quite a Night!" *London Review of Books*, September 30, 1999.

Woolf, Virginia. *Mrs Dalloway*. London: Hogarth Press, 1925.

————. "The Cinema" (1926). In *The Captain's Death Bed and Other Essays*. New York: Harcourt Brace Jovanovich, 1950.

ACKNOWLEDGMENTS

This book was the brainchild of Mike Jones at Bloomsbury and my agent, Laura Morris. They say they thought it up over a lunch. But I had been having lunch for years, without ever dreaming of such an idea. So I am in their debt for the enormous pleasure I had working on the book, and for the way it returned me to a childhood interpretation of the cinema that adult years had largely blown away. Thus, I had come to realize that movies belonged to directors, to writers, to producers and production systems, and to intricate schemes of collaboration or contest. There's truth in all of those ideas, but they tend to blind us to the most obvious and early ways of reading the medium—that pictures belong to actors, and to us, and they make a strange phantom love affair between us.

Mike and Laura demonstrated the best kinds of support and encouragement throughout the process of the book, and I hope they realize how important they were to its ultimate achievement—whatever that may be. In America, at Knopf, Jon Segal was the book's editor, and he did excellent, useful work at every stage, despite many difficulties that I threw in his way. As the book went along at Knopf, it was carried by the enthusiasm of many other people at the house—old friends by now: Kathy Hourigan, Kevin Bourke, Anthea Lingeman, Kathy Zuckerman, Carol Carson, and Anke Steinecke —my thanks to them all.

I was fortunate at every stage that a number of key people in Nicole Kidman's working life elected to help me in answering questions and in talking generally about the actress. And so I owe a large debt of gratitude to David Hare, Sam Mendes, Jonathan Glazer, Jean-Claude Carrière, Baz Luhrmann, Anthony Minghella, Robert Benton, Laura Ziskin, Robert Towne, Joyce Maynard, Susanna Moore, Buck Henry, Walter Murch, Richard Eyre, Stephen Frears, Virginia Campbell, and Christopher Hampton. There were also several people in Australia who talked to me and who asked to remain unnamed. I should also thank two very important people in the vital but anonymous role of publicists: Leslee Dart of the Dart Company and Catherine Olim at PMK were supporters of the project—not least with Nicole Kidman herself.

I thank Ms. Kidman for talking to me, and for answering all my questions. This doesn't mean she approves of the book, supports it, or would agree with everything in it. I daresay she will have objections. But I hope it is a book that even she may read with some interest and benefit. Above all, I thank her for her courage, her determination, and her ingenuity in just being "Nicole Kidman."

Beyond that, as someone who has been thinking about actresses for some sixty years, I know that this book was helped along the way by people who were dead before they had a chance to see a Nicole Kidman picture, and by people with whom I have talked about the movies: I am thinking of my parents, and my grandmother, Violet Thomson, who was an actress—every minute of the day; I am thinking of Kieran Hickey, Patrick McGilligan, Michael Powell, Jim Toback, Irene Selznick, Richard and Mary Corliss, Tom Luddy, Mark Feeney, Steven Bach, Lucy Gray—companions in argument; and many others, including notably the body of French actresses or actresses in French films, from Falconetti to Deneuve, who mean more and more as the years pass and to whom this book is dedicated.

INDEX

A Note About the Author

David Thomson has taught film studies at Dartmouth
College and served on the selection committee for the
New York Film Festival. He is a regular contributor to *The
New York Times, The Nation, Movieline, The New Republic,*
and *Salon.* He lives with his family in San Francisco.

A Note on the Type

The text of this book was composed in Palatino, a typeface
designed by the noted German typographer Hermann
Zapf. Named after Giovanni Battista Palatino, a writing
master of Renaissance Italy, Palatino was the first of Zapf's
typefaces to be introduced in America. The first designs
for the face were made in 1948, and the fonts for
the complete face were issued between 1950 and 1952.
Like all Zapf-designed typefaces, Palatino is beautifully
balanced and exceedingly readable.

Composed by North Market Street Graphics,
Lancaster, Pennsylvania
Printed and bound by R. R. Donnelley
Harrisonburg, Virginia
Designed by Anthea Lingeman